Intellectual Property Strategy

A Practical Guide to IP Management

Consulting Editors **Alexander Korenberg** and **Stephen Robertson**

Consulting editors
Alexander Korenberg and Stephen Robertson

Managing director
Sian O'Neill

Intellectual Property Strategy: A Guide to IP Management
is published by

Globe Law and Business Ltd
3 Mylor Close
Horsell
Woking
Surrey GU21 4DD
Tel: +44 20 3745 4770
www.globelawandbusiness.com

Printed and bound by Gomer Press

Intellectual Property Strategy: A Guide to IP Management
ISBN 9781911078074

© 2017 Globe Law and Business Ltd

DISCLAIMER
This publication is intended as a general guide only. The information and opinions which it contains are not intended to be a comprehensive study, nor to provide legal advice, and should not be treated as a substitute for legal advice concerning particular situations. Legal advice should always be sought before taking any action based on the information provided. The publishers bear no responsibility for any errors or omissions contained herein.

Table of contents

Introducing IP strategy

Alexander Korenberg
Kilburn & Strode LLP
Stephen Robertson
Metis Partners Ltd

If you are new to the topic of intellectual property (IP), by owning this book you've taken that important first step towards gaining a better understanding of what constitutes an IP strategy, learning the importance of it in business and taking on board some of the key considerations and matters that ought to be incorporated into an IP strategy. For those that are already involved with the topic, this book will enable you to deepen your knowledge and hopefully provide some interesting points of view.

There is no rule book that says an IP strategy must look like this, incorporate that or even achieve the following. An IP strategy is often just about deciding what works for your business in IP terms, based on the resources you currently have, are likely to have in the future, and your business objectives in the short and long term.

It may be a little clichéd but we're going to use a medieval castle analogy and its fortification to present an effective business IP strategy. The analogy starts with the moat that surrounds the castle which acts as the first line of defence – or deterrent – against enemies and puts out a clear message that an effort has been made to protect what's inside the castle. If we view the moat as being similar to registered IP assets such as patents or trademarks, both the moat and the registered IP assets are visible to attackers or infringers, and further investigation is needed to better understand how strong a defence each may provide. Potential attackers to the castle don't know how deep the moat is or what dangers lie under the surface until they investigate it further, similar to the diligence required on a patent portfolio by competitors to allow them to work out ways to cross or get around these first barriers.

The next line of defence in the castle analogy is the castle walls. These are visible to the outsider but it's harder to make an informed assessment of their quality or strength until further and more complex diligence is undertaken, such as in relation to how thick they are, what they are made of and the structure of how they were put together. The castle walls are here viewed as being similar to business IP assets such as brand and reputation, software, or even critical business partners. These important business IP assets act like the castle walls as they are visible but it's difficult to understand their value to the business without further diligence.

Of course, the owner of the castle will rely on the skills of the archers and knights for defence and, if they are organised and well trained, this will define how good a defence they can provide and will differentiate the castle from others. In business terms this is similar to the critical know-how of key employees and how that individual know-how is shared amongst the team to make the business more robust and scalable.

Furthermore, the castle and its occupants may have created some additional castle fortifications or barriers such as clever countermeasures in the form of carefully designed arrow slits, setting traps for or dropping hot oil or scalding water on attackers. In business IP terms, these are the trade secrets and innovations that a business creates and protects, which are often unknown to competitors and can create real unique selling propositions (USPs) or barriers to entry.

Of course, defending the castle involves the occupiers of the castle working together as a team, particularly when under attack, as everyone recognises that castle protection is for the common good. All castle occupiers can lend a hand, feeding and nurturing the more skilled defenders and providing them with weapons and ammunition. In business IP terms, that's analogous with building an IP culture across the business, which recognises that everyone can play in part in developing an IP strategy which has a positive impact on the business strategy and the financial results of the business.

All of these medieval strategies may be 'defensive' in nature. There were, of course, offensive tactics that could be deployed including having 'lookouts' going out and observing the movements of potential attackers and having outposts in other villages in the region to provide warnings of potential threats. These activities could be viewed as similar to business IP strategy which may incorporate 'offensive' elements including analysing competitor activities, reviewing their patenting strategy and utilising patent landscaping techniques, possibly entering into licensing discussions and asserting rights at some point.

Finally, castle owners used to earn 'rent' from farmers who paid for the right to graze their animals in safety outside the castle, behind the protection of the moat and within the safe gaze of the archers. In business IP terms, this is similar to IP assertion and out-licensing the IP to third parties on the basis that you have invested time and money creating strong IP rights, creating the opportunity to earn revenues from your IP assets in different commercial ways, much like the castle owner.

So, now we've set the scene, got you accustomed to the concept and given you a useful analogy to get you familiar with IP rights and their usefulness, let's return to the business world. While, historically, intangible assets (which include not only IP rights but also internal knowledge and the human resources that embody them, a customer base, market position and so forth) only made up a small fraction of the value of a business, this has changed dramatically over the last few decades. Intangible assets have now overtaken tangible assets (such as bricks and mortar, machinery and inventory) as the critical assets in a business. The UK Intellectual Property Office (UKIPO) reported that, in 2011, the UK invested circa £127 billion (rising to £133 billion by 2014) in knowledge assets compared with an investment of £88 billion in tangible assets for the same period. As a result, the investment in IP and its subsequent, albeit often hidden value should, therefore, be on everyone's agenda.

Thus, IP matters are now critical to most businesses and few business strategies can afford not to incorporate an IP strategy. This book focuses on IP strategy relating to registered rights, in particular patents. The reason for this is that while rights that exist automatically, such as copyright, are certainly useful – and even vital – as a tool to prevent competitors from free-riding on your investment in creative activities by copying your works, and underpin important economic sectors in particular in the creative industries, registered rights are more under your business's control. What is more, patents in particular have taken on huge importance in all aspects of technology businesses, from attracting investment at an early stage to creating revenue streams for later stage businesses. This also means that, since registered rights like patents and trademarks are true monopolies, the rise of, in particular, patents in the high tech sector puts pressure on businesses to assess the risks that may be associated by others. Both aspects (IP as valuable assets and IP as business risks) are considered in this book.

This book aims to cover most aspects of IP strategy, at least as far as it pertains to registered rights, at a level that is accessible to anyone without specialist legal knowledge. It would be unrealistic (and undesirable) to attempt to teach all details and nuances to an audience that is more likely interested in an overview and the chapters are therefore pitched at a level that enables business decision makers to understand the main issues at a strategic level, to understand where more advice may be needed and to converse with their advisers, both internal and external to the business. In short, this book aims to provide business decision makers with an oversight enabling them to set and execute IP strategy in collaboration with their advisers, lawyers and IP professionals.

The book starts with a primer on all IP rights. This is followed by a series of chapters on the creation and management of patent rights and the assessment of risks associated with those rights held by others, a chapter on exploitation of IP by licensing and chapters focusing on brands and trademarks, and trade secrets (often a precursor or alternative to patenting). Topics covered in this book range from the creation to the exploitation of registered IP rights, touching on business areas that involve operational, legal, financial and human resource issues. An integrated IP strategy thus requires a wide-ranging skill set and an integrated team of a number of officers or directors in a company. That said, some chapters may be more relevant to some than others, and the table on the next page provides suggestions as to which chapters of this book are most pertinent to particular aspects of a business.

What this table suggests – and, we say, reflects reality – is that IP strategy is a multi-disciplinary undertaking, requiring engagement and input from all areas of the business outside legal and research and development (R&D) functions. For example, human resources will have much to say about such aspects of setting up an IP strategy and IP generation as putting the right teams in place and incentivising and motivating innovators. Input from finance will be required in, and finance needs to take note of, areas such as resourcing and managing a portfolio, licensing and the influence of IP in areas such as tax and merger and acquisition activities. And, of course, the contribution of IP to a firm's assets and bottom line beyond these areas will be of interest to finance. While marketing functions may most naturally be interested in branding and the use of trademarks, input from marketing will be invaluable when it comes to information and intelligence about competitor activities that are relevant to policing IP rights and the risks posed by third-party rights. Marketing will also need to be aware of trade secrets and the implications of confidentiality or lack thereof, where interests of creating and maintaining IP value can conflict with promoting aspects of a company's products or activities. We suggest that, given the importance IP now has in terms of creating and maintaining value in a business, IP strategy should not make dull reading for anyone involved in aspects of running a company.

	Research & Development	Operations	Risk	Marketing	Finance	Human Resources
IP value		✓	✓		✓	
Encouraging and supporting innovation	✓	✓	✓			✓
Developing an IP strategy	✓	✓				✓
Portfolio management	✓	✓			✓	✓
Protecting your brand			✓	✓		
Trade secrets	✓			✓		
Freedom to operate	✓	✓	✓	✓		
IP policing	✓	✓		✓		
IP licensing			✓	✓	✓	
Non-practising entities		✓	✓			
IP and tax strategy		✓			✓	

Intellectual property: A primer

Lorna Brazell
Osborne Clarke

1. Introduction

It is easy to forget that property ownership is a system of legal rights. Although occupation of a house, or having a coin in one's pocket, feels like owning property, physical possession alone does not give the legal right to knock the house down, or spend the coin: those are rights conferred by the law only on that subset of occupiers or holders of objects who are by law the owners of the property in them. Nevertheless, generally speaking most people understand that each place or object does have a legal owner, and that they as passers-by or temporary holders of the object have little or no right to decide what is to be done with it. Intellectual property (IP), similarly, is a system of legal rights, with the distinction that the subject matter, unlike a house or a coin, is intangible and therefore less easily recognised as subject to legal rules. IP divides up creative work into a number of categories and provides rules by which a person or a company can claim property rights over that work. If something has the legal status of property, then it can be bought and sold, licensed, mortgaged to raise funds or inherited just as physical assets can be. Thus, ownership of IP gives the owner the ability to control the use of ideas and the products of the human mind in all its manifestations: from technical inventions through to the ingenuity of traders in improving their position in any market and the works of artists and performers in all fields of the arts.

Some rights which are commonly called IP, such as know-how or trade secrets, are not in law property rights and so cannot be dealt with in this way. Instead they are protected by a range of other laws.

Note that while IP rights give the ability to control the use of works, they are not self-enforcing and there is no public system for enforcing them. The owner of the rights has responsibility for tackling infringers by bringing civil court proceedings for an injunction and damages. Assistance from public authorities such as local trading standards officers can be called upon in some circumstances, but these departments are highly unlikely to take action without being notified.

As industries have evolved using ideas and other intangibles differently, a number of different kinds of rights have been devised over the years. It is important to be clear in any IP management strategy as to which rights are actually relevant to the business in question.

The best-known IP rights are patents, trademarks and copyright. These have some characteristics in common but are different from each other in other ways. For instance, some IP rights, such as patents and registered designs, are absolute monopoly rights. Even someone who comes up with the same product or design wholly independently can be prevented by the right holder from exploiting his own work. These are very powerful, and therefore valuable rights. Other rights, such as copyright and rights in confidential information, are only partial monopolies, which means that anyone who honestly comes up with the same product independently of the earlier creator has the right to exploit his own work regardless of the prior right holder. Such rights can only be used to stop those who have in some way derived benefit from the right holder's prior effort, such as through copying, and so the ability of such rights to deliver genuine market exclusivity may be lower.

The formalities associated with the various rights also differ widely. Some rights, most notably copyrights, arise automatically as soon as the new work comes into existence, whereas other rights such as patents have to be applied for and come into existence only when registered with a government authority. Some rights, again most notably copyrights, are effectively global rights by virtue of international treaties; others, namely European Union trademarks and European Community design rights, may have limited international effect; but most are strictly national rights. Very few businesses today can be satisfied with rights limited to a single jurisdiction, so it may be necessary to apply for and obtain equivalent national rights in many countries.

There are numerous additional species of IP which have been introduced to protect particular interests in particular industries. For instance, semiconductor topography rights, plant variety rights and performers' rights are special forms of IP relevant to the semiconductor, agriculture and entertainment industries respectively. They apply exclusively to those specific industries and will simply never be relevant except to businesses operating in those industries. As regards these, all that the non-specialist needs to know is when they might conceivably be relevant, in order to do further research or seek expert advice if necessary.

It is also important to appreciate that IP rights do not give a positive right to do anything. Thus, a patent over an improved form of wheel does not give its owner the right to make and sell the wheel if, in doing so, he would be using pre-existing spoke technology that has been patented by someone else. A licence would be needed under the earlier patent. Similarly, a brilliantly creative adaptation of a children's book into a computer game may well attract copyright of its own, but it will also infringe the copyright in the original book and cannot be made and sold without the permission of the holder of that copyright.

2. National and international rights

The harmonisation of IP rules worldwide began in the 19th century, with the Berne (copyright) and Paris (patents and designs) Conventions.[1] As a result of these and subsequent revisions and additions, culminating the Agreement on Trade-Related Aspects of Intellectual Property (the TRIPS Agreement) under the World Trade Organization (WTO), the national laws of all major markets follow a similar set of

---

1   Berne Convention for the Protection of Literary and Artistic Works (1886; as amended by the Paris Act 1971) and Paris Convention for the Protection of Industrial Property of 20 March 1883 (as variously revised and amended).

basic principles, though national implementations are not identical. There are also some regional agreements which govern specific rights in specific jurisdictions, such as the European Union's EU Trade Mark and Community Design. Other than these exceptions, for any given work the owner of the IP rights over it is actually holding a bundle of similar but not identical national rights, which may require constant vigilance to remain effective.

In view of this it is important to be aware that very few countries have courts which are really familiar with this branch of commercial law. Regardless of the theory, in practice the scope of rights and the appropriateness of remedies can both be misunderstood, leading to inadequate enforcement or even in the worst case scenario to complete loss of rights. Low levels of judicial expertise have a far greater impact upon IP assets than upon a business's other assets. The English courts have developed significant expertise in IP issues over recent decades and represent one of the most sophisticated systems available globally for determining related issues.

3. Ownership of IP

Ownership of any registered IP right is generally uncontroversial: the party which is named on the relevant register as being the owner, is the legal owner. (There are, of course, occasions where a right has in fact already been assigned to a new owner but the change has not yet been registered.)

Ownership of the various unregistered forms of IP right is a different matter. The statutes which establish each form of property right stipulate who will be the first owner of that right when it arises. But this is generally in the form of a cascade of options. Thus, for example, the first ownership of a copyright work depends upon whether or not the author created the work in their capacity as an employee (in which case the employer owns the copyright) or in their own right (in which case the author owns the work). In contrast, first ownership of a commissioned design may belong to the commissioner, but if the work was not commissioned then the designer's employer (if any) owns the rights. Only if the designer was freelance will they own the rights themselves.

The effect of these rules is that frequently an organisation believes that it owns rights only to discover when that ownership is challenged either that it does not own it, or cannot prove ownership. Records need to be kept as to who created what materials in what circumstances – something which is rarely thought about at the time of creation, and so may prove to have been overlooked when the question first comes to be asked, several years later.

The greatest source of confusion, however, is the widely held belief that a commissioner of a copyright work – whether text, or artwork for a website or other material – owns the copyright in that work. This myth derives from a failure to understand the national nature of IP rights. Under US law, copyright in a 'work made for hire' does indeed belong to the paying (hiring) party. But under English and other European laws there is no such rule. Accordingly, a company which commissions work and does not expressly take an assignment of the copyright, will have the benefit of a licence to use the work for some purposes but will not own the copyright itself. This is a frequent source of disputes.

Where works are produced through collaboration, ownership can also be problematic. Joint ownership may arise automatically (as in the case of copyright) or be agreed (such as when patenting the fruits of joint research), but this is rarely a suitable solution in commercial terms. Once again, US law is the source of misunderstanding here, since US laws permit joint owners to act separately in respect of their individual shares. Under the European approach, however, joint owners need to act jointly in order to assign or license the rights, and over time as the parties' interests diverge this is likely to become less and less possible to agree. In practical terms, it is more effective to have one party own the rights with others having such licences as they may need for their own future exploitation of the rights.

The following sections outline the characteristics of the principal forms of IP rights.

4.   Copyright

Copyright is both the most widely known and the most widely held form of IP. There is no system for registration of copyrights in most jurisdictions, although registration is an option in some including the US and China. However, even in these countries copyright subsists without being registered; registration is principally a precondition for enforcement. The common expression 'copyrighted', implying some action has been taken to obtain copyright, is a misleading hangover from an earlier era when registration was required.

All businesses and almost certainly all individuals as well own copyright in numerous works, since copyright arises automatically whenever someone writes or draws an original (not copied) sentence or scribble. All that is needed is to be able to show who it was that created the work and when. But most of these 'accidental' copyrights have no market value whatsoever. It is principally in industries which rely upon some form of artistic creativity, whether as a product in itself (such as newspapers, fashion or music), or as a tool for other purposes (as in advertising) that the copyrights have any commercial significance. Copyright in operating manuals for industrial processes can also be valuable, as the only source of technical know-how outside the heads of the current employees.

Copyright is also important in protecting computer software. This has for decades been a source of contention, since copyright protection is less strong than patents, but despite much discussion it has not been possible to reach a widespread consensus as to how software should be protected under the patent regime.

Copyright confers on the owner of the right exclusivity as regards various acts such as making copies of the work, issuing copies to the public or adapting or performing the work. Anyone who does any of these 'restricted acts' without permission infringes, and a court can grant an injunction requiring them to stop as well as an order for damages and payment of legal costs. Proving copying is not always easy: even an identical work does not infringe unless it has been derived directly or indirectly from the original. Unless the copy is exact, such as a pirate copy of a film or photocopy of a newspaper article, then there is often scope for argument as to whether or not the amount copied is sufficient to infringe. The test is one of quality not quantity: has a substantial part of the original been copied? The many rules of thumb bandied about as to how much it is safe to copy without permission are all unfounded in law. The Court of Appeal recently ruled that a series of eight second extracts from a two-hour broadcast of a cricket match infringed, as they were the most interesting and hence most valuable parts of the recording.

There are a limited number of exceptions to copyright, such as the right to quote from a work in the course of genuine criticism or review. But it is important to be aware that these exceptions are purely national: the US general exception for 'fair use' is much broader and more flexible than the closest equivalent exceptions under European copyrights. Accordingly, a use of a copyright work which may be permitted in the US risks being found to infringe in the EU.

The protection given by copyright is the longest-lasting of any IP right other than trademarks. For literary (written), musical and artistic (graphic) works it lasts for the entire lifetime of the author of the work, and for a period thereafter, which varies from country to country but is generally between 50 and 70 years. As a result, it may be necessary to look further back through the annals of a business in order to be sure that all relevant rights have been identified and assigned, than will be needed in relation to shorter-lived forms of IP. Keeping records of who produced valuable copyright works is thus an important component of protecting its value: if the work is infringed 50 years after its creation, the owner needs to be able to identify the author and whether they were an employee of the business, or else point to an assignment or other proof of ownership. Modern businesses are not always set up to retain such records.

5. Trademarks

While copyright protects the actual work in which it arises, trademarks are all about protecting the goodwill of a business, and may be used with a single product, a range of products or all products emanating from that business. Any sort of mark which a trader uses to distinguish its goods or services in the eyes of the relevant public can function as a trademark. Words (KODAK), logos (picture an apple with a bite out of it) and sounds are commonly used. Trademark rights may accrue to these even without registration, provided they achieve a sufficient level of consumer recognition.

Brands of all kinds are very valuable in many industries, but particularly in consumer goods and services, where the underlying product may be practically identical to its competitors but command twice the price if it carries a prestigious label. The extreme example of this is in the highly technical field of pharmaceuticals where, once patent protection has expired, a trusted brand can retain market share because of its recognition among patients, in the face of very substantially cheaper and chemically identical alternatives.

Of all forms of IP, trademarks are the only one which potentially lasts forever. Provided that a trademark remains in use and the mark does not become the generic term for the products it is used to promote (for example, biro), it can continue in effect indefinitely.

The strength, and hence generally speaking the value, of the rights obtained under a trademark depends upon whether or not it is registered.

A trademark can be registered either nationally (through the UK Intellectual Property Office) or for the EU through the European Intellectual Property Office. A registered trademark confers an absolute monopoly on the use of the same mark for the same goods and services as those listed in the specification of the trademark application. Ignorance of the registration is no defence: anyone can check the register, and so is taken to have notice of the trademark owner's rights. The registration also enables the holder to prevent the same mark being used on similar goods or services, or to prevent a similar mark being used on the same or similar goods or services, if as a matter of fact consumers are likely to be confused by such use.

In contrast, the rights of a proprietor of an unregistered trademark depend upon the level of recognition of the mark among the relevant public, which is infinitely variable. WTO Member States are required to provide protection to 'well-known' marks even if these are not registered in their territory. What is required to achieve 'well-known' status is, however, a matter left to each Member State to decide, however, and as a result the test is highly variable. The Mercedes badge is apparently one of the most widely recognised marks in the world; few other trademarks are recognised across all continents and Mercedes trucks are used everywhere for their durability and longevity. Such a level of recognition could confer a standard of protection similar to that of a registered trademark. Other unregistered marks with a lower consumer recognition level may only be able to retain exclusivity in a restricted geographical area, or for a very limited category of goods or services. The UK Supreme Court recently ruled that the mark NOW used by a well-established Hong Kong broadcaster, including promotional material available globally on YouTube, did not have the right goodwill in the UK to prevent Sky from launching its own UK broadcast channel under the mark.[2]

6.   Designs

Good design is key to the success of many consumer products, from household cleaning appliances to fashion or luxury cars, but less important in industries where function or simple cost dictate the choice of a product.

Unfortunately, there is less international harmonisation for design law than for any other category of IP, so that the protection available in Europe is materially different from that in the US, for example. The terminology is also different: the US has a system it calls design patents (as opposed to utility patents which protect technical inventions) whereas the European systems refer to them simply as designs.

New designs in the UK can be protected by a series of potentially overlapping rights: registered Community and national rights, unregistered Community and national rights, and in some aspects, also by copyright. This adds up to a surprisingly complicated regime even within the EU. For the purposes of IP portfolio management and strategy, registration is always preferable where possible.

6.1   Registered designs

Registered designs, like the other registered rights, provide an absolute monopoly.

---

2   *Starbucks (HK) Ltd & another (Appellants) v British Sky Broadcasting Group plc* [2015] UKSC 31.

This can be used to prevent manufacture, import or sale of any product incorporating a novel design which creates the same overall impression on an informed user of products of that kind.

A design can be registered either for the UK alone, at the UK Intellectual Property Office, or for the entire EU (a registered Community design), at the European Intellectual Property Office. Unlike the process for registering trademarks or patents, there is no examination of an application to register a design, which means that this very strong right can be obtained simply by completing the appropriate forms and paying a filing fee. It will, however, be more vulnerable to validity challenges throughout its life than patent or trademark rights precisely because it has not passed any formal verification process. Design rights can therefore be harder to value accurately than other registered rights.

The rights last for up to 25 years (subject to payment of renewal fees). In consumer products, this will in many cases be longer than the shelf-life of the product. These are therefore potentially very powerful rights – and in the case of the Community registration, effective throughout all Member States of the EU.

6.2   Unregistered design rights

In contrast, unregistered design rights (whether Community or national) are more like copyright in that they arise automatically but provide only a partial monopoly, protecting against copying, not against independent development of the same design. Other than these common features, they fall into two categories of differing strength.

The unregistered Community design right lasts only for three years. It is intended for very short-lived products such as fashion items, or to enable a company to 'road test' its design before deciding whether to invest in a design registration.

The unique unregistered design right under national law in the UK on the other hand lasts up to 15 years, though subject to a compulsory licensing regime for the final five years. It is intended to provide protection for relatively utilitarian designs which may not meet the standard of novelty and individual character required in order to register a design right. The design must also be original and "not 'commonplace in the design field in question".

7.   Patents

Patents, which protect technical inventions, are traditionally considered the strongest, and in many cases the only effective, form of IP. A patent provides an absolute monopoly against either copying or independent development of the same invention, which is defined in the claims, and gives a relatively harmonised level of protection wherever in the world applied for. Subject to payment of renewal fees, protection lasts for up to 20 years from the filing of the application (save in the case of pharmaceuticals, biotechnology and agrichemicals, where an extension of up to a further five years may be available).

Their principal relevance is to manufacturing industries of all kinds, where they protect inventions either in the form of processes or products, and to the delivery of services which depend on technology, such as telecommunications networks.

Patents can also be obtained over some computer-related inventions; the notorious divergence between the US and the rest of the world over the kinds of computer inventions which can be patented has narrowed in recent years.

A patent is obtained by filing an application and subsequent process of prosecution of that application (negotiation with the relevant patent office), which often takes several years. The patent office must be persuaded that the invention is new, contains an inventive step (is not obvious) and is capable of industrial application, and does not fall within a short list of excluded subjects. Exclusions include: scientific discoveries, business or mathematical methods or varieties of plants or animals produced by traditional breeding techniques. The list of exceptions varies from country to country, which may significantly affect the value of the patent in each territory. No enforcement is possible in most countries while the patent application is 'pending', but once the patent has been granted damages can potentially be claimed back to the date of filing. Using a technology which is subject to a patent application is therefore risky, even if there appear to be grounds for expecting only a relatively narrow claim to be granted.

Partly because they relate to technological developments and partly because of the legal conventions surrounding their drafting and interpretation, patents are seldom easy to understand. The accurate distillation of a technical idea from its description over tens or hundreds of pages is fraught with difficulties. Few non-specialists make any effort to understand specific patents despite their high market value, treating them simply as a 'black box'. This frequently leads to misleading claims being made as to the actual scope of the monopoly under a patent or group of patents. It can also translate into a failure to take care to ensure that the formalities, of registering assignments and making sure renewal fees are paid, actually get executed. Patents regularly lapse through apparent oversight in these matters, and can be restored to the Register only in very limited circumstances.

Despite the existence since 1975 of a European Patent Office (EPO), unlike the position for trademarks and designs there is as yet no such thing as a unitary European patent. An application can be made either nationally or centrally, but at present even a central application results in a bundle of identically worded national patents. This may be about to change. Although somewhat uncertain due to the UK's decision to leave the EU, it may soon be possible to register a European Patent with Unitary Effect and to enforce European Patents in a single pan-European Unified Patent Court.

8.   Confidential information

Like copyright, most businesses will generate some information which they consider holds sufficient value for it to be worth protection through maintaining confidentiality. Some information may have only transient value, for instance plans leading up to a new product launch, while other information may represent the core of the holder's business, as in the case of the famously secret formula for Coca-Cola.

Unlike copyright, there is no particular category of business for which confidential information is more or less likely to matter. These rights need to be considered in any transaction, in any context.

Unfortunately, under English law, despite increasingly frequent references to 'owning' data there are in fact no property rights in confidential information or trade secrets. The legal rights in information as such are purely rights to prevent the unauthorised use or disclosure of the information as a matter of equity. Rights in confidential information cannot be assigned or mortgaged in the usual senses. This is in contrast to the rights under the laws of various States in the US, where statutory 'proprietary information rights' may exist and be assigned, mortgaged and so on as property. It is particularly important not to allow IP definitions to include proprietary information as a substitute for a clause specifically addressing confidential information as it is recognised under English law, although in practice this can be difficult when faced with a precedent of US origin and a counterparty which does not appreciate that difference in laws. Other European jurisdictions have very disparate regimes for protecting confidential information, which may be seen as a branch of employment law or even criminal law. These are in the process of being harmonised to an approach similar to the English system under a European Trade Secrets Directive, which is due to come into effect once implemented into national laws by July 2018.

Again like copyright, confidential information is only a partial monopoly right: an independent development leading to the same information cannot be prevented. The monopoly is only effective against the use or disclosure of information if it has been obtained (directly or indirectly) from the person to whom it is confidential. It is, however, potentially even weaker than copyright, in that a business which wishes to assert that information is truly confidential needs to be able to demonstrate that it has made at least minimum efforts to ensure that it is kept confidential and that employees are aware of this. Mere assertion is not enough. Consequently, not only legal policing but practical measures need to be in place if confidential information is to retain its status and thus its value. Information maintained unencrypted on a computer network which is linked to the internet may simply not qualify. Nevertheless, if real steps are taken to ensure the information is protected then information can remain confidential indefinitely. But a single instance of information reaching the public domain may result in confidentiality being lost forever.

9. Database rights

The newest form of IP is a custom-designed legal right to prevent the extraction or reutilisation of information which is held in a database. This was introduced by the EU in 1998 in recognition of the increasing importance of technical and commercial data in businesses of all sorts.

Like copyright and rights in confidential information, database right is only a partial monopoly. It protects the investment made in putting the database together, so prevents others from short-cutting that investment by taking the data out of the database. But if another business makes its own database and includes exactly the same information, it will obtain its own database right and using the data in that form it will not infringe any rights in the first database.

Database right has not proved as valuable and effective in all cases as the drafters may have hoped since databases comprising data created by the database holder (rather than compiled from pre-existing data) have inadvertently been excluded from protection. Thus, a database of information about the performance of a vehicle engine collected through the vehicle's sensors as it is being operated might not attract database right in the hands of the vehicle's manufacturer; but a database of comparative information about vehicle performance collected by a third-party researcher by buying the data from several manufacturers would be. Accordingly, for the time being any business holding a database of valuable data which it has created needs to be aware that the most effective protection for the data is its confidentiality.

10. Conclusion

As this brief overview shows, there are a range of different IP rights and the differences are important. Although some rights arise automatically, a registration process is necessary for others but the added initial cost and effort of registration normally translate into stronger rights which are easier to enforce, if enforcement is required. The exact scope of rights, whether registered or unregistered, depends upon local (national) laws, so that a management strategy should focus on identifying exactly what protection is available in the specific markets where a product is expected to be launched. Within the EU, harmonisation is in progress through initiatives such as the Digital Single Market programme relating to copyright, the Agreement on a Unified Patent Court and the Trade Secrets Directive. These will make enforcement easier over time. But harmonisation beyond the EU borders is unlikely to be reached for many years to come.

11. Chapter summary

- The distinction between registered rights providing true monopolies versus unregistered rights enabling only the prevention of copying is significant for valuation.
- You need to police and enforce your rights yourself.
- Rights are creatures of national law: different rights may be available in different countries and rules may vary.
- While some harmonisation has occurred, and is ongoing, the differences between countries is likely to be a feature of the IP system for the foreseeable future.

IP value and intangibles: a critical corporate resource

Stephen Robertson
Metis Partners Ltd

1. Introduction

This chapter focuses on the 'value' of intangibles and intellectual property (IP) assets. The fundamental reason to have IP assets and an IP strategy that recognises and manages them, is because of the value these assets bring to your business. In this regard, 'value' of course has many meanings. For example this could be the price paid to acquire IP assets, the capitalised value of IP assets on the balance sheet or an independent valuation of IP assets or even the amount of money borrowed against the revenue streams associated with IP assets. These are all expressions of value.

Taking this further, since IP assets are indeed a resource controlled by an entity for the purposes of earning some future economic benefit, should we not view them in the same way we view other key corporate resources like factories, machinery, technology and workforce? Should investment in IP not be subject to the same project appraisal processes that are adopted for expanding the workforce or building new manufacturing premises? Should its estimated value not be available to support securitised lending as it is for other assets?

The answer, of course, to the questions above is an emphatic 'yes'. The challenge is that all of the aforementioned corporate resources are tangible and visible like the tip of the iceberg is, and most IP assets are intangible and sit below the surface of the water as shown in Figure 1.

It is widely acknowledged that intangible assets now account for the majority of the value of corporates and in some sectors, such as technology, it's estimated that the intangibles amount to up to 80% of the value of the business. The fact that it's difficult to get this value recognised on the balance sheet means many corporates fail to recognise this value and so do not manage it properly. As a result, IP assets are often seen by corporate managers as representing a 'cost' of doing business rather than as an investment. They are often seen as the cost/investment related to the following:

- Overcoming barriers to entry that exist in a market, for example achieving Food and Drug Administration (FDA) approval for a drug or CE approval for a medical device can be very time consuming and creates expensive and labour-intensive hurdles which innovators have to overcome (often designed to protect consumers).

- Creating hurdles or barriers over which competitors have to climb or work around, such as those created by investing in and securing granted patents around an idea or innovation.

Figure 1: The intangibles iceberg

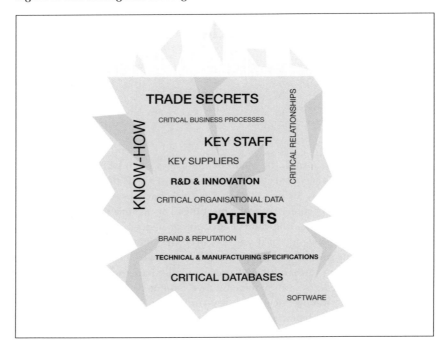

- The investment in the unique selling points (USPs) of the business that set it apart from others, for example the Perspex brand is synonymous with plastic sheeting and was built on an innovative patented process over 50 years ago. Current investment around the Perspex brand is focused on product innovation and investment in manufacturing processes is protected by trade secrets.
- Driving mergers and acquisitions (M&A) strategies and transactions, for example at the end of 2016, Sports Direct plc sold the Dunlop brand to Sumitomo Rubber Industries of Japan for 28 times profit, a price significantly above the book value of the IP asset – it was described as a 'strategic acquisition'.

The above examples demonstrate that IP assets could be viewed as both a cost and an investment. This will now be explored further.

2. IP assets: cost vs investment

There is an ongoing debate around what makes a cost become an investment. Recognising that the money spent creating IP assets can be linked to the generation of revenues or the protection of margins and can therefore be turned into a return on investment ('ROI') decision, is a good way to start the debate. The most obvious recognition of the value of IP comes from linking the IP to the revenues it currently generates or is likely to generate in the future, and this is often an easy way to get anyone interested in corporate success on the same page, no matter their role or their agenda. For example:

- an HR director passionate about the investment people, since people and their know-how are often a key asset in business;
- a technical director focused on driving technical advancements in the business and recognising that investment is key to innovation and retaining key members of the team;
- a sales and marketing director responsible for sales targets, building USPs and looking for inspiration and insight into the return on marketing spend;
- a finance director looking for ways to cut costs and perhaps pruning or trimming a costly portfolio of registered IP assets such as patents, trademarks or designs; or
- a chief executive recognising the importance of key IP assets in increasing the valuation and exit price of the business that's been promised to investors.

The company resources spent on IP assets are often only reflected within costs incurred. This enables us to identify what is potentially being invested in IP but without an indication of how these IP assets are critical to business processes or directly contribute to the generation of revenue streams. How then are we to reliably assess whether the spend is appropriate or worthwhile? The absence of a related asset on the balance sheet (or statement of financial position) means we have no indication of future value that the IP may bring.

3. IP assets: an inventory

Of course, if we are to begin to manage these new kinds of assets then we need to be able to recognise them. Creating an inventory is a good way to start. Often drawing easy-to-understand pictures of the IP assets in a business is a good way to get every director onto the same page and build an initial inventory of a firm's IP assets and how and where they are utilised or not.

Take Figure 2 below. It simply narrates in simple terms three key areas of a business: first, back-end resources; secondly, middle section processes; and thirdly, front end outputs to capture the IP assets or resources used or created in each of these three areas. It keeps things relatively simple but allows many people in the business or stakeholders to see where IP assets exist and are important to a business.

4. Intangible asset taxonomies

Of course, none of this is new. Academics, consultants, practitioners and corporate executives have been writing on this subject for many years and in many forms and guises. As a result, there are many existing taxonomies and labels for intangible assets and here are a few, from the broadest to the narrowest:

- intellectual capital (human, relationship and organisational) – often viewed as the broadest range of intangible assets a company can access;
- intellectual assets (the intangibles a company might own); and
- intellectual property rights (patents, trademarks, designs and copyrights).

Figure 2: IP assets – business context

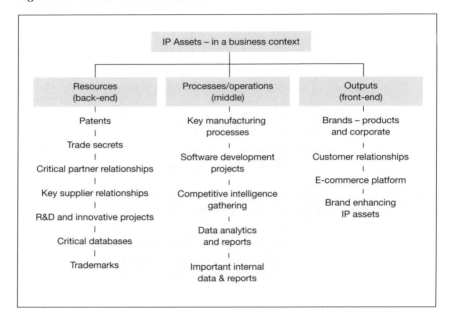

The key underlying theme is finding a common language that recognises 'spending money in the creation or acquisition of mostly intangible resources that vary in importance to the business' as they help generate revenues in the business. By identifying these resources and then turning them into 'assets' and recognising their contribution to a business an ROI can be measured. Like assets, many of them can be owned, managed and transferred from one party to another.

In Figure 3 below, a taxonomy is used to create an inventory of IP assets under different headings to confirm their existence and allow further analysis relating to their use and importance. This example focuses on the idea that there are a number of IP assets across the business that, first, are business value drivers, secondly, underpin the creation and sales of products and services and, thirdly, generate income and forecasts. The point is that there are various ways of visualising IP assets and acknowledging their existence and impact across a business and often the six types in the dotted circle are considered to be the most important ones in a business. There is no 'one size fits all' solution.

5. Revenue growth versus margin protection

This chapter has discussed the link between intangible assets and the products or services they underpin. Often, when it comes to IP assets, it's worthwhile making the distinction between revenue generation and margin protection – patents are intended to keep competitors out and so allow you to keep margins high/increase margins. This is clearly demonstrated in the pharmaceutical sector which is dominated by big corporates who leverage or exploit their blockbuster patents over

Figure 3: IP assets – a business taxonomy

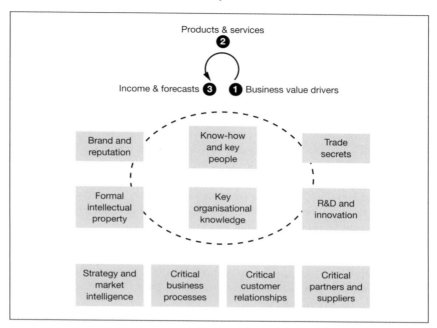

the life of those patents. Patents also allow corporates to cross-license and secure favourable partnerships with others.

Brand and reputation can encourage customer loyalty and revenue generation for many businesses, thus helping to maintain high margins and keeping competitors out. For example, the Intel brand is a well-known technology brand and consumers often look for the 'Intel inside' brand when buying a PC because of the trust that has been built with consumers around the quality, reliability and performance of Intel processors.

For other corporates, trade secrets and secret recipes are critical to products and services and protecting market share. Software IP assets, it could be argued, might allow you to save on the margin if developing the software yourself is less expensive than the cost of licensing it in from someone else.

Other larger corporates recognise that a mix of IP assets is the key to their commercial success, for example Apple relies on its brand and reputation and is recognised as an innovator and as a producer of very high-quality, hi-tech goods. It also has unique and constantly updated software for the iTunes platform and trade secrets around some of their manufacturing and product protection processes, for example waterproofing mobile phones. Apple also relies on its patents to fight off competitors and this rich mix of IP assets help drive sales and increase margins.

6.   Accounting rules and regulations – we cannot ignore them.

Despite all the evidence, there has been a reluctance, to date, to acknowledge IP value. Or rather we do acknowledge that IP has value, but we perhaps do not trust estimates of its value. This may appear to be too subtle a distinction but IP valuation still suffers from the stigma of being the 'poor relation' of physical/tangible asset valuation. Yet investment in IP has, over the last decade, significantly outweighed the corresponding investment in tangible assets. The UKIPO reported that even in 2011 the UK invested circa £127 billion (rising to £133 billion by 2014) in knowledge assets compared with £88 billion investment in tangible assets for the same period.

Current accounting rules have not helped the cause, with accounting practices, adopted in the US, the UK and internationally, not permitting companies to recognise many of the IP assets they have invested in or created internally, for example in the case of brand. The recognition criteria set out in accounting standards for an asset to be included in the financial statements essentially has three elements, all of which must be satisfied for the asset to be reported in the financial statements. First, it must be controlled by the entity; secondly, it must be expected to generate future economic benefit as a result of that control; and, thirdly, the value of it must be able to be reliably measured.

It is this final requirement that results in many IP assets being absent from financial statements, although certain IP assets such as software and R&D costs can be capitalised in certain circumstances. However, they are only capitalised at cost, not market value, since historic cost meets the criteria of 'reliable measurement' under the accounting rules.

For those readers unfamiliar with accounting statements and the underlying accounting rules, the absence of IP value from corporate reports might simply infer that IP assets are less relevant than other corporate assets. Yet, corporate transactions imply something different, especially since IP assets, such as brands' innovative technologies and patents, are frequently the primary drivers for M&A – how often could that be said about plant and machinery or inventories?

The accounting rules exclude many IP assets from recognition on the grounds that their value cannot be measured reliably and yet is their valuation any less reliable than say the market value of property, plant and equipment, or the estimate of the net realisable value of inventories for resale in say the retail sector? An asset on the balance sheet is by definition an indication of the future income streams (economic benefit) from either its use or sale. Techniques used for IP asset valuation (discussed in more detail later in this chapter) adopt the same accepted valuation methodologies used for other assets, including property and financial assets, and yet are deemed to be less reliable. How can we expect users of accounts to make informed decisions about the potential future performance of an entity if there is no indication in the financial statements as to the key resources, the IP assets that the entity will use to achieve that performance and create value?

Furthermore, there is a significant difference between the treatment of internally generated IP and acquired IP assets which adds to the potential confusion when comparing entities, their resources and their key performance indicators. The sale of the 'Dunlop brand by Sports Direct plc at the end of 2016 is one such sale that demonstrates the independent value of a brand and the inconsistencies in the reporting rules. Dunlop was generating revenues of circa £43 million and Profit before tax was £4 million when the brand was sold to Sumitomo Rubber Industries of Japan for circa £110 million. The sales price represented 28 times profit. The value of the Dunlop brand was not reported in Sports Direct's balance sheet prior to this sale and so users of its financial statements could not have foreseen that it could generate this level of return. As a result, we might ask the question: how reliable are the financial statements and are they really useful to investors?

7. IP value – do the diligence

The business community has to be willing and capable of ensuring that they can account for IP value in all the business decisions they make, whether the accounting rules are helpful or not. This requires that they take an active role in assessing critical IP assets in a business and appreciating how they will contribute to future performance – because these assets are of real value. It is important to identify how much of the expense associated with IP assets is in fact the cost of gaining or maintaining the IP rights, versus the amount that is being invested in IP and therefore expected to bring a corresponding return. This will be different for each IP asset type and different again depending on the sector in which that IP asset is being monetised.

This process is relevant for many, if not all, stakeholders in a business. The stakeholders it is relevant for include the following:

- *Investors* – when comparing potential targets for investment, investors must consider all the assets that the entity owns and relies on in order to generate future returns. Investors must identify entities that will typically rely on IP to generate future returns to enable them to compare these meaningfully to other investments that have, for example, significant levels of tangible or financial assets.

- *Sellers and acquirers* – M&A activity relies on the identification and valuation of core IP assets. Sellers often have to showcase key IP assets and demonstrate how these assets underpin revenue streams in order to secure the best exit price. An estimate of the value of these IP assets is critical in price negotiations. Acquisition strategies are often focused on IP drivers and few deals are struck because the target has great premises or up-to-date machinery. It is more likely that the target is attractive because it has patented technology or a brand that could extend the acquirer's geographical or product reach. An assessment of the value of the target's IP will be part of the project appraisal process in deciding whether or not to proceed with the acquisition or when comparing more than one target.

- *Partners and joint ventures (JVs)* – commercial arrangements that involve parties committing vital corporate resources to projects should prompt the parties to identify, 'ring-fence' or separate and assess the value of those committed resources. Furthermore, IP-leakage is an issue in such arrangements. Imagine a vital trade secret or recipe being lost in a JV. This could impact on all future revenues that the partnership (and IP asset) was intended to generate because 'you can't put the genie back in the bottle'. In addition, valuing IP assets that are being introduced into or committed to a

JV vehicle or partnership, will ensure that you negotiate for a return that is commensurate with your contribution to the project.

- *Lenders* – an increasing number of lenders are now acknowledging that if it can be demonstrated that IP assets underpin future revenue streams then they can be considered for securitised lending. By clearly separating or ring-fencing IP assets in an insolvency remote vehicle, and demonstrating how they can be protected and managed and then assessing their value, often by way of an independent valuation process, they can provide sufficient comfort and security for lenders to provide IP-backed lending solutions.

8. IP valuation

Moving on from IP value and the variety of ways that it is recognised by different parties, the chapter now considers some important aspects of IP valuation. Of course, when it comes to traditional or tangible assets, the valuation is broadly, by definition, an estimate of the future return that an item is likely to generate. This return could arise from:

- its use in the business, like plant and machinery;
- its sale, like inventories or assets deemed for disposal; or
- its recovery, like financial assets and receivables.

However, many people view value as being an estimate of future return, which is by its nature, uncertain. Users of financial information will still place reliance on the valuation of assets provided in a set of accounts, for example irrespective of the fact is has been estimated. This is likely to be because the information is relevant for our future decision making and because we take 'comfort' that the value is reported in the financial statements by someone 'in the know' (the preparation of financial statements is the responsibility of directors), whom we believe is a professional, adhering to an ethical code, adopting generally accepted principles and methodologies for valuation or what we might call standards.

IP valuation does not currently have a specific set of standards; however, it adopts the same accepted valuation methodologies adopted for other assets and if the valuation is performed by a professional and reputable person, with transparent and supportable assumptions, then it can be relied upon to underpin transactions and inform decision making.

The methodologies accepted for the valuation of IP assets (and used for other assets including tangible and financial assets) are:

- *cost method* – based on the principle that the value of IP assets can be represented by the cost to either recreate or replace the assets;
- *income method* – based on the principle that IP assets can be valued using a variety of methods built on the income that the IP assets are believed to help generate or underpin; and
- *market method* – based on the principle that IP assets can be valued by benchmarking them against similar IP assets sold in the open market.

You will of course recognise that each of these methods can result in a different valuation amount for the same IP asset. Therefore, do not underestimate the importance of selecting the most appropriate valuation methodology (or asking a suitable professional to perform it for you) that suits your IP valuation needs whilst being compliant with the accounting guidance. Naturally, when it comes to valuing assets, the market method is seen to provide the most reliable measure of value; however, since there is no active market for the buying and selling of IP assets and very little transparency around the sale or licencing of IP in the current market, this method is rarely used in practice. Yet, that may change in the future if there is more transparency and reporting of IP related transactions and valuations.

The appropriateness of the selected methodology will often be determined by the corporate scenario in which the IP asset is being used, for example a pre-revenue company with no reliable income forecasts is likely to value their patents using the cost method rather than an income-based method; an estimate of the value of a company's brand is more likely to be performed using the income method as the cost of developing the brand (sales and marketing costs) is likely to be less relevant than the future revenues that it is expected to generate.

However, as the importance of IP assets is now being recognised, so too is the valuation of IP assets. IP valuations are being relied upon more often, particularly where those valuations are performed by reputable professionals and are transparent, defensible, justified by reasonable assumptions and which adopt appropriate methodologies. As a result, IP valuations are now being seen to extend the options for IP value recognition, including being used to:

- underpin a range of corporate transactions, including individual IP asset sales, M&A and JVs and partnerships;
- form the basis of negotiations for licensing agreements for IP assets;
- ensure sellers can demonstrate the maximum potential value of the entity on exit;
- make key internal decisions about allocation of resources and investment based on IP mapping and related future revenues from IP assets; and
- provide comfort where IP assets are being used as security for external investment and financing.

9.   IP monetisation principles

Monetisation of an IP asset can be viewed as making money directly from the IP assets. This might involve either assessing its monetary value or the monetary context of the value of the IP assets. That requires an understanding of the various ways to recognise the monetisation of IP assets, whether that's the cost of creation, the cost of acquisition, income from licensing out the IP or simply monetisation by using IP assets to borrow money.

I would say that the most common expression of IP monetisation is putting a value on it and then using it to generate cashflow through a sale and leaseback arrangement. This would involve putting a value on the IP assets in question using one of the three aforementioned cost, market and income valuation methods and then selling the IP assets to a separate corporate vehicle and licensing them back for use.

As noted above, the term 'monetisation' of IP assets can mean different things to different people but in essence it is about expressing the value of IP assets in a way that's represented by some monetary figure, such as a transaction for the purchase/sale of a piece of software for say £500,000: agreeing an appropriate royalty figure (eg, 3%) for the licence of the software and that royalty rate is to be paid as a percentage of sales (underpinned by that software). This may facilitate borrowing from the lender based on the royalty cashflow the IP assets (software) now generate. That borrowing could be two times annual cashflow/royalty.

For example, let's say a small engineering business supplying precision-engineered products and turning over £10 million, secures an independent valuation of its corporate brand. This brand is used on all products, packaging and marketing and let's say the brand is valued at £500,000 on an income-based method. Ignoring the potential tax implications (often tax is not payable on the sale of the IP assets to a related company) the brand is then sold to a separate IP Company (IPCo) and subsequently licensed back to the trading company for an annual royalty, based on an agreed percentage of sales/turnover, let's say 3%. The trading company will pay the IPCo £300,000 in annual royalties assuming the turnover remains static at £10 million per annum. Now this is monetisation; as the IP asset (brand) has been independently valued at £500,000 and is now generating £300,000 in annual revenues through the royalty rate-based arrangement. This rate must be a 'reasonable royalty' and is often referenced in the initial valuation (particularly if they used the income method) using third-party comparable royalty rates. In addition, a process needs to take place to assess the quality of the brand in relation to the 'comparables' and make any reasonable adjustment to the royalty rate.

Now let's assume the trading company wins a big order one year later and this increases turnover to £15 million per annum. The royalty rate remains the same but the level of royalty income will increase by 50% in line with the increase in turnover. The royalty income is now £450,000 per annum. This income could be further monetised by borrowing money against this trading income (£450,000 per annum) of the IPCo, ie the annual royalty, linked to the owned IP assets (the brand). Any lender now has a much clearer understanding of the value of the brand to the trading company, can get security and control over it through the IPCo and in certain circumstances may then offer to lend an amount up to two times annual income, so £900,000 (2 x £450,000 annual royalty). This improved visibility and the ring fencing of IP assets in IPCo's can both provide comfort to lenders and help the trading businesses better recognise the true value of IP assets.

Turnover £10 million – Year 1	Balance Sheet (income-based valuation) £500,000 Annual royalty (3%) £300,000 Cashflow valuation (based on royalty x 2) £600,000
Turnover £15 million – Year 2	Balance sheet valuation £500,000 Annual royalty increases to £450,000 Cashflow valuation (based on royalty x 2) £900,000

In brief, the balance sheet implications of the above transaction are that the brand was never on the balance sheet of the engineering business as you cannot capitalise the cost of an internally generated brand. However, by putting a value on that IP (brand) and creating a transaction by selling it to a separate company (the IPCo), that does add (in this case) £500,000 to the balance sheet of the engineering business which sold the brand. It also puts both an acquired intangible asset value of £500,000 and a liability of £500,000 (the amount owed for acquiring the brand) onto the balance sheet of the IPCo and so it has a nil effect on the IPCo. If they are related companies, then there is often no tax to pay on this transaction.

In short, IP value, management, strategy and valuation are now being prioritised within businesses and form a vital element in all corporate strategies. Stakeholders should consider if they are basing their business and investment decisions on the tip of the iceberg only (the physical assets) as shown in Figure 1 (above) or have they really considered the biggest driver of value in the business, the IP assets 'below the water level'.

10. Chapter summary

- Intangibles are widely regarded as key corporate resources of successful businesses, yet measuring their value is not easy.
- A board of directors, though perfectly aligned on the vision and goals of the business, are often misaligned on the importance and value of IP assets in achieving those goals.
- Developing an inventory of IP assets is critical to understanding better the value of the IP assets to a business.
- Proper diligence is required to understand the full extent and condition of the critical IP assets and their value to the business.
- IP valuation is a well-established practice despite variations in its approach and application, furthermore it is becoming increasingly important to strategic business decision making.
- IP monetisation is often about exploring sophisticated ways of leveraging an investment in IP assets and creating a monetary stream through different corporate structures.

Encouraging and supporting innovation

Alex Tame
Tame IP Ltd

1.   Introduction

Before diving into the area of innovation and exploring some of the aspects that help to create a sustainable innovation pipeline, the term 'innovation' needs to be defined.

As a recently qualified graduate I started my professional career working in the shipbuilding industry and as part of my rotation scheme, I spent three months working on continuous improvement initiatives throughout the shipyard. We incentivised all employees across the organisation to submit their ideas to help improve working practices, their environments and identify ways to reduce manufacturing time (without detriment to quality). We had engagement for this from across the business. I spent many hours listening to a wide variety of initiatives and ideas from the relatively obvious (such as moving litter bins to more appropriate locations) to the ridiculous. No idea was rejected without first listening to the employee and our team always provided a fair assessment and maintained a continuous line of communication to the work force to ensure that ideas kept flowing. One specific idea for time saving when cleaning ships managed to save over 400 man hours of labour. The solution was somewhat obvious in hindsight; simply tilt the ship 45 degrees when cleaning to enable the water to run off and aide the cleaning process.

A few years ago, I asked two corporate chief executive officers (CEOs) for their view on innovation and to provide a few innovative examples from within their organisations. Both agreed that good innovation has the 'surprise' factor, something that they don't expect to see. One CEO pointed to a new business unit that was developed from an employee's single idea that had been raised ten years previously. The individual had been circulating his idea to a number of senior directors and executives, each time being rejected. Then one director finally spotted the potential in the idea and helped him to realise it. Today that business unit is turning over a significant return. In another example, a CEO suggested moving the cash registers in their retail stores from above to under the counters to create more space.

These examples, and many others, highlight the challenge faced when considering the term 'innovation'. Quite simply, innovation has many differing facets and has different meanings to different people in different companies and cultures. In other words, finding a single/one-size-fits-all solution to the innovation challenge in the corporate world is virtually impossible and it's therefore not so much an activity that can be adopted or rolled out within the corporate structure but more of a cultural mind-set: a way of 'being' and 'behaving'.

I've frequently seen and heard CEOs attempting to launch new innovation challenges. This normally ignites the organisation to insert the word 'innovation' into a range of job titles, start a recruitment drive and update employee objectives to ensure delivery of new 'innovations'. This often leads to failure and before long the enthusiasm dwindles and the organisation returns to normality.

Typically, large organisations, especially the more the traditional ones, struggle to change the culture of their businesses. When it comes to innovation, we are experiencing a growing number of disruptive innovators who are causing the more traditional players to reconsider their response to the changing dynamic. The hi-tech industry in particular has been affected by these changes; especially as more disruptive innovators break through into the corporate world. Companies such as Dropbox, Spotify, WhatsApp and Uber continue to deliver fresh innovation and while they shift from start-up to small/medium enterprises (SME) to global corporates, they somehow manage to maintain a strong ethos and culture of innovation.

Successful corporates with a strong culture of innovation (for example, Apple, Amazon, Facebook and Google) have worked hard to maintain the small 'start-up' mentality that they started out with in the early days. Their culture of innovation is something that is valued, protected, encouraged and supported throughout all levels of the organisation. Initiatives, such as Google's well documented '20% time' and other similar concepts help to remind managers to preserve an innovation mind-set through the employees as it develops and expands.[1]

There may not be a quick approach to cracking the challenge of innovation within the corporate world but there are a number of lessons to learn from those who are experiencing success and pitfalls to avoid from those who struggle.

2.   The importance of innovation

It may sound obvious but unless there is a clear vision and focus regarding the desired output then the initiative will be doomed to failure from the outset. There are two important questions you need to ask. What is the overriding purpose? What are you hoping to achieve? Some answers might include:

- solving customer problems;
- winning new customers;
- entering new markets;
- creating new products;
- improving internal processes;
- improving efficiencies;
- raising brand awareness;
- repositioning image; or
- developing a global good.

---

1   To read more about Google's '20% time', see the Forbes article on the topic, available at www.forbes.com/sites/johnkotter/2013/08/21/googles-best-new-innovation-rules-around-20-time/ #22543a8768b8. The article suggests a range of guidelines and rules that could be adopted.

Ultimately, an innovation strategy, as with a corporate business strategy, must be laser focused and clearly communicated to ensure that it has a chance of success. If the scope is unclear then attempts to innovate will only lead to distractive innovation with little or no value. It takes time to get it right.

A senior director once mentioned to me that he instructed his research and development (R&D) team to "fail more". He viewed failure as a positive step on the innovation journey. He thought that failures should be encouraged and rewarded, provided that lessons are learned so that truly innovative ideas and concepts will flourish.

3.   The importance of community

The innovation community is the critical component that will determine success (or failure) and in corporate world, knowing who the key players are is vital. R&D, product development, marketing and technology areas all offer different elements that, depending on the mission, will help determine where you focus your energy.

Corporates will also have certain 'known' individuals who you might want to target, those who are known for being creative and innovative in their approach: lead engineers, chief designers, master inventors, notable patent inventors, subject matter experts etc. This group of individuals form an important function within the innovation community. Not only do they offer a useful and rich source of innovative ideas but they will have a positive and influential impact on the wider community.[2]

An important point to note on community relates to the role that the central/global function plays versus the local market where IP is being created. Many corporate businesses are structured with a hub and spoke model and this can lead to R&D or product development teams being spread over different locations and with different reporting lines. Depending on the wider business strategy, an effective innovation programme needs to consider the cultural impact and decision-making rationale in this context.

There are many books available that cover the topic of business culture[3] and the differences can be quite striking, especially in term of communication. The *Harvard Business Review*[4] highlights four categories that can impede success:

- direct versus indirect communication;
- trouble with accents and fluency;
- different attitudes toward hierarchy and authority; and
- conflicting norms for decision making.

I would also add a fifth category to highlight the difference between cultures that are centred around the success of the team (ie, Japan) versus the success of the individual (ie, the US).

Take for example a company with the R&D team split across different countries

2   To further explore this area, see IBM's 'Master Inventors', available at https://en.wikipedia.org/wiki/IBM_Master_Inventor.

3   www.trainingindustry.com/blog/blog-entries/4-types-of-communication-challenges-in-multicultural-organizations.aspx.

4   https://hbr.org/2006/11/managing-multicultural-teams.

such as Japan and the US. The approach to innovation on the two sides will be quite different as Japanese culture is based around a value system whereby respect and honour (to superiors) and pride in the work ethic is integral to the ethos of the team. By contract, self-accomplishment and confidence are traits that would be prevalent on the US side. This presents a challenge for communication and recognition (or reward) of success in any innovation programme. Sadly, many innovation initiatives fizzle out early on in the life cycle as cultural differences across the organisation are not addressed, especially in terms of the communication channels.

4.   The importance of communication

Many innovation programmes fail within months of grand launches, and the reason behind this is clear: a lack of communication and inactive engagement to keep the community up to date and informed.

Communication needs to be regular and consistent with clear service-level agreements (SLAs) at every stage in the process. When communication stops, people lose interest and fail to engage or offer support when the initiative is relaunched at a later date.

The type of media used for communication within the organisation is another important factor that is often overlooked. The traditional view with respect to using email or paper newsletters and memos is no longer sustainable. Email continues to swamp work lives, and as inboxes fill up with more urgent work matters, corporate communications are (more often than not) left unread and/or deleted.

Different corporate organisations will each have a different view as to what works best in their organisation but it's well worth giving consideration to the wealth of new and innovative digital communication channels that are emerging. Above all, face-to-face interaction is the best means of communication.

5.   The importance of key contacts

In large organisations, it's essential to know who the key contacts are, especially the stakeholders/decision makers who will inevitably determine the level of success of an innovation programme. Running a successful innovation pipeline requires the leader to be a master of the corporate political dynamic, managing upwards, while at the same time managing the innovation flow and effectively communicating within the network.

For companies with multi-site locations it is worth considering who the key innovation supporters and influencers are. This group can be invaluable as they are the ambassadors. So spending more time with this group of employees will be beneficial as they are the people who spread the innovation message across their own personal networks.

Human resources (HR), payroll and the finance teams also need to be actively engaged, especially when it comes to reward, recognition and remuneration.

6.   The importance of support

Companies adopting a successful innovation programme give due consideration to the various support mechanisms that are involved, especially in terms of the balance of in-house resource versus outsourced support. Whatever the balance, the key is to keep focused on the innovation pipeline and the desired successful outcome.

Assessing the need to bring in external resources to remove administration and other barriers from the process, speed up decision-making and source expert consultancy all need due consideration.

7.   The importance of intellectual property

Intellectual property (IP) is a by-product of any innovation programme, but ultimately IP will be created; and this can take a variety of forms from copyright to trade secrets to know-how to patents. Many of these topics are covered in more detail elsewhere in this book. The remainder of this chapter considers the role of patents, the considerations required in the corporate environment and the key players involved.

8.   Key players – the inventor community

The inventor community are arguably the most important players in the corporate setup. Engineers, technical experts and R&D personnel provide the innovation pipeline with a stream of ideas and inventions that feed into the patent filing system for subsequent commercial and technical assessment. Many of these ideas will flow from the innovation projects and programmes undertaken across the organisation.

As ideas flow across the organisation, the key to success is to establish a process that is supported by the necessary resources and software tools to manage the workload effectively. Get this balance wrong, and you can quickly drown under the volume of ideas flowing and mismanagement of inventor expectations. Get the balance right, and you will reap the rewards of a fully functional, well-oiled process that ensures that good quality inventions are progressed while quickly rejecting those ideas that are not suited to the strategy.

The key to success with the inventor community (as with the other key players in the process) is to build a healthy relationship. The IP manager who builds a solid relationship with their inventor community, understanding their motives, drivers and interests will ensure that the filing programme runs smoothly. Engineers enjoy talking about their work, so spending time listening and finding out about their projects and programmes helps to build a healthy relationship and an open and honest dialogue. This approach, while time consuming, helps the IP manager to understand the various types of innovation that are happening 'on the ground' and starts to build up a picture of where the most valuable IP is likely to be generated across the organisation. Through this system of open dialogue, the IP manager is also able to manage expectations with the inventor community regarding the status of their inventions. Too many invention processes fall down when inventors submit ideas into the central system but then fail to receive any feedback or, when they do, they find that projects have moved on, or worse still, a disclosure has occurred. Every inventor will claim that their ideas are the most valuable and the most efficient. IP managers should ensure that they avoid reacting to the 'he who shouts loudest' syndrome and stick to the process SLAs.

IP managers must also be mindful of those inventors who leave their idea submissions to the last minute, forcing the IP team to prioritise their submission due to impeding deadlines for disclosure. Building a healthy relationship with the inventor community will ensure that such pitfalls are avoided as far as is possible.

9. Key players – the IPR coordinators

As mentioned above, building a healthy relationship with the inventor community can be time-consuming, especially in a large corporate setting with inventors spread across multiple national sites and different countries. Face-to-face time with inventors to learn and listen is incredibly important to ensure you have an efficient process that is meeting the needs of the inventor community and managing expectations. However, in large organisations, there is a growing trend of intellectual property rights (IPR) coordinators being appointed to support the IP manager, offering assistance 'on the ground' with local inventors and management.

These IPR coordinators are becoming a critical part of the IP set up as they are able to facilitate engagement at a local level by managing and coordinating new ideas/inventions to the central team and by liaising in patent attorney engagement, IP promotion and education.

For some companies, these IPR coordinators are appointed as full-time employees, located in strategic departments, areas of high level strategic importance or where there is an active inventor community. Other companies look to their inventor pool for those engineers who have an interest and passion in IP, offering a small percentage of their working time to support the central IP function.

This network of IP coordinators is critical to the success of the IP function, and the more efficient IP managers will spend most of their time building strong relationships with this community, educating and keeping them fully informed and up-to-date with changes that are going on centrally to ensure that the local IP coordinators are able to spread the message to areas of the business in a quick and efficient manner.

In some cases, where new ideas/inventions are in plentiful supply, these IPR coordinators are able to help triage and push forward those ideas that are deemed a higher priority to the business and this in terms helps to relieve pressure of the patent engineers.

10. Key players – patent engineers

Patent engineers are an incredibly valuable resource to the IP function. Whilst Patent attorneys have specialist skills in claim construction and patent filing and drafting etc, the patent engineer is able to sit down with the inventors and flesh out their ideas in more detail, extracting the key technical components and helping to shape the invention in a manner that can be passed over to the patent attorney in order to make their work more efficient and focused.

Typically, patent engineers are experienced inventors who can very quickly understand and grasp the technical components in a variety of circumstances and in many cases, these patent engineers are able to help improve the initial idea and strengthen the invention.

To some extent, the role of the patent engineer could be viewed as an outsourced component of part of the patent attorney. Generally speaking, good quality patent attorneys are in short supply (and in high demand) so the role of the patent engineer is an effective and efficient way to assist with the overall process. As a result, patent engineers are becoming more prominent in large organisations.

The cost of filing a patent application is expensive, and the ongoing cost commitment over the coming years is a significant investment for any company to consider. To that end, many companies are now running novelty and prior art searches for ideas that they deem suitable for potential filing and these searches offer a number of advantages.

First, for a relatively modest cost you can determine whether there is significant prior art already in existence that would limit the value of proceeding with a filing. This would obviously save significant cost in the long run. Secondly, the search will provide an indication of the state of the art and help to identify areas of potential white space, in other words, where the skilled patent attorney should focus the claim of the application.

As for the patent engineer, they can facilitate this process either by using an outsourced supplier, or by using one of the many software tools that are available and running the searches in-house. Quite quickly, the patent engineer is able to eliminate those ideas that would otherwise have been filed and provide real cost savings to the business.

Moreover, the patent engineer can help to manage the inventor community and assist with stakeholder management and reporting, as they will have a good handle on the invention flow, possible cost management downstream and the shape of the portfolio going forward.

11.   Key players – stakeholders

In many large organisations, there are multiple stakeholders that need to be engaged with and managed in regards to the patent operation. This will range from the Chief Executive Officer (CEO), to the Chief Technical Officer (CTO), finance directors, R&D personnel, strategy personnel etc.

Many companies have established patent committees to facilitate decision-making. Decisions such as patent filing, foreign filing, patent office responses and brokerage are among the many decisions required and patent committees can be highly effective within an organisation, but equally, they can stifle progress as decisions made by committees require consensus and they take time, invariably slowing down the overall process.

The most efficient organisations appoint a trusted decision maker who is empowered and supported to run the process; to be accountable and responsible for the decisions, and entrusted to seek advice and input from various stakeholders prior to making the final decision.

There are plenty of management books available which talk about stakeholder management; the principle is the same whether its related to IP of any other business matter – they key is to learn the language of the stakeholders and communicate with them on their terms and in a language they understand, keeping points short, simple and to the point. Bring recommendations rather than problems and provide regular high level updates.

It's also worth giving consideration to the priority that IP is given within the senior levels of the organisation. For some companies, IP is a highly strategic matter that needs to be discussed on a regular basis across the C-suite; for others, it is merely an activity that is used to encourage and motivate the engineering community.

12. Key players – subject matter experts

The area of subject matter is often much overlooked in the corporate environment. If this area is utilised appropriately it can offer great value to the IP operation of the organisation. Larger corporate organisations face a continual challenge for those employees who are destined for management versus those employees who are on more of a technical career path. It is often the case that brilliantly gifted technical engineers are forced into managerial roles and within a short space of time they fail in their new role. These engineers require career progression that rewards and recognises their technical capabilities rather than being forced on to a managerial ladder for which they are not suited.

Some large engineering and high-tech firms have recognised this challenge and the last few decades has seen the emergence of Technology Academies and Technical Career Paths that have been specifically designed and tailored to support and meet the need of those employees within the engineering community. This is enabling engineers to move up the technical career ladder towards distinguished and master engineer status or even fellows of the technology community.

This esteemed group of technical experts, especially those who reach the higher levels within their organisation, are a vital and very important component of an officially run IP organisation. Typically, this group of engineers are world experts in their field, known beyond the boundaries of their corporate organisations and are frequently tapped up by recruitment head-hunters.

In a large corporate environment where ideas are steadily flowing into the central IP team from across the organisation, the challenge is always to identify quickly and efficiently those ideas which offer significant potential value to the organisation's portfolio. Using this group of technical subject matter experts enables the organisation to ensure that higher 'value' ideas are protected and improves the overall value of the IP portfolio. If the subject matter expert gives a particular idea the green light, then with an element of confidence you can be sure the idea is strong and worth investment.

Furthermore, to ensure effective portfolio management, these technical experts are able to give guidance regarding the direction that the patent application is taking and apply that knowledge to their specialist technical field to ensure and help get the best value of the patent application for the business.

Typically, this select and elite group of subject matter experts are influencing the technology strategy of the company and are in frequent dialogue with senior directors. As such, they are fantastic ambassadors for the IP message and in many cases, they will be prolific inventors within the organisation.

13. Key players – patent attorneys

Patent attorneys play an essential role within the innovation set-up across the organisation. Where possible they should be treated as an extension to the team and involved in the innovation programme from the beginning. After all, your patent attorney will be looking to get the best possible protection for your innovation and ensure its commercial alignment to the business.

From my experience, more successful innovation programmes are those where the patent attorneys have been fully engaged from the start and there has been an open, honest and transparent dialogue and flow of information across all parties.

This can prove challenging where the attorneys' support is outsourced, but as with many aspects of business, success comes from building and developing a closer working relationship.

14. Reward and recognition

Reward and recognition comes in many shapes and forms and cuts across different cultures and different age ranges. It has different meaning to different people and overseeing any type of reward and recognition scheme within an organisation can be time-consuming, complicated and a drain on resources.

However, it is a vital component of the central IP function and one that must be taken very seriously to ensure that you are running and overseeing a successful IP function.

14.1 Reward

The key to success when it comes to reward is striking the right balance between the remuneration offered to inventors and ensuring that it drives the right behaviour from across the organisation.

Most companies will offer a monetary reward payment to their inventors who are named on patents that get filed. The amount paid will vary from company to company but invariably the challenge is to set the amounts at the right level to ensure that it drives the right behaviour from their inventor community and fairly rewards those who contribute the most value to the IP portfolio.

If the monetary reward is set too high, the IP processes may get flooded with frivolous ideas that will absorb significant resources from the central team and subsequently the vast majority will be rejected. If the reward level is set too low, then engaging the engineering community to come forward with their ideas for consideration will be a struggle and it is also highly likely that the more valuable ideas will go unseen and, worse, perhaps be leaked from the organisation.

There is also a cultural component to the reward mechanism which needs to be considered: for example, a key question is: do you set a global (one size fits all) reward policy that covers your entire company or do you tailor the reward policy offering differing monetary awards in differing locations or countries? While a single central reward policy is easier to manage, it will drive different behaviours in different locations. Take for example an organisation with research engineers located in Turkey, Germany and South Africa. A central reward policy in this example could potentially encourage a plentiful selection of ideas to be submitted from Turkey and South Africa but may stifle engagement from the German research engineers. The balance comes from looking at reward in the context of the overall company strategy, identifying where the most strategic ideas are likely to originate and structuring your reward programme to encourage inventors working in those programmes and areas to come forward.

The second level of reward that is typically offered by companies is triggered when a patent first reaches its granted status. The challenge here is again to set the reward at an appropriate level for the organisation, considering that grant is likely to occur several years after the initial filing took place. The issue is that some inventors may have left the organisation, and recognising that the value of a granted patent is likely to be deemed higher than at the time it was filed needs to be considered.

Finally, there are examples of companies that pay inventors for patents that are deemed to be in use. This is a highly complicated area and invariably there are a variety of methodologies for determining value and working out the most appropriate amounts to be paid to inventors.

It's also worth noting that depending on the nationality of the inventor, their employment status and location may have an impact on their reward and remuneration. German inventor law, for example, is highly complicated and as with other countries it's worth checking the national inventor laws as part of any inventor reward programme.[5]

14.2   Recognition

Recognition is often a much overlooked area and it is surprising how, with a little effort, you can have a big impact in the corporate world regarding recognition.

In 2015, I commissioned a piece of research to benchmark reward schemes in different sectors and in different companies; the results were quite striking. In general, engineers and inventors who were new to an organisation or relatively new in their career were certainly more motivated by the monetary reward aspects of inventory award programmes. However, for engineers and technical experts who were the more seasoned inventors, monetary reward was less appealing than recognition. This group of inventors are generally more driven and motivated by recognition within their organisation and across their peers especially when they are seen as leading technology experts in their field.

From an IP management point of view, this value can be harnessed through the various IP communication channels that are reported around the business. Examples might include highlighting top inventors on regular reports and issuing news updates to the inventor community, with a focus on particular engineers and inventors.

Some companies feature a patent wall in prominent office locations as an open reminder to all employees (and visitors) of the significance that IP places within their organisation. Qualcomm's patent wall is perhaps the most well-known across the industry,[6] although other companies, such as Tesla, are taking a slightly different approach to showcasing their innovation.[7]

---

5   To explore the area of reward and recognition in more detail see the results of the CMS "Employee Inventor Rewards Survey", available at https://cms.law/en/content/download/78468/2996037/version/1/file/Employee%20inventor%20rewards%20survey.pdf and associated articles that have been written since its publication, available at https://cms.law/en/AUT/News-Information/CMS-Survey-on-Reward-Schemes-For-Employee-Inventions.

6   http://pwe.qualcomm.com/.

7   gas2.org/2014/06/23/the-tesla-patent-wall-before-and-after/.

From my experience, the patent wall serves an important purpose; for inventors to see their name in lights on the patent wall is a very powerful motivation tool for the organisation to use. Other examples might include hosting an annual dinner with the C-suite for the top inventors, handing out trophies and plaques featuring inventor patents etc. Whilst many of these recognition ideas may seem a little quirky, the power that these have for inventors should not be underestimated, especially in the way that they are presented to the individuals and seen among their peers.

Several years ago, I handed over a patent plaque to an inventor located in Spain; as part of the presentation I had arranged for the local CTO to pop down and spend five minutes presenting the plaque and talking to the inventor. That inventor still recalls that moment with pride and will probably remember that significant milestone in his career for many years to come.

There are cultural elements to reward and recognition too; in some cultures, such as in Japan, there is a very strong team ethic so it is worth giving consideration to how you can reward and recognise the team contribution rather than simply highlighting a specific inventor. By contrast, in the UK, Germany and the US for example, the focus is much more on the individual contribution.

Above all when it comes to reward and recognition, remember that it's not just about the financial reward.

15. Portfolio management

Portfolio management is a critical component of the central IP function and in a corporate organisation with a large portfolio of patents, decisions need to be made frequently and each one will have an impact on the IP budget and resources required to carry out the necessary actions.

Decisions are needed at every step of the process from invention capture through to management of the granted portfolio of patents. Invariably, throughout the process, IP functions are continually looking to automate as many decisions as possible to ensure the smooth running of the portfolio management function.

Consideration needs to be given to a range of factors, such as whether the patents are relevant to competitor products. Key questions are: could they be leveraged against other entities that are seen as a threat to the business? How are the patents being utilised within the organisation? It's also imperative to have a good understanding of the value that your patent portfolio presents to the business, not just in terms of direct licensing or sales revenue potential but also as an asset class that adds value to the overall business.

15.1 Invention harvesting

As inventions and ideas flow into the central IP function it's important to triage very quickly and eliminate any ideas that are less interesting/strategic to the business and focus resources on ideas that are deemed more 'valuable'. One of the dangers facing IP departments at this early stage in the process is spending too much time and energy exploring frivolous ideas with inventors that, whilst they may be patentable, are of little strategic use to the business. Adopting a process and methodology to assess ideas quickly and triage inventions as they float through the pipeline is critical to avoiding causing unnecessary bottlenecks and tying up valuable resources that could otherwise be utilised more effectively elsewhere in the process.

As ideas are accepted into the system, patent engineers and IP managers will start to have more in-depth discussions with the inventors and engineers, unpacking their initial idea in more detail. This will in many cases involve novelty and landscape searches etc. During this process, the IP manager will need to be continually assessing these ideas against a set of criteria that will determine whether the idea still fits the profile required for the portfolio.

The criteria used to assess ideas will differ from company to company, and today, many corporate organisations have developed their own in-house ranking and scoring methodologies. Understandably, most organisations keep their scoring methodologies a tightly-guarded secret, but in general these methodologies will typically address the following type of technical and commercial questions:

- How different is the invention to the state of the art?
- Is the invention a game changer/market disruptor?
- How financially sensible would it be to implement the solution?
- How easy is it to detect the solution?
- How long is the proposed invention likely to be used?
- Will the end customer have a better experience specifically due to the invention?
- What is the size of the market specifically related to the invention?
- Who are the key IP holders in this technology area?

Some companies have developed scoring mechanisms related to their internal assessments; setting a level that if reached commits the idea to filing or abandonment if the score falls short of the target. For other companies, these assessments are used as the basis for a discussion with the patent committee where a consensus view is sought before making a final decision.

Software companies and service providers are also developing scoring methodologies to assist their client's effective portfolio management.[8]

Patents are a long-term investment and whilst there is an initial cost for filing and drafting, the central IP team must consider the long-term budget impact of committing an idea to a filing. It's also worth noting that from my experiences, companies and inventors find it very difficult to abandon patents later in the process when a significant cost has already been committed. To that end, it's well worth considering alternative options to filing such as publication and keeping the invention as a trade secret.

However, if an organisation chooses to harvest, rank and score it's ideas and inventions, the key is to ensure you have a harmonised and consistent approach.

---

8   A couple of interesting examples include the Patent Asset Index™ by PatentSight, available at www.patentsight.com, and the Ocean Tomo Rating™ system, available at www.oceantomo.com/ratings_uspto.

15.2   Patent prosecution

After the initial patent application has been filed, the IP team will need to consider the foreign filing strategy required for the invention. This can be a costly exercise as the more broadly you choose to protect your invention, the more expensive the initial outlay (drafting, filing and translations for each country chosen) and long-term cost commitment. To that end, many companies are spending more time and effort reviewing their patent applications around 10 months after first filing to ensure more effective and efficient cost management, and in some cases, patent applications will be abandoned rather than protection expanded. The decision-making criteria will be somewhat similar to the points raised in the previous section, but by this stage, they will take into account the search results presented by the patent office as a significant factor regarding next steps.

Throughout the prosecution phase, the assessment criteria will need to be re-applied as the various patent offices respond with their examination reports and other various office actions need to be considered. Each of these can be costly and, fundamentally each decision made by the IP function will have a knock-on effect that needs careful consideration.

15.3   Granted patents

For organisations with large patent portfolios the annuity bill is the costliest aspect of the IP budget and as such, is usually under the scrutiny of the finance department on a regular basis.

From a portfolio management perspective, the IP function is required to review the granted patents in the portfolio on a regular (typically annual) basis and assess whether they are still fit for purpose. There are now many software tools available to assist with this process (eg, PatentSight, Patsnap and Questel Orbit). In some cases, scoring and ranking algorithms have been created and these can be especially helpful when dealing with a large corporate portfolio.

An additional factor that may be considered at this stage of the process is the monetisation potential of the patent. Patents deemed not suitable for retention may have market value and therefore may be worth retaining for subsequent sale.

16.   Conclusion

Innovation has a variety of interpretations, and different companies will deploy different strategies around innovation specific to their business requirements. The key to running a successful innovation programme is to ensure senior-level support from the very beginning, to be laser focused and to ensure that your organisation has realistic expectations as to what the programme will deliver.

IP is a by-product of the innovation programme and requires a clear focus on building strong relationships with the stakeholders, the inventor community and those needed to support the overall IP operation. The challenge for any IP manager at the centre of this function is to manage expectations from across the business, communicating with both senior stakeholders and the inventors while establishing and managing resources to efficiently process the flow of ideas and management of the patent portfolio.

17. Chapter summary

To ensure you build a sustainable innovation programme you need to do the following:

- ensure there is a clear vision and focus for the programme from the outset;
- ask who the key players are that will determine its success;
- maintain regular and consistent communication as this will help to manage expectations and ensure continual engagement;
- ask who the contacts are that the programme lead should focus 80% of their time, effort and energy with for maximum benefit;
- gather additional external support from software, service and legal providers as this can help ensure internal resources are used more efficiently;
- consider the fact that IP is always a by-product of innovation; and
- finally, remember that the incentive to innovate isn't just about future revenue.

Focus on the key players when managing the central IP function:
- the inventor community;
- the IPR coordinators;
- the patent engineers;
- the stakeholders;
- the subject matter experts; and
- the patent attorneys.

Developing an IP strategy

Gareth Jones
SwiftKey

1. Introduction

There are many ways to set up an intellectual property (IP) strategy, and there is no one 'right' way. The aim of this chapter is to provide inspiration using a series of four suggested steps. It is hoped that when setting up an IP strategy for your business or for your client, the guidance given here will prompt you to consider aspects of the IP strategy you might not have otherwise considered.

Figure 1: The steps to an IP strategy

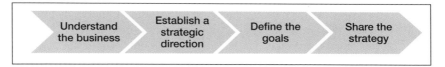

The four steps proposed in this chapter when setting up an IP strategy are shown in Figure 1. What constitutes an ideal IP strategy is entirely dependent on the business, and so the most important thing to do when setting up an IP strategy is to understand as much about the business as possible. Before you can consider the detail of what needs to be done, it's important to decide why IP is important to the business and what exactly it is you are trying to achieve in the form of a strategic direction. Only then can you start to identify the specific goals that will advance the business in the intended direction when achieved. You will probably then need to share the strategy with the wider business, whether to seek approval or to encourage the collaboration necessary for an efficient implementation.

2. Understand the business

Figure 2: The steps to an IP strategy: understand the business

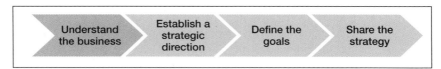

Businesses can differ in many ways, for example, by size, market, technology, business

model, geography and culture. To add significant value to a business, the IP strategy should be very closely aligned with the wider strategy of the business, and therefore IP strategies can differ as much as businesses can. Even if two businesses appear to be very similar, the most valuable IP strategy for one may be vastly different from the ideal strategy for the other; this may be because they have different definitions of success, different approaches to implementation or something else is subtly different about the context of the business. It is unlikely that you will develop a useful IP strategy without first learning as much as possible about the business itself.

The aspects of the organisation that are most relevant to the IP strategy will vary from business to business, so you'll need to understand as much as possible and probably more than is necessary, in order to determine what is actually important. Two things that will always be paramount are, first, to learn about the business strategy and, secondly, to determine the current IP position. To determine the other relevant aspects, it is important to understand the business context.

2.1 Learn about the business strategy

Without understanding the business strategy, you won't be able to understand the direction in which the business is heading and you won't be able to align the IP strategy in the same direction. Whilst the output from IP activities can sometimes drive changes to the business strategy, it is the business strategy that fundamentally drives the IP strategy. The term 'business strategy' is used here in the broadest sense, to encompass the mission, vision, goals and operating plans of the business, over all time periods, and for all products and divisions. Each of these may have an impact on IP strategy.

Business strategies can focus on various corporate goals, including increasing profit, increasing market share, growth, liquidity events for investor exits or simply survival. The implementation of the strategies themselves can also be wildly different, for example, vertical integration across the buyer or supplier chain, horizontal integration through diversification or acquisition, price-skimming, product differentiation, divestiture, retrenchment and liquidation. IP strategy can support these different strategies in many ways:

- to increase profit an IP strategy could focus on risk reduction and outbound licensing, and potentially sacrifice feature exclusivity (assuming the impact on market share would have less of an impact on profit);
- to increase market share IP enforcement could be used to drive feature exclusivity and brand value, and win over customers;
- to increase growth an IP strategy could underpin prospects in new markets through IP asset acquisition, either to gain access to new technology or improve freedom-to-operate positions;
- to boost the chances of a successful exit for private equity investors an IP strategy may be focused on risk reduction and freedom to operate, targeted organic portfolio growth to appeal to potential acquirers, inorganic portfolio growth to satisfy IPO investors, a licensing-based fall-back strategy for a failure to achieve commercial success, or any combination of these; or
- to support business survival an IP strategy can use indiscriminate sales or

licensing of assets to secure revenues, asset securitisation to obtain capital, or asset divestiture to reduce costs.

A business may have a very simple strategy, or it may adopt a more sophisticated one. Sophisticated business strategies can comprise a number of different complex strategies and multiple objectives; these may relate to different divisions or products, some may be dependent on each other and some may conflict and even be mutually exclusive. The strategy objectives may differ over different timescales, such as, cost control in the near term or market leadership in the long term. Having a complex business strategy is not necessarily related to the type of business, and may simply be due to the strategic approach taken by the leadership team.

A single business strategy may have a number of possible likely outcomes, whether intended or not, and they should all be considered, as IP can often still provide value for the negative business outcomes; for example, recuperating returns on IP investment through asset sales or licensing during times of instability or uncertainty. It's unlikely to be efficient to consider all possible outcomes, but some will be more likely than others and it's these on which you should focus your IP strategy. There may be some low likelihood but high impact outcomes that should also be considered, and so you may find it useful to rank outcomes by both likelihood and impact to aid your selection.

2.2   Determine the current IP position

Following consideration of the business strategy, the other key area on which to focus (because it has such a direct relevance) is the IP position of the business. The current IP position of a business will guide the IP strategist on areas of weakness and strength, and therefore on which IP goals or activities will most likely improve the IP position.

One way to obtain a complete understanding of the IP position is to undertake an IP audit. There are many ways to do this, from simply searching for IP audit or due diligence checklists and doing it yourself, or engaging a specialist such as an IP consultant or patent attorney to perform one on your behalf. IP audits will not only help to identify and document all IP assets and risks, they can also identify the strengths and weaknesses that will directly inform an IP strategy.

The state of the IP position may be defined by various factors, including the size of the IP asset portfolios, the geographical and product/feature/brand protection these portfolios provide, other factors affecting the quality and value of the portfolios: how much the business has invested in IP to date, maturity of IP processes and management, internal IP awareness and culture or even just how fundamentally important IP is to a particular business.

As well as an inward-looking view on the IP position, it's important to consider issues from an external point of view. The factors above defining the state of the IP position should be considered against competitors, suppliers, customers, partners and adjacent markets and similar technology areas. You should also ask a number of questions: which third parties own patents in the same technology or solution areas? Which third parties operate in which jurisdictions with similar brands, even if in different goods and services markets? Who has the most significant patent portfolio for the product's primary features? Who has the most valuable employees and know-how? Finally, who appears to have trade secrets that protect key product aspects? Understanding the fundamental IP strengths and weaknesses, and how these compare with the outside world, will be helpful in identifying areas of focus for an IP strategy.

The IP risks also need to be evaluated. IP is not just about building portfolios of valuable assets, it's also about reducing risk. When deciding what to include in your IP strategy you need to understand what the primary IP risks are to the business, and what the sources of those risks are (for example, internally from all employees or specific teams or externally from competitors, suppliers, or other third parties such as domain or trademark squatters,[1] or Non-Practising Entities (NPE)[2]). Once you understand the risks, you can consider how to reduce or mitigate those risks, for example, how to leverage your IP assets or how to design around infringement issues.

2.3   Understand the business context

As well as the business strategy and the IP position, there are many other factors that might help to better understand the business and influence the IP strategy. Some areas of business context you may want to consider include: an understanding of the different product lines, the competitive/geographic/technology markets in which the business operates, the financial position of the business, corporate risk and organisational structure and culture.

(a)   *Different product lines*

A business may have a single product, or it may have many different product lines produced by different divisions. Understanding more about the products will make your IP strategy more relevant; for example, knowing the relative importance of each product will help to prioritise product-specific IP activities. An understanding of the technologies used by each product will help with the understanding of potential overlap and efficiencies for patent related matters, as well as with identifying other potential markets to direct patent scope and increase value. Appreciating how branding is used and shared by different products will help you to understand which brands are most important for trademark matters.

(b)   *Competitive, geographic and technology markets*

Understanding the various markets in which a business operates will help you to identify sources of commercial risk and opportunity, and hence where IP support may be most beneficial. Knowledge of the competitive positions may also help with understanding which competitors can impact multiple product lines and therefore help to prioritise competitor-specific IP activities like freedom-to-operate risk reduction, or enforcement and licensing. If a market is new and emerging, then freedom-to-operate activities may be more important in that environment compared to in mature markets, the latter which may be more suitable for outbound IP licensing. Understanding market

---

1   Entities that register internet domain names or trademarks in bad faith, with the intent to profit from the goodwill belonging to someone else.

2   This varies in definition, but usually means a patent holder that doesn't manufacture products or supply services related to their patents. Other related terms include Patent Assertion Entity (PAE) and the pejorative 'patent troll'.

growth and shrinkage forecasts and rates of change and likely strategic directions to be taken by competitors will help prioritise longer-term IP activities.

(c) Financial position of the business

The financial position of a business can impact IP strategy in terms of prioritisation, budget management, IP risk and revenue activity value and fundamental direction. Understanding which areas of the business are most profitable, which divisions are growing or shrinking in terms of revenue and costs (and forecasts for these) can help with prioritisation decisions. The cash flow situation, knowledge of regular fluctuations and future forecasts can help align an IP budget expenditure to more preferable timing (and ease those difficult budgetary discussions) and inform timing and value of IP risk reduction and revenue earning activities. Whether the business is publicly or privately owned, and whether it is funded by angel or venture capital or other private equity investment, might affect the fundamental direction and goals of the business, as well as identifying who might provide helpful input to the IP strategy.

(d) Corporate risk

Understanding the various risks to each of the products and to the business itself, and their likelihood and potential impact, will help to identify areas in which IP could reduce or mitigate the risk. For example, a competitor providing significant commercial risk to a particular product line may actually be in a weaker patent position, and this could be used as leverage to reduce their competitive edge, either through feature removal, product injunctions or increased costs via licensing. Another example might be cash flow risks at a specific point in time, and IP could be used as collateral in debt financing to temporarily alleviate the issue.

(e) Organisational structure and culture

The internal organisation itself may have some influence over IP strategy, whether through hierarchy, politics, culture, headcount, pressure or risk aversion. A complex management or budget-controlling hierarchy, or a highly political environment may make decision-making difficult, and therefore affect which IP activities will be approved and supported by groups within the organisation; there may be less value in committing to activities that won't gain traction from internal teams. Factors such as headcount and high pressure environments may also make it difficult for other teams to support IP, thereby limiting the feasibility of activities that require collaboration. The culture of a business may affect engagement with IP issues, and therefore the need to provide employee incentives such as invention reward and recognition programmes. Lastly, understanding how the business generally perceives and mitigates corporate risk may influence how much IP risks should be reduced or even ignored.

Checklist:
Understanding the business
- Learn about the business strategy
- Determine the current IP position
- Understand the business context

3.   Establish a strategic direction

Figure 3: The steps to an IP strategy: establish a strategic direction

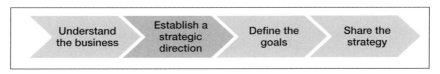

Whilst there are many different perspectives on what exactly should go into an IP strategy, the development of a strategy is likely to involve most or all of the following: mission, principles, vision, goals and operating plan.[3] These can be considered separately or together, and you can start at the top with the mission and work down to the operating plan, or vice-versa. Each of these levels of perspective will form part of the IP strategy to some extent, even if the same exact terms and definitions aren't used directly. When setting the high level direction of an IP strategy, you need to consider the IP mission, principles and vision; this section explains the relevance of these aspects of strategy, but actually applying them to your business is something that only you can do.

3.1   Determine the IP mission

In business strategy, the purpose of the business is often summarised by the corporate mission statement – why does the business exist and what is it trying to achieve? The same can be done with IP strategy – an IP mission statement can be written to explain why IP matters to the business, and the purpose of undertaking IP activities and managing IP assets. Depending on the business, an IP mission might consist of phrases such as:

- to increase business value and stability;
- to protect investments and ensure freedom to operate;
- to generate competitive advantages using IP;
- to use IP to deliver the broader corporate strategy; or
- to provide cost-neutral IP-generated value to the business.

An IP mission might contain a combination of the above, and also many others.

Determining the IP mission for a business is essential, as all other aspects of IP strategy will be derived from it, and all IP activities will help the business move towards the mission. Whether in statement form, a one-page document or simply the way you talk about the IP function, articulating the purpose of IP will help others understand how to best align with the IP strategy. The IP mission is something that should rarely change, and probably only with significant changes to the context of the wider business; for example, dramatic changes in business models, fundamental market disruption or after long-term maturity.

---

3   Splitting IP strategy into these different levels of perspective was inspired by the horizons of focus in D Allen, *Getting Things Done: How to achieve stress-free productivity*, Hachette Digital, 2001.

3.2 Define the principles

Principles are important for a business as they form the definition of how it operates, its internal culture and values and the way it manages relationships with the outside world. It is through principles that you ensure consistent decision making, even when delegating throughout the business, as principles can be used as a set of rules that people can follow.

Principles can be related to all aspects of IP and can be used to mark out the hard-line boundaries that the business doesn't want to cross. Or they simply set the tone for how the business wants to operate, for example:

- respecting third-party IP rights;
- assessing business value for every investment in IP;
- decision making in collaboration with the business units rather than in isolation;
- willingness to enforce IP rights against competitors; or
- encouragement of open source usage and contribution.

Like the IP mission, the IP principles will rarely change; they define the rules for how the mission will be fulfilled.

3.3 Establish a vision

The IP strategy vision defines the desired IP position of the business in the long term, perhaps within three to 10 years. Unlike the mission, which states the direction in which the business wants to head, the vision is more a concrete definition of what success will look like.

The ideal long-term IP position will vary between businesses; it might be one of the following:

- to have the largest patent portfolio in the technology area;
- to have a highly engaged internal IP culture;
- to be confident in a freedom-to-operate position and counter-offensive strength against the primary competitor; or
- to have achieved a successful exit for investors on the basis of the IP position.

The vision can be defined in very high level statements or could comprise very specific metrics that are measured regularly, to track how close you're getting to success and how fast you're achieving it.

Checklist:
Establishing a strategic direction
- Determine the IP mission
- Define your principles
- Establish a vision

4.   Define the goals

Figure 4: The steps to IP strategy: define the goals

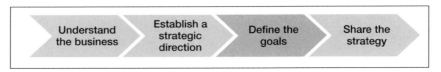

The strategic direction (as defined by your IP mission, principles and vision) is a path to success that is likely to consist of many intermediate steps. The IP strategy goals define the first of these steps. The goals stipulate the things that need to be achieved over the short to medium term, perhaps within the next one to three years.

Goal-setting is a standard business activity so there are various techniques to ensure the exercise is valuable, for example using SMART criteria.[4] For IP strategy goals it is recommended that they at least fit within the IP mission, conform to the IP principles, contribute towards the longer-term IP vision and are measurable and time-bound so progress can be tracked. Examples of IP goals might be:

- increase the size of the patent portfolio in technology area X by 30% within the next two fiscal quarters;
- establish a new inventor reward and recognition scheme by the end of the year;
- expand brand protection to include the 20 most commercially important jurisdictions;
- implement a trade secret policy and processes, and have identified the five most valuable secrets in each division by the end of the third quarter;
- establish a brand watch service, monitoring trademark offices, domains, web pages and application stores by year end; or
- initiate an IP monetisation programme that is profitable within three years.

To define the goals for the IP strategy, you need to first identify a number of possible goals that fit within the strategic direction. Then you need to determine which of those goals are most valuable and select them for inclusion in the IP strategy.

4.1   Identify the possible goals

If a business already has an active IP strategy, or if significant time has been spent understanding the business with IP strategy in mind, a number of IP goals will already be obvious candidates for inclusion in the strategy. However, it can sometimes be difficult to complete that set of possible goals for initial consideration. Inspiration could be sought by first considering how different categories of IP value could each benefit the business. It is also recommended that you consider how different aspects of the business itself might affect IP goals.

---

4   en.wikipedia.org/wiki/SMART_criteria.

4.2 Use IP value categories to identify goals

There are many different ways in which IP can add value to a business. One way to consider as many of these as possible is to think in terms of four value categories.[5] Each category defines a type of value that IP can provide and the various activities that can be used to generate that value. Considering each of these categories and how the related activities can add value to your business may provide inspiration for goals to include in the IP strategy.

(a) Financial

IP activities that contribute financial value are primarily those that add to the top line of the balance sheet, reduce costs or improve cash flow.

Adding value to the top line means generating revenue from IP, perhaps through divestiture and the out-licensing of IP assets or through financial damages and settlement figures from enforcement of IP rights.

IP can generate cost-savings through activities such as reducing quantities of IP assets to reduce maintenance fees, reducing tax liabilities from regimes like patent boxes,[6] slowing portfolio growth to reduce asset creation expenditure or simply by reducing all IP activity and therefore budget and headcount needs.

Improvements to cash flow can be achieved through IP-backed debt financing, where IP assets are used as collateral, or by leveraging IP to improve the ability to raise capital through equity financing.

(b) Defensive

Defensive value is generated by IP activities that reduce risk to the business and therefore reduce any associated costs or losses that may be incurred in future. These risks are usually related to infringement of third-party IP, and activities are those that either reduce the risk likelihood or impact.

Reducing the risk likelihood includes activities such as buying, licensing or designing-around IP rights, including those that are currently infringed, those that may be infringed in the future or perhaps those that are simply a litigation risk because they have an aggressive owner.

Activities that reduce potential risk impact include acquiring or creating IP rights that read on current or future products from the holders of high risk IP rights, either for counter-assertion or cross-licensing purposes. Bear in mind that the impact of IP risk can actually be reduced by owning anything of interest to the IP rights holder, whether IP assets or otherwise.

(c) Strategic

IP can add strategic value to a business in many different ways, primarily through generating competitive advantages.

Competitive advantages can be created from IP by protecting or increasing market

---

5   Inspired by the IP value extraction levels in R Laurie, 'Constructing a holistic corporate patent monetisation strategy,' *IAM* magazine, issue 72.
6   This is a special tax regime to incentivise research and development (R&D) by taxing patent revenues differently from other commercial revenues.

share or increasing competitor costs. Market share can be affected by the enforcement of IP rights, providing feature exclusivity or injunctive relief (and subsequent revenue increases from price premiums). Competitor costs can be increased by damages or settlement figures from enforcement, or through fees from the licensing of IP rights.

Another type of strategic value is reputational; this can be generated with shareholders, investors, customers, partners, suppliers and the press, by building the kind of innovator brand strength that IP-rich companies can inspire. Other strategic values from IP can include value from spin-outs and joint ventures that leverage company IP assets, supply chain concessions from outbound licensing and access to new technology from inbound IP licensing.

(d) Enterprise

Enterprise value is where the fundamental value of the business is increased, whether the value is the publicly traded stock price, an IPO price, prices for merger and acquisition actions, for pre-money investment or any other economic value for a business.

Examples of IP activities that generate enterprise value include undertaking an IP audit in preparation for due diligence, establishing an employee IP training programme, documenting the business's 'IP story' for potential investors, creating IP with the interests of specific potential acquirers in mind, acquiring patents in quantity to appease the needs of the IPO investor and monetisation of IP assets to satisfy activist shareholders. Another more complex value-generating activity is the creation of Special Purpose Vehicles (SPVs), where IP assets are assigned to a subsidiary or independent company. SPVs can generate value in many different ways, including reducing tax liabilities, obscuring asset ownership, mitigating against broad outbound portfolio licensing terms, raising finance without insolvency risks and creating collaborative IP asset pools.

4.3 Use aspects of the business to identify goals

Using the four value categories will probably generate a significant enough number of possible IP goals to form a highly effective IP strategy. However, sometimes other goals that could provide additional value are missed, perhaps because they are less obvious or simply because they don't register for one reason or another. For this reason, you should consider a number of other factors related to the business, using these to either filter the current set of possible goals or to identify and inspire more specific versions of the broader possibilities. Some business factors that could be used for this purpose include: business unit needs, timescale, business type and maturity, possible futures and types of IP.

(a) Business unit needs

The IP needs of each business unit, division or product may vary significantly; they may even be dependent on one another or they may conflict, either with each other or with the broader IP needs of the company. Treating each of these business units as a separate business in its own right may lead to a number of very different and previously unconsidered IP goals.

(b)   *Timescale*

Duration will naturally have an effect on IP strategy; the results you'll want in six months will probably be very different from those in six years, but it may be necessary to start working towards both sets of results immediately.

To identify goals across different timescales, it is recommended that you divide time into several buckets. Simply dividing the buckets into short, medium and long term will work for most, but some businesses may have event-driven buckets specific to their operations, for example, before and after an exit for venture capital funded start-ups, before and after government approval of a core pharmaceutical product or before and after a particularly key business strategy has been implemented and proven.

(c)   *Business type and maturity*

The type and maturity of either the business, its IP processes or the markets in which it operates can drive IP towards either creation or maintenance. Creation goals are those that are more focused on creating or acquiring new assets and processes, whereas maintenance goals are those that include updating, modifying and disposing of existing assets and processes.

A mature market-leading business in an established market may find maintenance IP activities sufficient, but a newly-created start-up in an emerging market will almost certainly be focused on creation. A mature business in a market being disrupted by innovation from new market entrants might find goals related to its IP processes remain focused on maintenance, but asset creation goals are becoming essential for survival.

(d)   *Possible futures*

A business may have more than one possible future, and the goals to effectively encourage, discourage or capitalise on each future will vary.

For example, a start-up business may identify three feasible futures: long-term growth and an IPO, an acquisition or a failure to achieve commercial success; very different IP goals may be needed to improve the likelihood or impact of each of the desired outcomes and to reduce the likelihood or impact of the undesired one. Another example might be the future market position of a business after entering a new market: domination and monopoly, oligopoly, perfect competition or underdog; again, the ability to encourage or discourage the different outcomes may require very different IP goals.

(e)   *Types of IP*

Different types of IP are perceived differently and provide value and reduce risk in different ways. Considering the different types of IP separately may identify additional IP goals, especially when considering IP not commonly used or strategically managed by the company.

For example, a patent-oriented company where business value is primarily created by product innovation, such as a pharmaceutical or technology business, might benefit from goals related to using trade secrets to complement their product protection. A business that highly values trademarks, such as those with high-value brands or franchised chains, might benefit from using registered copyright to further protect aspects of their brands. Other IP rights to consider include utility models, registered designs and database rights.

It is also worth considering these aspects of the business against each other and against the four value categories. Perhaps enterprise value activities are important for an acquisition future, but strategic value is important for an IPO future. Maybe Subsidiary A in an established market needs to focus on maintenance but Subsidiary B in an emerging market needs more creation. Patents may be important to obtain investment in the short term, but trademarks are more valuable in the long term to protect the brand.

4.4 Select the most valuable goals

Armed with a set of possible IP goals that fit the high-level direction of the IP strategy, you next need to determine which of these goals are most valuable to the business, and therefore which will be included in the IP strategy. Firstly, you will need to divide any goals of varying scope. Secondly, you need to prioritise the goals based on the return on investment they are likely to generate. Lastly, you need to select the final set of goals based on available resources.

(a) *Divide any goals of varying scope*

Some goals may vary wildly in terms of potential scope, either because there are multiple alternative implementations or because there are multiple configurations for a single implementation. For example, a goal to acquire patents in a particular technology area might vary significantly in cost and value if implemented as a one-off US$250,000 purchase, compared to a US$10 million acquisition programme over several years. A goal to increase trademark protection might vary according to the number of brands, the types of marks to protect and the geographic scope of protection sought.

Goals of varying scope should be divided into more specific alternative options to simplify the subsequent comparison against other goals. This division can be done in many ways, for example, by selecting high-, medium- and low-cost options, or the two most likely candidates. However, the division of a goal may not be obvious as there might be many suitable options. One common example is selecting geographic coverage for patent portfolio growth for which there are as many options as there are countries. Factors that might affect this particular decision include: the current, future and potential sizes of the different markets; the countries where competitors manufacture, transport and import their goods; the cost of filing, translating, prosecuting and renewing a patent application; and the IP enforcement environment within each country (for example, litigation costs, plaintiff/defendant-friendly courts and damages awards).

(b) *Prioritise the goals based on likely return on investment*

To be able to determine whether a goal is likely to provide enough of a return on investment to be included in the IP strategy, you need to be able to estimate what it would cost to achieve and the likely value it will generate. This will involve considering the resources needed to implement any activities involved, the costs associated with those resources and the value to the business of the intended outcome. Depending on the sophistication of the business, this cost/benefit analysis could be achieved with a very simple relative categorisation (for example, high, medium and low), or high-level financial estimates, or by using detailed financial models. Once these estimates have been made, the goals can be prioritised against one another.

(c)   ***Select the final goals based on resource constraints***
Once you have a prioritised set of goals with cost estimates, you can start allocating available resources such as budget and headcount against those of highest priority. When you run out of resources, you have a candidate set of goals for inclusion in the IP strategy.

Bear in mind that some goals may conflict with others, either because they are mutually exclusive or because the value may change when used in conjunction. For example, enforcing patents to obtain feature exclusivity and licensing patents to competitors to generate revenue, or growing a patent portfolio organically and through asset acquisition, where coverage may overlap and therefore provide diminishing returns. In these instances, you may need to generate multiple candidate sets of goals and either calculate their cumulative value or make a judgement call on which set is likely to generate most value for the business.

Checklist:
Defining the goals
- Identify the possible goals
- Select the most valuable goals

5.   Share the strategy

Figure 5: The steps to IP strategy: share the strategy

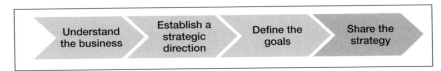

Getting buy-in is essential for any IP strategy, either for its fundamental approval from the relevant stakeholders, or to ensure it can be implemented effectively from accepting collaborators across the business. An effective way to get buy-in is to talk in the simplest terms, use the language of those who will hear the message and focus on the value the buy-in will provide to them. It's also worth remembering that you are selling the outcomes supported or generated by the IP strategy, not the IP strategy itself; rarely is an IP strategy of interest to those outside the IP department.

5.1   Get approval from stakeholders

With senior management it is often useful to demonstrate the value your IP strategy will generate using the language of finance, as executive performance will probably be measured against financial performance metrics, and so these will have an impact on their personal compensation and job security. Articulate the value provided by IP in terms of the impact on things such as the balance sheet, profit and loss, cash flow, share price and market capitalisation. One way to do this effectively is to go back to the four value categories: financial, defensive, strategic and enterprise. If your IP strategy has been generated or defined in terms of these value categories, they can each be mapped to corporate financial terms and be articulated appropriately, as follows:

- financial: this is the most obvious mapping as IP activities in this category are providing direct financial value in terms of adding revenue to the top line (and perhaps reducing intangible asset value), reducing expenditure through cost-saving and tax reduction or improving cash flows (and perhaps increasing liabilities);
- defensive: value generated by defensive IP activities is likely to reduce risk, and hence reduce significant future costs or ensure future revenues (whilst perhaps increasing near-term cash outflows);
- strategic: as the most complex value category, many financial aspects are relevant to strategic IP activities, whether adding to top line revenue from price premiums, market share growth and new market opportunities, or increasing cash flow from damages awards or increasing bottom line revenue from supply chain concessions; and
- enterprise: the value of a business is always financial and so activities in the enterprise area are easy to articulate in terms suitable for the C-suite, whether increasing stock price and market capitalisation, or share price and business value for mergers and acquisitions (M&A) or the value for pre-money investment.

5.2   Get support from collaborators

Once buy-in has been obtained from the stakeholders, the effort needed before actually implementing the IP strategy doesn't end. It is important to understand which areas of the business will be key collaborators in the various IP activities, and hence could become difficult roadblocks or bottlenecks; this list of people and departments will be entirely dependent on the chosen strategy. Once the likely collaborators have been identified, they need to be convinced of the value in the IP strategy, possibly before it has even been approved by the stakeholders in some business cultures. Some of this may come from the senior management in a top-down approach, some will need to come from inter-departmental knowledge sharing and some from grass roots engagement. The approach will need to be similar to that of the buy-in process with stakeholders, but perhaps with less of a focus on financial metrics, and more on the direct impact to individuals (for example, inventor reward and recognition incentives) and departments (for example, reputation and strategic alignment). This will help smooth the collaborative environment when work needs to be undertaken by those outside the IP department, by increasing engagement through appreciation and increasing efficiency through comprehension.

Checklist:
Sharing the strategy
- Use financial language to get approval from stakeholders
- Share the strategy widely to gain support from collaborators

6. Chapter summary

Figure 6: The steps to IP strategy

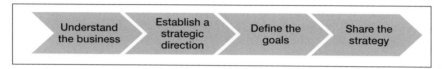

- It is important to remember that IP strategy cannot be defined in isolation, and that understanding the business in as much detail as possible is what will help make your IP strategy as effective as possible.
- Use this knowledge and an understanding of the many types of goals that IP can help to achieve to determine the right strategic direction and goals for your own business, based on a cost/benefit analysis that you know will stand up to opinions across the business.
- Ensure you get buy-in from the relevant stakeholders, by talking in their language and explaining how the business outcomes from your IP strategy will provide value to them and their areas of interest; you can't define an IP strategy in isolation and you can't implement one in isolation either.
- If you understand the business and you understand the value IP can provide, the IP strategy will easily fall into place.

Portfolio management

Peter Cowan
Northworks IP
Paul Kallmes
Metis Partners Inc

1. Introduction

Many ventures grow their registered intellectual property (IP) portfolios – trademarks, patents and designs – over time as branding and technology grows with the business. Yet, as the business expands, often the state of a business's IP portfolio may not keep pace or scope with continual changes in the marketplace. As such, the approach to portfolio management needs to focus on the registered IP being continually aligned with both current and future IP needs. Regular actions of trimming, refocusing, and possibly acquisition of IP assets, should be considered to secure the desired coverage and levels of protection.

Within these actions, and as the IP portfolio grows, often the question considered is: what is best practice when managing and growing an IP portfolio? But perhaps the better portfolio management question to consider is: what components of the IP environment influence decisions and processes surrounding portfolio management? What are the practical steps that a chief executive officer (CEO) or IP manager should consider to enable the best portfolio management possible? Understanding and acting on portfolio management in the context of the broader business environment will allow for more efficient management efforts which create long-term benefits for the organisation. Thus, the trimming, refocusing and IP growth actions are more likely to benefit the business.

So where does the IP manager or executive start? To answer and understand this question it is important to address the IP portfolio management considerations and IP strategy in parallel (see section 2 below), and understand how they interact with each other (see section 3). Next, it is key to understand the associated costs and benefits in order to set the framework for the best portfolio management decisions to be made (see section 4). In any business there are resourcing considerations in setting up a portfolio management process (see section 5), and then ongoing processes and the key decisions that will occur along the way (see section 6).

2. Aligning IP portfolio management and business strategy

Portfolio management is more than following a simple process, as any management decisions need to be considered with the entire IP ecosystem of the business in mind. Therefore, it is necessary to undertake any IP portfolio management not in isolation but rather through linking up with relevant business and IP strategy inputs and decision points. This enables any portfolio manager, chief IP officer (CIPO), or CEO to synchronise the long-term IP process decisions with the company's overall business strategy. Without a proper business context, any business may be unable to make the appropriate decisions to generate quality IP filings or plan for structural adjustments in a growing portfolio.

In practice IP managers and CIPOs oversee a process that addresses the critical aspects of IP management: ensuring the IP is codified and secured as legal rights where possible; decisions on types of IP asset protection from the numerous risks they face; managing the assets in alignment with stated business strategy; and keeping stakeholders focused on the long-term creation of value from IP.

Understanding the desired business-led strategies and outcomes is key for any IP portfolio-management process – it ensures quality inputs to portfolio management and provides a framework to make business decisions which maximise exploitation of that portfolio.

It is likely that a company's IP strategy will evolve as the competitive landscape shifts, as market conditions change, as internal support evolves and so on. The astute IP manager will take all relevant internal and external factors into account and adjust the company's portfolio management decisions and processes, while keeping all essential management, C-level and board level stakeholders informed and involved. Likewise, the C-level leaders (such as the CEO and chief financial officer (CFO)) will ensure the portfolio management decisions being made align with the broader business needs. Figure 1 illustrates the influences on portfolio management and its processes.

Practical application number 1
It is important to create and understand the IP portfolio management influences for your organisation. To assess if a portfolio has the "best" IP for the business, it is critical to see where and how the portfolio connects with the business strategy. As a practical step, no matter how a company's IP strategy may start out, it will pay to revisit and refine it regularly and realign any IP management processes to support it.

3.   **IP strategy as a driver for portfolio management**
In more detail, a clear, concise plan for IP management is critical for successful patent, trade secret and trademark portfolio management decisions. This clarity will occur with a connection between business and IP strategies, both strategies having influence on how portfolio management is handled, and finally in turn what results are generated. Considerations behind portfolio-management decisions and process are covered in more detail in other chapters but in summary they include:
- Technical sophistication of your company and reliance on IP:
  - Are patents a fundamental necessity to protect products?
  - Is the product offering complex and does it require heavy use of trade secrets?
- IP activity in your industry (licensing, assertion, cross-licensing):
  - Are licences in or out necessary for a successful venture?
  - Will having little or no IP put the business at a disadvantage or have no consequence?

Figure 1: Portfolio management influences

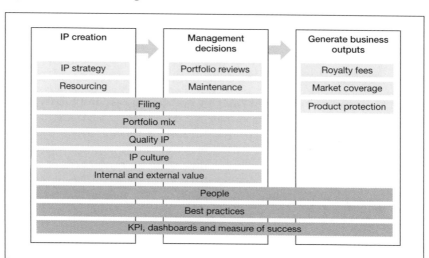

- General reliance of industry players on IP:
  - How are the incumbents using IP as a business tool?
  - Is an IP-based partnership (licence) a substitute for building your own portfolio?
- Resource availability for IP creation and deployment:
  - Are sufficient resources available to support IP over the long term?
  - Is there sufficient cooperation among necessary departments, such as the technical, legal, financial and executive functions?
- Offensive and defensive strategic objectives:
  - Are the primary business drivers for IP offensive, defensive or both?
  - Are the risks and rewards of each approach properly understood?
- Competitor activity in new product introduction and market entry:
  - How rapidly do you and your competitors introduce products?
  - What kinds of IP are needed to support product introduction?
- Market position vulnerabilities and remedies:
  - Can the portfolio be used as a sales tool, and is the sales team aware of this function?
  - Will patent ring-fencing around core technologies protect your market position?
- Desired exit strategies:
  - If by acquisition, what kind of portfolio contributes to better opportunities?
  - Does the portfolio have a stand-alone value to the company or a buyer?

A company-specific prioritisation and resource allotment for these and other strategic categories will directly influence the direction and the weight of decisions a company takes with its portfolio-management processes.

Practical application number 2

It is important to create and understand the IP strategy drivers for your organisation. Utilising the questions above, you can create a structured criterion for making portfolio decisions. This criterion is then a framework to refer to in IP review meetings to understand which IP filings to let lapse, proactively trim or actively seek out to purchase and divest.

4. Managing for portfolio value by evaluating cost and benefits

Portfolio management is more than just advancing IP through a decision process and doing so within a defined budget. It is about generating tangible portfolio value or creating some level of measurable business benefit. Yet stakeholders who interact with an IP team vary greatly and, thus, so do their definitions of the 'benefit' IP portfolio management brings: internal research and development (R&D) managers rationalising their budget or resources, a CFO looking for increased venture valuations or royalty revenue, licensing executives performing royalty audits or a CEO managing investor needs.

In short, management for 'IP portfolio value' will be based on a different definition for each business and the stakeholders inside the businesses. One CEO may value IP to be used for business and negotiation positions, while another stakeholder may value IP that can be enforced and generate royalties for the venture. For all, what is the most prudent way to return top-level IP value via portfolio management consistently while supporting all stakeholders? To determine this, the portfolio-management process must briefly define how 'value' is measured and use that as a variable for all management decisions.

4.1 Management for value over cost

For all businesses is it good to be aware of traditional models, while focusing on the overall IP benefit guides positive portfolio-management decisions. The critical point to contemplate is that the portfolio management process that drives value for any stakeholder is continually evolving. As a result, any cost and evaluation to define an internal or external value must evolve continually to account for the changing risks associated with patents, increased pace of market evolution, business globalisation and current business environment. This is where the step past the traditional models is required.

As an action for the business, portfolio management decisions that continually consider IP in the context of future IP-business requirements will link the IP-management process to the creation of real 'business value' for the stakeholders to support. To accomplish this a business should consider at least two consistent base drivers in the evaluation of costs and benefits: firstly, the cost to create IP and, secondly, the business opportunities it generates.

Portfolio value = business opportunity – cost to create and maintain

Measuring portfolio value can be seen in terms of the above equation: the business opportunity the portfolio brings minus the costs required to create and maintain the portfolio – the latter being the key point a portfolio manager can have influence over.

Costs to create and maintain can be both tangible and intangible. Within the IP process tangible costs include hard costs required to generate and maintain IP: attorney, R&D, marketing and IP team management time. For technology-specific companies, R&D costs can be heavy, but for brand-heavy ventures, the marketing and trademark costs are often the key drivers. In addition, annual annuity payments mark a tangible cost required for at least trademarks and patents, which can have a global impact (both in terms of currency and coverage). These annuity bills may be the only cost of a registered piece of IP once it is granted, but left unchecked, annuity bills can impact portfolio value negatively if IP is maintained in countries where no value or benefit can be seen or calculated, ie, no products or services are being sold. The intangible costs to portfolio value lie mainly in the strategic aspect of IP. A typically untracked cost comes in the form of the time and resources of both the IP manager and the business leaders. It is valuable to illustrate at the executive level that the generation of portfolio value comes at a cost, however small, of the business leaders' time as well. This is time to help prioritise inventive concepts, validate portfolio scope and growth and confirm foreign filing decisions.

Considering both tangible and intangible factors moves a portfolio manager from strictly calculating monetary cost, to presenting business costs for portfolio management – the true cost of portfolio management.

Business opportunities can be both tangible and intangible; yet, again, the portfolio manager must understand that the definition of 'benefit' depends on who is asking. In practice, it can be seen that boards, executives, investors, R&D managers, inventors and IP managers all class opportunity differently and, thus, consider portfolio value differently. For some, the benefit rests on the quality of IP; for others, the benefit lies in global brand protection; and for yet others, the gain is business knowledge they can wield during a licence negotiation. Understanding the 'business benefit' required, guides an IP manager in prioritising specific IP management and portfolio decisions. Relevant considerations for a business include topics such as fundamental technical or brand protection of the product, defensive position against competitors who have licence programmes, competitor exclusion, stronger negotiation positions, increased sales opportunities, restricting new entrants etc.

Practical application number 3
It is important to define and regularly update the 'portfolio value' definition utilised in the business. Understanding this will enable portfolio managers to realise when divesting IP assets that are of no value needs to occur, when acquisitions need to occur or when licensing or technology transfer into or out of the marketplace is possible.

4.2 Balancing short and long-term value creation
The difficulty many IP leaders face in today's business environment is the increased pace and globalisation of the marketplace. This translates into some markets moving faster than IP can be secured and increased costs for securing global rights, both of which can directly impact portfolio value.

This section looks at portfolio coverage of business opportunities from the long-term perspective. Keeping in mind patents have a 20-year life, geographic coverage should take into account future market moves, competitive positions and potential adaptations in patent law. As an example, historically, having US patents was considered the driving value of a patent portfolio; yet now, licence entities are considering the global view – Europe, China and the United States as examples. This is a switch from as little as five years ago.

Practical application number 4

You need to define and separate short-term and long-term portfolio management goals, along with similar business goals. Long-term IP goals which require short-term financing and support may need a business case defined with clear business scenarios laid out for both the situation where the IP is registered and not registered. To increase stakeholder support you should also outline the future lost business rights if inaction is the decision.

Practical application number 5

Short-term vs long-term filing strategy decisions need to be aligned with long-term business use. An IP manager must understand the goals for the registered IP portfolio: Is it for offensive licensing? It is for defensive use against key competitors? Or is it for a business valuation increase? For example, a patent portfolio that resembles the makeup of a potential acquirer may stand a greater chance of acquisition at a higher valuation than a company's valuation.

Case study: evaluating value – small and medium enterprise

A small and medium enterprise (SME) high-tech venture is calculating the IP benefit of implementing a strong portfolio-management process. Positive business opportunities include market and global protection in advance of product launches, secured freedom to operate and increased investor confidence that funds are protected. The negative internal costs include legal fees, as well as time reallocated by the chief technology officer (CTO) and key inventors from the soon-to-be released technology. The ultimate business opportunities this creates are unknown but are expected to reap future benefits with licensing potential as market adoption happens and followers emerge.

For this venture, a strong, positive portfolio value can be managed around future value, but even then, it is mainly an intangible view: increasing incoming investor funds and protecting soon-to-be launched products from immediate copycats.

For the astute IP manager, this drives IP portfolio-management decisions that are tightly aligned with future market protection and require deep involvement from the legal, technical and business teams. Portfolio-management failure can occur if the IP moves through the process using only one or two of those teams and ensuring IP has a strong link to realistic future business opportunities.

5. Resourcing for IP creation and portfolio management

Long-term security in IP depends on a company's ability and willingness to commit the resources to create or acquire necessary IP. The creation of IP assets can be resource-intensive, with numerous realistic challenges likely to be encountered, such as resource availability, competitive activity, internal support issues, budgetary limitations and employee bandwidth. As a result, the responsible IP manager must gather and drive the necessary cross-business resources to meet portfolio creation and management goals, and the CEO must ensure such resources are available and that IP decisions are handled on a regular basis. If it is assumed that the company has an agreed-upon IP strategy linked with and supportive of the overall business strategy, how it is resourced is a factor in the successful deployment.

5.1 Staff resourcing

For many growing ventures the most underestimated resource constraint is often people – either due to incorrectly resourced skillsets or lack of engagement. In practice a company that creates its own IP portfolio must define and allot the proper trained personnel resources to meet its strategic IP objectives. This normally entails the participation of a mix of technical, legal, managerial and executive personnel who understand the impact of IP on the business. As in other business functions, the proper assignment of IP skillset, responsibility and accountability is essential to IP-strategy implementation. Note that this assignment of specifically skilled resources and the timeline to involve the resources will depend directly on the specific goals of a company's IP programme and the stakeholders involved. For example, a litigation-intensive management approach will probably involve substantial expenditures on IP policing, reverse engineering and legal skills, extraordinary patience and tenacity with slow-moving legal processes, and a CEO and CFO who understand the risk-benefit profile of IP litigation. A licensing-intensive approach might focus more on building goodwill in its industry and demonstrating technical competence that can support IP deployment to as many companies as possible.

Practical application number 6

Resource allotment needs to consider the skillet of the team to ensure the responsibility for execution lies with individuals that can accomplish the task. There are often cases where IP ownership may be added to a job description yet the training and skillset – or even time required to execute – do not align with the IP needs. Thus, a CEO should ensure that competence reviews and training should also be part of annual resource reviews for all involved in IP.

Practical application number 7

Resource allotment can often be spread beyond the functional IP team. For example, many ventures have allocated IP resources in R&D teams to work alongside the functional IP team, ie, 10% of R&D managers' job as a stakeholder is to manage the IP processes. Alongside this comes the need to keep these resources trained and educated on the processes, and how their daily R&D role is linked with the IP goals.

Practical application number 8

The judicious use of resources needs to be considered. Almost all decisions require regular reviews – some based on time (monthly, quarterly, annually) and others based on internal business actions (new projects beginning, project development stage gates, new product released to market) as well as external market changes (competitive product releases, new technology adoption). As noted earlier, stakeholders of business, legal and technical considerations are important for all decisions yet one group may be responsible for driving the process and keeping to the timing that aligns best with the business culture and goals.

5.2 Legal versus business control over IP assets

The ultimate goal of IP in any business is to secure a desired business outcome by using the legal tools of patents, copyright, trademarks or trade secrets. Historically IP was seen largely as a legal task and thus often fell under or evolved from an internal legal group, however this has shifted in last few years. IP is now seen as a business tool and the question of control is a valid one.

Often the legal department has some level of control of the IP portfolio, but the legal department may not always be in alignment with the individual or team responsible for executing the business oriented IP goals. In the case where the best 'legal' position of reducing risk is at odds with the best 'business' recommendation, the situation needs a careful assessment of the mix of legal and business input and authority and sound legal advice must be given to the context of the business needs. Without that business context, portfolio management will often result in a strong 'legal' portfolio with valid patents, globally protected trademarks and very secure trade secret processes. The potential danger is if this result has low business relevance for boardroom application in terms of the corporate goals and strategy/direction of the business.

There is no question that support from C-level and other senior management will be essential for IP managers in companies where the legal team is involved in decision-making processes for the IP portfolio. Thus it requires a balance. The question here is: how can this leadership balance best be managed? The scenario where business strategy and risks are not anticipated beforehand will often lead a business to deferring towards the lowest legal risk. However, adopting agreed business goals and how an IP strategy or IP processes will support these goals results in clear weighting of final positions, should they differ.

Practical application number 9

The balance of IP control requires the business and legal groups to collaborate closely to balance the legal and business impact of decisions and IP processes. The CEO will ultimately have the say in who will control the IP group (the legal group or a business unit) but it should not automatically default to one or the other based on history. Rather, it is best discussed and agreed on based on the corporate goals and business strategy, team competencies and business environment. Having a pre-planned sound IP and business strategy will enable this discussion.

6. Ongoing portfolio management decisions: vigilance, acquisition and maintenance

The key success factor inside the ongoing portfolio-management processes is to break out of the day-to-day 'management tasks' and continually validate the future impact of the portfolio is still occurring based on current IP management decisions.

To accomplish this requires a constant vigilance on internal and external IP issues, a view of portfolio growth through acquisition and a constant review of the overall costs of maintenance surrounding the portfolio. Having the team with the trifecta of business/legal/technical skills will be the difference between a portfolio that is managed to exist and a portfolio that is managed to create business value.

6.1 Invention selection and evaluation

A fundamental input to the IP portfolio management process is creating new inventions or launching new brands. Implementing harvesting sessions within a business for inventions allows for the identification of idea sources (new or existing products, new or updated technology, business solutions to customer pain points, technical solutions to market needs etc). As part of the ongoing process of portfolio maintenance, quality growth occurs by harvesting for inventions that have value to the business.

A question to ask at this point is: how is this harvesting of innovations linked to quality growth? The issue of value and benefits is discussed above – for every business it may be different, but by defining what creates 'value' for the business gives a CEO or IP manager the ability to review all innovations to make an informed business decision on which to move through the full IP process. This may be ensuring innovations related to 'patent protection on key products that have the characteristics of being easily detectable for infringement' are more often approved compared to 'patent protection on manufacturing processes which only add incremental cost savings to the product'. In practice the cross-sectional patent-review team is critical for ensuring the fully formed ideas that best meet the portfolio's strategic intent to move through the process.

Again, having the legal versus business control defined will be of immense assistance – while an invention may have legal value, if the scope of legal protection must be narrow to be valid but has no business relevance, it should not be acted on.

Practical application number 10

IP harvesting sessions should be consistently scheduled – either into product development processes or on a timeline basis such as monthly. This will ensure employees see IP as a regular function of the business. In addition, while all innovations are welcome, the criteria for decisions which innovations move into the patent process should be clearly defined. This transparency allows for both a clear process on why some innovations failed to move forward and why others did, as well as ensures that the highest value innovations are continually approved.

6.2   Portfolio maintenance decisions

IP is a dynamic asset class, particularly regarding the regular introduction of new patents and the removal of existing patents through expiration, abandonment and legal rulings. Additional contributions to IP dynamics include mergers and acquisitions (M&A) among competitors, legal precedent, activity by non-practising entities (NPE), failure of companies with relevant IP holdings, high levels of start-up investment and filings, patent factories filing large numbers of applications and so on. Both the CEO and the IP manager must keep watch on external activities that may affect the company's position in an IP landscape and plan accordingly. Failure to do so may result in setbacks from which recovery may be difficult and, in some cases, impossible.

In order to manage and make relevant IP decisions for a company's IP portfolio in a suitably strategic manner over the long term, numerous business-relevant portfolio decisions must be made. The term 'business relevant' refers to decisions that are not purely isolated to 'what is good for the internal business' but rather take into account the broader IP environment with knowledge employees at their side. In addition, part of 'portfolio management' entails protecting assets, which includes ensuring incoming and outgoing employees do not accidently undermine or damage the IP, such as by disclosing a trade secret.

Practical application number 11
Regular review of the IP portfolio's performance against targets and assessment of ageing patents is part of normal portfolio vigilance. The numerous considerations behind the portfolio performance include the points built on the portfolio, people and processes sub-topics. The timeline for a 'regular' review can vary by venture and portfolio size but deeper annual reviews should be the norm and quarterly reviews to update and verify direction is not uncommon. High growth ventures should consider even more frequent reviews to ensure that fast business growth is protected. Reviews should include internal as well as external evaluations (eg, competitors, market shifts).

At this point the question to ask is: how is this portfolio maintenance accomplished? Figure 2 outlines how portfolio reviews are built on people and processes, and the following list gives example actions for an IP manager to contemplate within these three topics.

(a)   *Portfolio reviews*
- Regular review of IP portfolio:
  - Reviewing progress against IP-creation targets and milestones, patent issuance frequency, patent mix for coverage of products or markets and IP mapping and landscaping to ensure gaps are filled and competitors are blocked.
- Assessment of ageing patents and relevance to product lines:
  - Assessing economic rationalisation to support increasing maintenance fees, technology evolution and effect on IP holdings, consideration of

Figure 2: Ongoing portfolio performance is built on people and processes

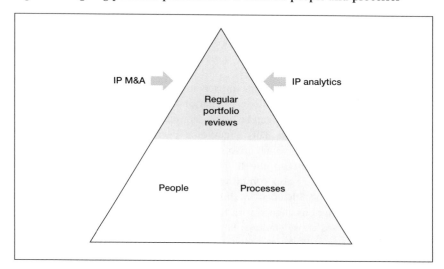

sale or abandonment of ageing non-core patent assets and expiration and abandonment effects.

- Expirations and renewals:
  - Managing renewals and expirations against economic returns, or the above IP benefits, to show support for or against paying maintenance fees.
- Active foreign filing and foreign-maintenance decisions:
  - Ensuring key markets, competitive manufacturing and key countries for business logistics are protected, while prioritising the list against the available budget.
- Patent prosecution for active market coverage:
  - Creating draft 'evidence of use' charts in the prosecution file to keep the prosecution team focused on the valuable claimsets and creation of divisionals and continuations from open applications with claims matching newly released competitor products.
- Patent issuance frequency:
  - Ensuring changes in issuance frequency are not attributed to an internal roadblock or process and monitoring issuance frequency against individual business units to assess a more discrete group.
- Competitive considerations:
  - Increasing new IP (trademarks, patents, copyrighted content) in areas where new 'fast follower' market competition is seen.
  - Monitoring of competition for IP.
- Technology evolution:
  - Ensuring evolving technologies have not rendered IP coverage useless.
- Mapping and landscaping:

- Ensuring gaps are filled, competitors are blocked and critical areas are identified to the IP leadership team.
- Patent prosecution against competitors:
  - Ensuring prosecution work continues with the competitive market space and evolution in mind, not with the intent of 'getting a patent'.

Note the following 'people impact' and 'process considerations' are key building blocks to successful portfolio maintenance yet they are covered in detail within other chapters. However, they can be briefly summarised as follows:

- People impact: This includes expectations regarding IP creation and deployment, which involves educating staff and teams on the expected involvement on the IP process by creating a common IP language for enabling. It also comprises efficient discussions on portfolio-management decisions. Included in this is embedding IP performance targets and job descriptions aligned with the IP process and goals.
- Process considerations: Both incoming and outgoing employees should be aware of IP duties and confidential IP access policies. In addition, processes are continually reviewed to ensure they have strategic fit with the company's goals. This includes assessment of resources expended, progress against specific milestones, successes and failures, necessary adaptations to strategic direction and stakeholder support and enthusiasm for continued programme operation.

6.3 IP analytics as part of the decision process

One key aspect of portfolio-maintenance decisions is to make relevant decisions based on the current IP environment. As noted above, external activities, which may affect the company's position, can be monitored using IP analytic techniques. It is important to note that IP-landscape information is not a prior art position but is a business view of the IP environment that may be used in management decisions.

While only as good as the data they are based on, IP analytics are an invaluable tool in the decision process for portfolio management. As an example, an IP landscape provides context to decisions on topics such as whitespace gaps to increase or expand patent filings, where to abandon foreign extensions or whitespaces to consider acquisitions (strictly IP or general M&A). Just as important for the decision process, an IP landscape also assists in communicating to internal teams how IP influences the competitive position within their non-IP roles. In practice, ongoing analytics and landscaping act as reference points for current IP decisions to verify if they are accurate or need to be adapted to how the competition is moving their published IP.

Practical application number 12

Portfolio management requires the use of IP analytics to be able to benchmark more accurately and compare the portfolio against the competitive marketplace. In practice analytics need to link the IP decisions to the bigger business picture – such as supporting why or how a business decision gets made. For example, reviewing the analytics to generate advance notice on where existing competition is moving or new competition is emerging, intelligence on tactical short-term branding or R&D shifts for specific technologies, relationships between competitive products or highlighting movement of key inventors in the technology space. This information creates actionable business and IP intelligence for the business leaders to act on.

6.4   IP acquisitions

It is common for companies to acquire IP through M&A and other business processes, at which point, the IP manager faces a potentially complex task. A number of questions need to be asked. What is the state of the acquired company's IP? Does it resemble the existing portfolio in claim structure and content, geographic distribution, age and so on? How large is the cost basis of supporting the acquired portfolio? Are there sufficient staff from the acquired company to support its integration into the larger company? Are there any liabilities associated with the new portfolio that may not have been identified in due diligence? If the registered IP is off target, can it be divested? The IP manager must address a substantial list of questions to ensure the new portfolio adds relative IP benefit or, at the very least, does not create unnecessary liabilities.

M&A often causes disruption in both the acquiring and acquired companies, so the time frame allowed to sort out any associated IP issues may be relatively short. If possible, the IP-management team should be included early in the due-diligence process, which will enable the team to ask these questions and highlight red flags uncovered in the process.

Other ventures may identify IP gaps in their portfolio and must search to fill them via acquisition. Unless a venture is building a licensing or offensive patent programme, such instances are relatively uncommon, so if a company's IP strategy includes growth through acquisition, a comprehensive IP monitoring or brokerage function must be put in place.

Practical application number 13

IP M&A goals need to be clearly defined to ensure acquired IP can be utilised as planned. Acquisition to assist in the defence of an ongoing IP litigation or as part of a licence payment or enforcement is one scenario which requires the buyer to ensure the IP is able to be leveraged, particularly around encumbrances.

Case study: IP filing management

An EU-based venture with a moderate-size portfolio has an allocated US$300,000 budget for new filings, ongoing prosecution and foreign extensions or annuity fees. A target of 10 new patent ideas are projected for this year by R&D, considering a flagship product is undergoing manufacturing review in China and is soon to be released globally. The IP manager does not have enough budget to file for protection on all patentable ideas, as well as continuing with prosecution and foreign filings for the existing portfolio.

Following a review with the marketing team, the IP manager realises that Europe, specifically the UK, Denmark and Germany, along with the US, make up 80% of the global marketplace. Key competitors are located in the US and Japan. R&D informs the team that partial manufacturing is often done in low-cost countries, such as China and India, but the US competition is soon to be shifting manufacturing to Mexico. As a result, the IP manager institutes a review process, limiting foreign extensions to European US, and Japan with China, India and Mexico flagged for only patents that can be aligned with the components being produced by an assembly facility. Immediately, this reduces the financial projection for ongoing prosecution and annuity fees in non-core countries and frees up funds for new filings.

Going forward, an IP-review committee implements a standardised review process to link each filed patent to business-relevant countries, as determined by the marketing and technical team. Ongoing prosecution and granted patents are reviewed to ensure differences in claims across jurisdictions still provide adequate coverage. All new patentable ideas are then prioritised to ensure they meet the criteria of commercial-product protection or slow competitive expansion. Finally, because manufacturing patents are determined to be difficult to enforce and of less strategic importance than device-specific patents, a limit of two new manufacturing specific filings is artificially set for the IP approval committee.

Only foreign filings in key countries are maintained, and the cost savings is reallocated to new filings. As a result, even with 10 patentable ideas presented by R&D, the IP manager passes only seven to the final filing process – lower than the target but decidedly higher relevance to protect the business.

7.   Conclusion

The management of an IP portfolio is a complex and challenging task. It is more than just implementing a process to follow. For success, three main points must be balanced: firstly, defining and understanding the IP strategy as it applies to the business; secondly, trading off risk and rewards with the implementation of the strategy; and, finally, coordinating a cross-functional team with defined processes that can deliver quality IP outputs.

8.   Chapter summary

Key considerations for successful portfolio management include:

- A clearly stated business strategy that includes IP as a fundamental component as it should actively drive portfolio management decisions.
- It should be remembered that 'portfolio value' as a decision maker is relative – having this defined will allow divestment, acquisition or filing decisions to be made with direct links to strengthen the business and its ability to achieve its strategy.
- A portfolio mix ensures all sources of IP (trademarks, patents and designs) are considered and managed.
- Defining a risk/benefit scenario for IP usage and decisions is necessary, including legal actions by or against competitors.

- Ongoing portfolio management requires regular reviews of the IP to ensure the business is still protected and IP gaps are continually addressed. The lead stakeholder may vary when making decisions but the business, legal and technical groups will almost always be involved.
- Monitoring for changes in the IP environment through IP analytics for supporting portfolio decisions to changing conditions is vital.
- IP M&A is often underestimated but if managed properly can be an effective strategy in improving the value of the portfolio to the business around key business events.

Protecting your brand

Ryan Pixton
Kilburn & Strode LLP

---

1.   **Introduction**

A brand can be made up of many elements. In addition to the name by which the company or product is known, a brand can encompass logos, straplines, colours, typefaces, container shapes and even sounds. Most of these can be protected through one or more forms of intellectual property (IP).

The IP right most commonly associated with brands is the trademark. A trademark is a guarantee of origin of a product or service. If you enjoy a particular chocolate bar, you want to be able to buy another product by the same manufacturer, knowing that it will be made in the same way, to the same standard and will boast the same taste as the bar you enjoyed. Equally, if you did not have a good experience with a company, you want to be able to avoid them in future. A trademark allows companies to distinguish their goods and services from others and provides that guarantee of origin.

Trademarks enjoy differing levels of importance in different industries. For a fashion house, the trademark is almost everything: without the House's name on the label, the garment is far less desirable. In heavy engineering, the quality of a machine will be more important to a potential user than the brand name. However, in both cases the purchaser of the goods will use a trademark as a means of determining who is behind the product.

A trademark can become one of the most valuable assets of a company. Consider the difference in attractiveness between an item of clothing carrying the Nike swoosh and one without. Such a trademark is worth many millions of pounds or dollars to its owner.

2.   **Trademark basics**

2.1   **Application for a trademark**

Trademarks are applied for on a territory-by-territory basis. Broadly speaking, a registration in one country will not give you any rights in another. Most registrations last for 10 years, and can be renewed every 10 years upon payment of a fee, in theory indefinitely. This makes trademarks a much longer-lasting IP right than patents or designs.

2.2   **Registration of a trademark**

Trademark registrations claim a list of goods and services for which protection is sought. The goods and services are divided into 45 classes in an internationally-used system called the Nice Classification. This has been adopted by most countries around the world. Generally speaking, the greater the number of classes, the greater the filing cost. Goods in one class can still conflict with goods in another (for example, beer in Class 32 will usually conflict with wine in Class 33), but the system allows for two identical marks to co-exist in completely unrelated fields.

3.   Trademarks for new goods and services

Whatever your industry, there are two items to consider when you are launching a product or service under a new name: Can the new name be used? Is it worthwhile protecting the new trademark?

This chapter will next look at the key considerations when answering these two questions.

3.1   Can the new name be used?

(a)   Domain name registration

When a company is first setting out, or planning a new product, the starting point is often to search for domain name registrations to see whether the key extensions (.com, .co.uk etc) are available or already in use. This can be a sensible first step, since if it is important to your business to trade online or be found easily online, you need a name that has freely available domain names for purchase. See below for further information on domain name considerations.

(b)   Researching the name

Having secured key domain name registrations, a company may then conduct searches for its new name using an internet search engine. This is a worthwhile step, since it costs nothing and can establish quite quickly that the exact name is already in use in the same field. If that is the case, a new name will need to be sought. Sometimes, you might find that your new name is already in use in a completely different field. You will need to be sure that you will not suffer any unfortunate associations with the name already in use – the existing use might be in an area of commerce which is wholly incompatible with the image you are trying to promote. For example, the name given to a mascot for Euro 2016 (Super Victor) was already being used for an adult sex toy, a fact gleefully picked up and reported by several newspapers. A few minutes' research might have avoided the embarrassment.

(c)   Checking the database of Companies House or equivalent

The next step might be to search the online database of Companies House, which is the central repository for company information in the United Kingdom or similar in other countries. If you find that the exact same name is registered by another company, that might sound the alarm that you need to tread carefully. However, a company name registration does not in itself confer the right to stop you trading under a similar name — you simply will not be able to register the same exact name at Companies House. A company name registration also does not tell you much about if or how a name is being used, and whether this company is likely to be a problem for you in establishing your brand.

(d)   *Checking the online database of IP authorities*

For those who have previously encountered trademarks, the next stop in checking out a new name might be the online database of the Intellectual Property Office in the UK or equivalent authorities in other countries. This allows you to check whether a third party has already registered your proposed new name, and if so for which goods and services. If you find a conflict at this stage, it would be worthwhile obtaining advice from a professional as to whether there might be ways around the risk.

(e)   *Trademark clearance searches*

For many new businesses (and quite a few existing ones launching a new product or service), the above steps are as far as they will go in checking out a new name. They are content to launch and take their chances. However, it is prudent to consider having 'trademark clearance searches' conducted prior to launch, for the reasons outlined below.

(f)   *Infringement*

If you start using a trademark that is identical, or similar, to a mark that is already registered for identical or similar goods or services, you might be infringing that trademark. Trademark registrations allow their owners to prevent others using a mark where there is a likelihood of confusion on behalf of customers. The fact that you did not know about the registration is no defence. Nor is it a valid defence to state that as far as you are aware, no one has been deceived and it was not your intention to deceive. Courts rule on the likelihood of confusion occurring.

(g)   *Penalties for infringement*

Penalties for trademark infringement include costs, damages, accounts of profits made from the infringement, delivery up or destruction of the offending articles and injunctions against continued use. Even in the best-case scenario, you would be likely to have to rebrand if you were found to be using a confusingly similar mark to a registered trademark.

(h)   *Trademark clearance searches*

A trademark clearance search is intended to clear a mark for use, as far as possible. It searches for any pending or registered trademarks that may be in conflict with your mark and have effect in the country concerned. For example, a UK clearance search will look for marks not just on the UK register, but also the European Union Trade Mark register and the International (Madrid Protocol) register. A professional will be able to advise you on the results and in particular, what risks exist and how to avoid or mitigate them.

(i)   *Timing and cost*

Whether to search, and the level of search performed, will depend on your budget, your plans to launch and your attitude to risk. It is not practical for a new business to have full clearance searches conducted in all key markets, because the cost will be too great. Most UK businesses are content to have a UK clearance search conducted, together with a screening search in other key markets. Screening searches only look for identical marks, so they cannot clear your mark for use, but they may flag up obvious risks.

If you have been using your mark for a couple of years, you have already taken the risk. In that case, a search might not be worthwhile unless you are considering expanding into new countries or new products.

Some businesses take the view that they will deal with any challenges to their trademarks as they arise, without conducting any searching first. That has the benefit of saving on search costs, but does entail risk. If a mark is intended for a time-limited promotion, a company may decide that they can accept the risk of infringement on the basis that they will offer to cease any further use if they are challenged. That is a risky strategy, however.

(j)   *Domain name registration*

Domain name registrations are inexpensive to buy, so securing them is a fairly quick and cost-effective starting point for many start-up businesses.

Owning a domain name registration does not give you much in the way of enforceable rights to the name. You have simply 'got there first' to acquire the domain name. Trademark registrations (see below) are far more powerful tools to prevent others using a name.

There are many domain name extensions now available (.com, .co.uk, .biz etc). Whilst it is tempting to secure them all upfront, a more pragmatic approach would be to purchase the key high-level domains such as .com and .net together with the country extensions of your key markets (.co.uk, .co.jp etc).

If a third party has got to a domain name first and is using the domain name honestly, then there may be little you can do to prevent that other than making them an offer to purchase the domain name. For example, www.beer.com might be an obvious and attractive domain name to acquire, and would be available on a first come, first served basis.

(k)   *If the domain name is taken*

If your preferred domain names are already taken but not in use, do not despair as it may be possible to acquire them cost-effectively. The case law has developed quickly to deal with cyber-squatting, where a third party obtains a domain name registration, purely to extract from the trademark owner of that name a substantial payment. If you have rights to a taken name, it might be possible to take action through the relevant authority (ICANN for .com cases, Nominet for .co.uk cases) to force the transfer of the domain name registration to you. For example, a domain name registration for marksandspencer was taken by a cyber-squatter. The only reason for obtaining that would be to extract money from the retailer, and the mechanisms for domain name disputes allowed the trademark owner to force the transfer of the registration to them.

Equally, a third party might be using a domain name registration containing your trademark either to sell unrelated products, or to disrupt your business. In those cases, take down or recovery of the domain name registrations should be possible.

3.2 Is it worthwhile protecting the new trademark?

Whenever a new name is adopted for a product or service, it is worth considering whether it is worthwhile protecting it through trademark registration. In some circumstances a registration might not be worthwhile. For example, if a mark is intended to be used for a time-limited, one-off campaign of just a few weeks, it might not justify the expense of registration.

(a) *Trademark registration*

Usually, however, a trademark registration is well worth considering. A registration is sometimes referred to as a negative right, in that it allows you to prevent actions by others rather than allowing you to do anything you would not otherwise be able to do. A trademark registration is a monopoly right. It gives you exclusive rights in the trademark in relation to the goods and services claimed, for that country. If others use or apply for marks that are identical or similar, for identical or similar goods and services where there is a likelihood of confusion, then you can use the trademark registration as the basis for taking action to stop them.

(b) *Unregistered rights*

If you have been using a name for some time, then in some countries (including the UK) you may have acquired unregistered rights through that use. In the UK, that is a passing off right. That would also give you a potential basis for preventing others using the same name in the same field. However, a registration gives you several advantages over reliance solely on unregistered rights. To begin with, a registration certificate is evidence of the existence of your right. You do not have to prove through evidence that you have rights to a name. In passing off actions (when someone is using your name or a very similar name), you first have to establish through evidence the existence of your passing off rights. If your records are not extensive or complete, that can be an onerous task. Furthermore, there can be some doubt as to the date your rights commenced, and in relation to which field of activity. With a trademark registration, on the other hand, the date your rights commence is not in doubt, nor is there any doubt as to the scope of protection as the registration claims a list of goods and services. The threshold for establishing trademark infringement is also lower than for passing off – the courts have to find that there is a likelihood of confusion, whereas in passing off the threshold is whether the other party have misrepresented themselves as you leading to damage for you. Finally, the existence of a registration may do the work for you. If others are conducting searches for a new name and see that you hold a registration for that name in their field, that may be enough to persuade them to choose a new name, without you having to become involved.

(c) *Licence agreements*

In some industries, a trademark registration is also a useful means of controlling licence agreements. If you have a licensee, you would like it to be clear that you are the rightful owner of the trademark, and that you are granting use of a specified right. There have been instances where licensees have registered trademarks themselves, and caused problems for the licensors.

4. The trademark registration process

4.1 Protection

There are some mechanisms that protect you across multiple countries, the most well-known being the European Union Trade Mark (EUTM). This covers the whole of the EU in one application, and is more cost-effective than filing national applications in each Member State. There are other similar mechanisms in other territories, including the Organisation Africaine de la Propriété Intellectuelle (OAPI) which covers various African countries. The Madrid Protocol also allows you to file one application designating multiple countries of your choice, which is effectively a basket of national applications. That can cut down on filing and administrative costs, though not every country is a member and there are some limitations to the system. If you are contemplating a multi-country filing programme, it is worth taking advice from a professional on the most cost-effective means of doing so.

4.2 Application for a trademark

It is worth giving some thought to how broadly you word the list of goods and services in an application. Too narrow, and you will not have protection for anything other than your core activities, which does not give you much room for expansion in future. Too broad and you increase the risk of opposition from owners of earlier rights.

A trademark application is filed with the relevant authority (in the UK, that is the Intellectual Property Office (IPO)). You will need to state the name and address of the applicant, the mark, the goods and services and pay the filing fee.

(a) What constitutes a trademark

The application is examined by the IPO for formalities (whether the above items are correctly identified, whether a fee has been paid, etc) and then substantively. That means that they will check whether the mark itself is capable of registration. There are some restrictions on this. In the first place, it has to be a specific and identifiable sign. Simply claiming trademark protection for, for example, a bagless vacuum cleaner does not fulfil that criterion. The mark must be capable of distinguishing the goods and services of one undertaking from those of others. In practice, marks that lack this ability will be refused. Examples include simple punctuation (a full stop would not be regarded as a trademark by most consumers), and banal slogans ('The people you want to do business with' could apply to virtually any business).

A mark must not be descriptive of the goods and services. 'Fresh' is unlikely to be accepted for soaps, because that would give the owner a monopoly in a term that others should be free to use in relation to their soaps. On the other hand, 'Fresh' should be capable of registration in relation to musical instrument stands, as it does not describe such goods.

A trademark must not be the generic name of a product. 'Paracetamol' is now used as a generic name for a type of painkiller, so does not designate the goods of any one manufacturer. Equally, a trademark owner must ensure that they do not allow their mark once registered to become the generic name of the product. A registration of Pina Colada was revoked because the owner had not taken steps to counter generic use of the mark as the name of a cocktail.

(b)   **Restrictions and considerations on choice of name**

A mark must not be offensive or contrary to public principles of morality. It is hard to imagine many instances where a trader would wish to use a mark that was offensive, but there are instances where, for example, a word is offensive in another language. If you are applying for an EU trademark, the fact that a word is offensive in German would be enough for the mark to be refused, even if you intended to trade only in the UK.

There are also restrictions on marks that contain royal arms and other heraldry symbols.

Shapes can be registered as a trademark, though they must still fulfil the functions of guaranteeing the origin of goods and services. They must not result from the nature of the goods themselves (a ball must be round), result from a technical function or give substantial value to the goods (a princess cut diamond gives greater value to the diamond so would not be a trademark).

Trademarks can consist of words, logos, colours (for example, the green in the BP logo), shapes and sounds (for example, the Intel jingle), amongst others, provided that they do not fall foul of the above restrictions.

(c)   **When there is an objection**

If the IPO raise an objection on the grounds given above, the applicant is given an opportunity to argue against it, either through written submissions or a hearing.

It is possible to overcome some (but not all) of the above objections by showing through evidence that the mark has acquired distinctive character through the use made of it. That usually requires at least five years' worth of use, and evidence that consumers have come to know your mark as denoting your goods and services only through that use. For example, Nestle managed to secure a registration for HAVE A BREAK. Normally, that mark would face a refusal on the grounds that it lacked the ability to act as a guarantee of the origin of the goods, but Nestle showed that through extensive use the public had come to recognise it as indicating Nestle's chocolate bar.

5.   Oppositions and challenges by third parties

Once an application has come through the examination phase, it is published in the official journal. In the UK, the publication period runs for an initial two months, extendible to three upon request by a third party. This gives owners of earlier rights the opportunity to oppose your application if they consider that it conflicts with their earlier mark.

It is very difficult to judge in advance whether your application will encounter an opposition. If you have run a clearance search, that might give you an idea of a particular problem lurking. Sometimes, however, the owner of an earlier right will oppose on what look to you like spurious grounds or a weak case. Although you might ultimately win the opposition, it is an additional cost and time for you.

5.1 What to do if there is an opposition

Oppositions follow a timetable of statements and evidence. You will be given the opportunity to argue against the opposition and present evidence. There may be a hearing at the end of the evidence stages.

Oppositions are most commonly fought on whether there is a likelihood of confusion on the part of the relevant consumer between your mark and the opponent's. That will take into account the degree of similarity of the marks and the goods and services. Occasionally, an opponent can prevent registration or use of a conflicting mark in a different field, if they can show they have a sufficient reputation that would be damaged. For example, a gin distiller successfully stopped the same mark being used for bleach, on the grounds that use on bleach would reduce the attractiveness of the gin.

5.2 The outcome of an opposition

If you are successful in defeating the opposition, your application will be allowed to proceed to registration. You will also be made an award of costs, though this will not be sufficient to cover all the costs you have incurred in defending the opposition.

If the opposition is successful, then your application will be refused. Sometimes, there is a partial win for both parties, which allows part of your application to make it through to registration.

It is common for oppositions to be resolved through negotiation. This usually takes the form of a coexistence agreement, whereby each party agrees restrictions on their use and registrations so that they do not come into conflict in future. Amicable agreements are often preferable for both sides than fully contested proceedings, since they are cheaper and have a known outcome.

6. Trademark registrations and use

6.1 Length of trademark registration

In most countries, trademark registrations last for an initial 10 years, and can then be renewed every 10 years upon payment of a fee. Unlike other IP rights such as patents, there is not limit on how long a trademark can remain in force. The UK register contains marks that are over 100 years old.

6.2 Use of a trademark

Most countries have a 'use or lose it' provision. In the UK and the EU systems, the relevant period is five years from the date of registration. After that time, anyone can challenge you to prove use of your mark. If you cannot do so, the registration will be revoked. The aim of this provision is to prevent dead marks clogging up the register. If you identify a mark that looks as though it will be a bar to your use or application, it is worth doing some digging to see whether it might be challenged for non-use.

If your application is opposed by the owner of a mark that is over five years old, you can put them to proof of use of their mark in the opposition proceedings. If they cannot prove use, their opposition will fail.

It is an offence to represent that a trademark is registered if it is not. For that reason, you should only use the R symbol for registered trademarks. You can use the letters TM for unregistered rights: this simply puts others on notice that you are using the mark as a trademark and that you consider it to be indicative of your goods or services.

A final bit of housekeeping: it is good practice to keep the register up to date if the name of the owner changes, or the mark is assigned. If you need to rely on the mark in a hurry (for example, you wish to obtain an interim injunction against another's use), you do not want to have to go through the various formalities to record changes of name or ownership prior to taking action. By ensuring the register is up to date at all times, you can act quickly.

7. When to apply for trademark registration

It is too easy to view trademark registration as an unwelcome drain on your resources, particularly if you are a start-up business. Trademarks do, however, have one key advantage over other IP forms such as patents, which is that there is no time limit on when you can apply for a trademark registration. You can have been using a mark for years and still obtain a registration, unlike patents where use may destroy the novelty. For that reason, a sensible strategy is to apply for protection in countries at the stage when it seems viable you might be ready to use there. That helps to spread the cost over several years. It is also unlikely that you need protection in every country of the world. There are around 220 separate jurisdictions, and protecting your mark in all of them would cost a great deal. Pick your key markets and aim to protect yourself in those first.

Be wary of 'first to file' countries. In those (such as China), it is the business that files for an application who has the earlier right, even over a business that has been trading there for longer. That means that you could be shut out of a market for your key trademark. Obtaining protection in good time will mitigate that risk.

7.1 The priority system

You can also take advantage of the priority system. This enables you to file your first application on the first day, then applications in other countries over the next six months claiming priority of the first application. This means your rights in those countries will be backdated to the date of the first filing. In this way you are able to spread the load if you are contemplating multiple countries for a filing programme.

8. Designs

Designs are a separate right from patents and trademarks, and they exist in both registered and unregistered form.

8.1 The function of designs

Designs protect the appearance of a product (for example, a perfume bottle or a shoe).

Unlike patents (which typically protect things or processes) and trademarks (which identify the origin of goods and services), designs are intended purely to protect how things look. If you manufacture a dining chair that is identical to a registered design, you will infringe the owner's IP in that design. Designs are more commonly used in some industries than others. If your product sells partly because of its original and aesthetically pleasing appearance, then design rights might be worth considering. They are often used by car manufacturers, furniture designers and fashion labels whose highly desirable products are copied and imitated.

8.2   Registered and unregistered designs

In the UK, there are two concurrent systems for both registered and unregistered designs that exist alongside each other, which makes for a complicated mixture of potential rights to consider. The existence and duration of unregistered rights is furthermore a very grey area, which depends on a host of factors including when the design was first recorded in a document, when a product to the design was first marketed, and where. It would take a book in itself to explain the various permutations, so the following is a basic guide. If you are ever in doubt as to whether you have a protectable right, it is worth discussing with an IP professional.

Unregistered design rights in the UK (usually called 'the design right') last either 15 years, or 10 years from the end of the year in which a product to that design was first marketed. An EU unregistered design exists for three years from the date on which the design was made available to the public within the territory of the EU.

A UK registered design and an EU registered design both provide protection for up to 25 years. It is necessary to pay fees every five years in order to keep it in force for the full term.

8.3   When to register

In order to be capable of registration under either system, a design must be novel. That is, it must not have been disclosed to the public anywhere in the European Economic Area prior to the application date. There is a 12-month grace period, so in practice you can file an application for up to a year after you have first disclosed the design to the public.

8.4   What constitutes a design

Not everything can qualify as a design. Methods or principles of construction are excluded, as is surface decoration (for example, a paint finish on a product). 'Must fit' and 'must match' articles are often excluded from protection. For example, if a product must be the shape it is in order to fit another existing product, it will not qualify for registration. Equally, a design of a component part (for example, a car door) that is the way it is in order to match the rest of the product (for example, a car) cannot be protected.

A design must also create an overall impression on the informed user that is different from that created by an existing product. What qualifies as 'different' can appear trivial to a lay person, so it is worth taking professional advice as to whether a design is being infringed.

8.5   **Where to register a design**

In practice, most businesses in the EU use the EU Registered Design if they are considering registration of their designs. That is because a pan-EU right can be obtained cost-effectively and very swiftly. A design can achieve registration in a matter of days. The validity of the design (for example, whether it is novel, whether it is a 'must fit' etc) will only be tested if the owner seeks to rely on it in an action against a third party (example, if they sue a third party for infringing their design).

9.   **Chapter summary**

- Whatever your business, it is worthwhile considering trademarks.
- You should check as far as possible that your intended use will not infringe another party's rights. That can save you a lot of headache and cost further down the line if you come to the attention of the owner of a conflicting right. Emotional attachment is often developed to a preferred name for a new business, which can lead to business owners making poor decisions to continue with a name in the face of potential threats. If you conduct checks on your name upfront, you are more likely to take a dispassionate view as to whether the risks for that name justify keeping it, or whether your life would be simpler and less costly by choosing a different mark.
- You should consider trademark registration. This is mainly about protection:
    - allowing you to prevent others using your mark in relation to your goods and services;
    - controlling a licence agreement; and
    - ensuring that you are free to use in 'first to file' countries.
- Like other IP forms, a trademark registration is a property right. It can be sold either together with a business or as a part of a business.
- The level of searching you conduct, and the extent to which you protect your marks, will depend on your business, your budget and your attitude to risk. It is worth obtaining the advice of a professional if you are unsure about any aspect of the process.
- Depending on your business, designs are another area worth exploring. You can obtain registered protection swiftly and cost-effectively, which provides a deterrent to others thinking of imitating your designs. Care needs to be taken that you do not rob yourself of the change of securing design registrations by disclosing your design to the public before registration. If you are about to exhibit at a trade show, pause to consider whether there is anything about to be unveiled for the first time, and whether there is a design worth protecting.
- As with trademarks, designs are a property right that can be licensed or sold. They can be a valuable asset of your company, but they require robust internal processes to ensure they are captured and protected at the right time.

Trade secrets

Nicholas Mitchell
White & Black Limited

1. Introduction

People equate patents with secrecy; that secrecy is what patents were designed to overcome. That's why the formula for Coca-Cola was never patented. They kept it as a trade secret, and they've outlasted patent laws by 80 years or more – J Craig Venter, geneticist

Trade secrets and confidential information are not generally regarded as intellectual property (IP) rights. By definition they are not known to the public, in contrast to many IP rights which protect works that have been disclosed to the world through publication, production or by disclosure as part of a registration process. Despite that distinction, trade secrets are closely linked to IP rights and offer similar advantages to a business over its competitors.

This chapter explores the following elements:

- the nature of trade secrets protection and other protections for confidential information;
- the pros and cons of relying on these forms of protection;
- the nature and extent of duties on employees, ex-employees and which arise in other contexts;
- civil remedies available for breach;
- upcoming changes in trade secrets law across European Union Member States under the draft Trade Secrets Directive and under the Defend Trade Secrets Act in the United States;
- criminal liability for breach of trade secrets;
- practical steps to protect trade secrets and confidential information in a business context, including in respect of corporate transactions and current and departing employees; and
- exploitation of trade secrets and confidential information.

2. A definition of a trade secret

Valuable confidential information held by a business may be technical (such as a secret formula, technology or process, or research and development (R&D) data) or commercial (for example customer or supplier lists, financial information and documents relating to bids).

A broad definition of trade secrets in an international context is contained in Article 39 of the Agreement on Trade-Related Aspects of Intellectual Property Rights (the TRIPS Agreement) for 'undisclosed information', being information which:

- is secret in the sense that it is not, as a body or in the precise configuration and assembly of its components, generally known among or readily accessible to persons within the circles that normally deal with the kind of information in question;
- has commercial value because it is secret; and
- has been subject to reasonable steps under the circumstances, by the person lawfully in control of the information, to keep it secret.

The above definition will soon become more important in EU Member States, as it is used in the European Union's Trade Secrets Directive as a definition of 'trade secrets' (see further below). However, whilst there is a general consensus on the importance of trade secrets, there is no uniformity between different jurisdictions on either legal concepts or methods of protection. There is much greater international variation than in the context of registered IP rights.

In a UK context, the use of the term 'trade secrets' can be misleading. It is most commonly used to describe a class of confidential information covered by an implied term of confidentiality, which prevents employees from using or disclosing the information after their contract of employment has ceased. In this context, 'trade secrets' comprise a narrower class of information than that which the employee would have been impliedly prevented from disclosing during their employment. The law of confidence also applies to a much wider range of confidential commercial (and indeed non-commercial) information, depending on the circumstances. This chapter aims to address the protection of confidential information in a commercial context, as the protection of that wider class of assets is of interest to businesses generally.

3. A definition of confidential information

A wider class of confidential information (sometimes referred to as 'mere confidential information') will be protected, for example, by express terms in a current employment contract or non-disclosure agreement to that effect.

However, a contractual relationship is not a prerequisite to an enforceable duty of confidentiality. The law will provide a remedy to such a breach of duty, subject to limitations, where it can be shown that:

- the information is confidential;
- it was disclosed in circumstances giving rise to a duty of confidentiality; and
- there was unauthorised use of that information to the detriment of the disclosing party.

Any business must therefore ensure that their systems, processes and contracts support the conclusion that the information being disclosed is confidential and that this was made clear to the recipient of that information, whether they are an employee, a contractor, a professional adviser or a potential party to a corporate transaction.

4. Reasons to rely on trade secrets and confidentiality

Trade secrets and confidential information can protect a wide range of assets, for an unlimited time for minimal cost. They are present in most industries and are crucial for R&D activity. Employees whose roles are clearly defined as the development of new products and processes are almost always broadly aware of their duties of confidentiality and typically these are set out in express terms in their employment contract. However, such a duty will generally apply even where the contractual documents are silent.

Trade secrets, in the broad sense, will include many assets which will later be protected by unregistered or registered IP rights. Patentable inventions will go through a phase prior to filing where their primary protection is secrecy. Patent protection will not typically coexist in time with protection for confidentiality, given the public disclosures involved in a patent application.

The decision to apply for a patent should therefore involve a consideration of the consequential loss of confidentiality and the relative merits of patent protection over confidentiality in the asset in question (the section and the summary table below show the disadvantages). This is particularly the case where there is a risk that the application will fail and neither form of protection will survive.

By contrast, other forms of IP right can coexist with trade secrets. For example, the unauthorised downloading of a confidential customer list by a rogue employee or trespasser may give rise to remedies both for breaches of confidentiality and of a database right.

However, a limited category of information is best protected in the longer term by duties of confidentiality rather than by IP rights. Such works may include those which are simply inappropriate for other forms of protection, in that they do not meet the relevant tests (such as novelty). These may include search engine algorithms, minor improvements to an existing product or process or the 'secret recipes' of well-known foodstuffs.

Businesses may also choose to rely on trade secrets because of the potentially perpetual nature of such protection. Unlike time-limited monopoly rights, trade secrets remain protected so long as they remain secret and otherwise meet the test for protection, so a 'secret recipe' of a soft drink or fried chicken can retain its mystique and associated value for decades, rather than being provided to all on the expiry of a public filing. Similarly, a trade secret is confidential against the whole world, whilst patent protection is limited to those territories in which the patent is registered.

5. Disadvantages of trade secrets and confidentiality

5.1 Disclosure risks

The most obvious disadvantage of relying on confidentiality in preference to IP rights is the constant risk of secrecy being lost. Although there may be remedies in the short term against those who disclose or misuse confidential information, the ever-present risk of losing both practical secrecy and legal protection requires constant vigilance. Practical and legal measures that can help to ensure such protection are discussed later in this chapter.

5.2 Enforcement challenges

Breach of confidentiality is often more difficult to establish than infringement of IP rights. A trade secret is not a monopoly right in the manner of a patent or registered design, which can be enforced without the need to show copying. Unlike patents (and assuming no other IP rights exist in parallel), reverse engineering of a lawfully-acquired product will not be a violation, nor will the independent development of the same technology. In practical terms, enforcement will involve the challenge of establishing that a person who was bound by a duty of confidentiality breached it. The remedies available against innocent third-party recipients of trade secrets, where available, are limited in most jurisdictions.

5.3   International differences

Managing and enforcing trade secrets protections across borders can be more challenging than in the context of patents, where the TRIPS Agreement at least ensures the availability of patent protection as a single concept across contracting states. Although a requirement to protect 'undisclosed information', was also included in the TRIPS Agreement, there is significant international variation on how trade secrets are protected by law, even within the EU. This diversity of approaches results from the different ways in which trade secrets law has evolved from country to country, finding roots variously in contract, unfair competition law, tort and equity.

Table 1: Key differences between trade secrets and patent protection

Patents	Trade secrets
Last for 20 years from filing	Indefinite
Public disclosure	Must be kept secret
Require international registrations in key markets	No need to register; protected against the world
Filing, prosecution and renewal costs	Minimal costs related to confidential procedures and contracts
Monopoly protection	No protection from reverse engineering; must prove copying
Similarity between jurisdictions	Significant international variation in laws, protection and remedies
Must meet patentability requirements (eg, novelty, non-obvious/inventive step, capable of industrial application)	Must be secret and have value as a result

6.   Employee's duties

The development of trade secrets protection is the most applicable, and is most often tested by the courts, in the context of the duties of employees to their current or former employer.

Employees present the greatest risk of a breach of confidentiality, as they often have both:

- means, as they have access to confidential information by virtue of their role; and
- motive, in that, upon leaving one employer, they may find it extremely tempting to use that information for the benefit of their new business or employer.

In the context of corporate espionage, there are a number of known examples of individuals being placed within an organisation solely to obtain access to trade secrets for a rival business, including one case involving the seemingly straightforward business of car parks, as discussed further below.

In UK employment law, even in the absence of express terms in an employment contract, an employee is nonetheless bound by an implied duty of good faith to their employer during the period of their employment. That will often require that the employee may only use information given in confidence to them for the employer's benefit. However, once employment ceases, the implied duty of confidence is restricted to a more limited class of information: trade secrets or their equivalent (ie, information which is so highly confidential in nature as to merit protection as if it were a trade secret).

In order to determine whether a particular class of information merits protection as a trade secret or equivalent, the courts will consider the following issues:

- *The nature of the employment* – Employees in certain roles will habitually handle confidential material and can therefore be expected to realise its sensitive nature to a greater extent than employees who only handle confidential material occasionally or incidentally.
- *The nature of the information* – This may include secret processes of manufacture, but, as well as such technical information, may also include commercial data such as information about customers and pricing and other business strategy documents. The secrecy, or the value of such information remaining secret may be time limited, for example, as price lists change.
- *Whether the employer impressed upon the employee the confidentiality of the information* – An express statement that an item or category of information is confidential does not necessarily mean that it is, but it will assist when such warnings have been given.
- *Whether the relevant information can be easily isolated from other information which the employee is free to use or disclose* – Where confidential information is provided to the employee in a 'package' with non-confidential information, it will be harder to establish that it was clear to the employee what they could and could not disclose.

The courts will also apply these principles in respect of independent contractors or consultants whose roles are analogous to those of employees.

Case study: Faccenda Chicken

The key English case on trade secrets in an employment context remains *Faccenda Chicken v Fowler* [1987] 1 Ch 117. This case involved a business in which fresh chickens were sold from refrigerated vans at expected delivery times.

When an employee resigned, and set up a rival business, taking several employees with him, the former employer alleged breach of confidentiality regarding sales information, including details of customers, delivery times and the prices specific to different customers.

The Court of Appeal held that the sales information as a whole did not have the necessary degree of confidentiality to be protected by an implied term after termination of the employment contract, (ie, it did not amount to a trade secret or equivalent):

- the sales information for which protection was sought contained some information which was clearly not confidential;
- that information was not clearly severable from the rest;
- neither the sales information in general or the price information in particular was plainly secret or sensitive (although was potentially of some use to a competitor);
- the sales information was necessary for the employees' work and could easily be committed to memory;
- it was generally known to van drivers and secretaries at a junior level; and
- there was no evidence that the employees had ever been given express instructions that the information was to be treated as confidential.

7. Limits on protection: restraint of trade

Most jurisdictions recognise that, for public policy reasons, there must be limits on the ability of employers to impose post-contractual restrictions on each and every employee, in a manner that would prevent those employees from usefully building on acquired skills and knowledge whilst pursuing their careers elsewhere. In the United Kingdom and other common law jurisdictions such a concept arises from the common law doctrine against 'restraint of trade'. In other jurisdictions, statutory competition (antitrust) laws address this concern.

Express restrictive covenants imposed on ex-employees must be carefully drafted to be enforceable. The courts will decline to enforce covenants which attempt to restrain:

- ex-employees from using the skill, experience, know-how and general knowledge built up during their employment;
- the use of a class of information which is not confidential; or
- the use of information which is not a trade secret for an unusual and unjustifiable period.

Similarly, a term should not attempt to hold an employee to the same duty of confidence after their employment that they were held to during it. Confidentiality covenants in employment contracts should be drafted in such a manner so as to capture only that information which is capable of protection in the intended circumstances.

The restraint of trade doctrine does not just apply to employment contracts, but the relationship under which the covenant was entered into may be crucial to how legitimate a court will consider it. As a general rule, departing employees are protected from enforcement of broadly-defined covenants to a greater extent than the owner of a business after its sale.

8. Other contexts in which duties of confidentiality arise

Apart from in the context of employment, a duty of confidentiality can arise because of the circumstances in which the information is disclosed. It is not necessary that the relationship between the parties is contractual.

Whether a duty of confidentiality arises will depend on the precise facts. For example, courts have held that a duty arises in circumstances where confidential information is shared between the potential parties to a transaction that is not concluded, even though a written non-disclosure agreement was not entered into. This has been applied in contexts including between joint buyers in a prospective property acquisition and where an inventor discloses inventions for the purpose of entering into a related marketing or manufacturing agreement.

However, it is always advisable to require that a formal non-disclosure agreement has been executed before the disclosure of any confidential information to external parties. Some practical aspects of such agreements and corporate transactions generally are considered later in this chapter.

A duty of confidentiality can be imposed on third-party recipients of information even where there is no direct relationship with the disclosing party, but only when they are actually aware that the information is confidential, or have deliberately closed their eyes to an obvious indication that it is. This means that third parties are not strictly liable in respect of their dealings with confidential information or trade secrets, but may subsequently become liable, and may be restrained from using such information, if they are alerted to the fact.

9. Civil remedies and procedural issues

With the qualification that all remedies are at the discretion of the court, the following remedies may be available for breach of trade secrets or confidentiality generally:

- damages or an account of profits;
- a prohibitory injunction to restrain the use of confidential information;
- a 'springboard injunction' for example, to prevent the former employee dealing for a limited period with customers contacted by use of the employer's confidential customer information;
- a mandatory injunction requiring the disclosure of the use of such information;
- a mandatory injunction requiring the delivery up of infringing materials; and
- an order requiring the disclosure of the source of confidential information;

this may be subject to competing policy considerations such as the protection of whistleblowers and of journalists' sources.

The public nature of legal proceedings can present procedural challenges in successfully pursuing an action for breach of confidentiality in the courts. The ability to protect trade secrets during litigation is a problem in some jurisdictions, but English rules of procedure do provide a number of tools to do so, by agreement between the parties or on application to the Court. They include orders to:

- restrict the access of third parties to the court papers;
- require some or all of the hearing to take place in private;
- restrict access to certain sensitive documents disclosed during proceedings to named individuals;
- require that the names of either or both of the parties to the proceedings are not stated on an interim injunction (an anonymised injunction); and
- prevent the subject of an interim application from publicising or informing others of the existence of the order and the proceedings (a 'super-injunction').

By contrast to the position in the courts, arbitration (by bodies such as the International Chamber of Commerce or the London Court of International Arbitration) is typically a confidential process, in which many similar remedies, such as an urgent interim order, may be available to the parties. When commercial parties enter into a confidentiality agreement, it is therefore worth considering the benefits of including a suitable arbitration clause.

10. Current developments – the Trade Secrets Directive and the US Defend Trade Secrets Act 2016

The directive of the European Parliament and of the Council on the protection of undisclosed know-how and business information (trade secrets) against their unlawful acquisition, use and disclosure (Trade Secrets Directive) is intended to harmonise protection of trade secrets throughout the EU, which is currently inconsistent. An important aim of the Directive is to promote cross-border research and development, manufacturing and trade within the EU. It requires Member States to bring into force laws, regulations and administrative provisions to, amongst other things:

- make acquisition, use or disclosure of a trade secret without consent unlawful;
- provide fair, effective and dissuasive measures, procedures and remedies to ensure civil redress against unlawful acquisition, use and disclosure of trade secrets;
- provide procedures to ensure the protection of trade secrets in legal proceedings in which they are the subject, which might include restricting access to documents or hearings;
- provide for provisional judicial measures which amount to interim injunctions; and
- provide for remedies following a final judicial decision including damages, cessation of use, prohibitions on producing, offering, placing on the market, importing of infringing goods, recall, delivery up and destruction.

The requirement for harmonisation is treated as a minimum, with Member States able to apply stricter measures. The focus relates solely to civil, rather than criminal law. It has been noted that, regardless of future EU membership, the UK's trade secrets protections and procedures would have required only minimal amendment to bring it into line with the Directive's requirements. Nonetheless, the Trade Secrets Directive, when implemented, should give companies greater confidence when disclosing confidential information across borders within the EU.

At the same time, the US has passed the Defend Trade Secrets Act 2016. The Act creates a federal jurisdiction for litigation based on the misappropriation of trade secrets, which had previously been subject to inconsistent protections in state law. State law will continue to apply in parallel, but the new Act is expected to make enforcement easier.

11.   Criminal liability

In the US (for example, the Economic Espionage Act of 1996) and in the majority of EU Member States, there are specific criminal offences relating to the theft or misuse of trade secrets. That is not the case in all jurisdictions and, notably, in the UK, "the theft of the board room table is punished far more severely than the theft of the board room secrets", as Sir Edward Boyle MP memorably remarked in the House of Commons in 1968.[1]

Confidential information is not regarded as property for the purposes of the criminal law. So, for example, when a student dishonestly obtains a confidential exam paper, reads it and returns it, no theft is committed.

Other criminal offences may apply to the misappropriation of commercially confidential information, depending on the circumstances. Offences related to making infringing copies or illicit recordings under the Copyright, Designs and Patents Act 1988 may be of some assistance, as might the Data Protection Act 1998 where personal data is involved. The Computer Misuse Act 1990 makes it an offence to knowingly cause a computer to perform a function to obtain unauthorised access to any programme or data.

The civil law generally offers remedies that are primarily aimed at (and set at a level appropriate to) the compensation of damage rather than 'punishing' breach. Combined with the difficulties in proving breach, there is evidence that the civil law does not sufficiently deter those considering corporate espionage.

Case study: The National Car Parks case

The BBC described the National Car Parks case, which concluded without a conviction in 1993 following a two-month trial, as Britain's biggest industrial espionage trial.[2] This case illustrates the difficulty in establishing criminal liability in the context of confidential information under UK law.

---

1   Hansard HC Deb 13 December 1968 vol 775 cc802–28, available at http://hansard.millbanksystems. com/commons/1968/dec/13/industrial-information-bill.
2   BBC News website, "Millions for car park entrepreneurs", 24 March 1998, available at http://news. bbc.co.uk/1/hi/business/68904.stm.

The prosecution claimed that NCP had instructed Mr Hewitt, manager of a private security firm, to investigate the success of a rival, Europarks. The initial investigation established that there was no mole within NCP, as had been suspected. It was reported that the security firm then placed spies within Europarks' business, including one as a manager of a car park and another, a former army officer, as personal assistant to the managing director. Despite much reporting from within the organisation, shadowing of executives and searching of dustbins, little useful commercial information was ultimately obtained.

Mr Hewitt later gave an account of the operation to journalists from The Sunday Times, resulting in the matter becoming public. Civil action between the two companies was settled when NCP purchased Europarks. A criminal prosecution was brought against both the chief executive of NCP and Mr Hewitt. There being no specific crime related to industrial espionage, the principal charge was of conspiracy to defraud, which required both parties to have acted dishonestly. Both defendants submitted that they did not believe they were breaking the law in their respective actions and were acquitted by a jury.

12. Practical steps to keep trade secrets secure

Putting in place procedures and rules for the protection of commercially confidential information serves two purposes:

- prevention in protecting such information from actual disclosure and misuse; and
- enforcement in demonstrating to a court, in the event of an actual or threatened breach, that the information has the necessary character of confidence to merit such protection.

The next section proposes practical steps and considerations to ensure that trade secrets and confidential information are protected in respect of employees, competitors and third parties in general.

12.1 Know your own secrets

It is important for a business to identify what trade secrets it holds in order to ensure that it takes the steps required to protect them. Trade secrets should be treated differently to confidential information in general to ensure that they do not lose their special nature. To this end, a register of trade secrets will enable them to be treated appropriately as regards internal handling, distribution, disclosure under terms of confidentiality and the drafting of covenants in employment contracts and non-disclosure agreements.

12.2 Have a documented policy

Companies should adopt a policy for the protection and distribution of confidential information and ensure that all employees and contractors are made aware of it on their induction and at regular intervals. This ensures that practical steps to protect information are followed and will also emphasise the confidential nature of certain classes of information.

12.3 Mark documents as confidential

Documents known to be confidential should be stamped as such so that any reader, even a third-party recipient, is on notice that the author or owner of the documents considers it to be so. Instructions limiting distribution and copying may also be included on the face of the document.

12.4 'Need to know' distribution

The fewer individuals who know a secret within an organisation, the safer that information is from disclosure. If a piece of information is known to everyone within the business, from the caretaker up, it is more likely to be disclosed and it will be more difficult to establish the source of any breach. When considering enforcement, the courts are less likely to regard information known to even the most junior staff as having the necessary quality of confidence.

However, if a highly sensitive trade secret is known only to one or two people, there is a risk of its loss in an accident or it being held ransom in a dispute between the company and senior managers. Benjamin Franklin wrote, "three may keep a secret, if two of them are dead",[3] but if the third dies, there is no longer any knowledge to keep secret. The back-up and passing on of secrets should therefore be part of any business continuity plan.

For example, with some similarity to the security measures rumoured to be in place at The Coca-Cola Company, and perhaps aiming for a similar myth-making effect, it has been reported that only two people know the secret recipe for AG Barr plc's iconic soft drink Irn Bru, that they never fly together on the same plane and that it is also written in a document stored in a bank vault "somewhere in Scotland".[4] The Coca-Cola Company's own most famous trade secret has, since 2011, been locked away rather conspicuously in the interactive exhibit "The Vault of the Secret Formula" at a company museum in Atlanta, Georgia.

12.5 Consider what is reported publicly

Certain commercial information, including price lists and details of customers may lose confidentiality through marketing and PR activities. Businesses occasionally assert that certain information, such as key customers, is confidential when it is actually disclosed in widely distributed marketing materials and even on the company's website.

12.6 Physical and IT security

Confidential information will often be contained in both electronic and hard copy documents. Policies should require that physical files are stored securely, for example, being kept in a locked cabinet after working hours, rather than left out where they can be seen by colleagues, cleaning contractors or trespassers. Employees may also be restricted from taking confidential information from the premises to

---

3   Benjamin Franklin (as 'Richard Saunders') – *Poor Richard's Almanack* (1735), available at www.vlib.us/amdocs/texts/prichard35.html.
4   BBC News website, "Irn Bru secrets to be passed on" 25 May 2009, available at http://news.bbc.co.uk/1/hi/scotland/8066968.stm.

work on at home, but obviously this must be weighed against the business benefits of remote and out-of-hours working.

Electronic documents should be protected to an appropriate level to minimise risk. This may involve good network security and policies prohibiting certain higher risk practices such as the use of personal email accounts or USB memory sticks. Personal email accounts pose special risks not only because they may be more vulnerable to hacking and viruses, but also because the employee will continue to have access to the documents sent to and from their personal email account after they leave the organisation.

A vital form of protection against cyber risks generally is encryption, so that even if hardware or data is stolen or lost, a level of protection remains. Ensuring that laptops and portable memory devices are encrypted to an appropriate current standard will not only assist in the protection of trade secrets, but will also help data controllers comply with their statutory obligations regarding the personal data of employees and customers. Note, however, that encryption may also be broken, particularly if the person who desires to do so has sufficient resources and motivation or if the encryption method used is not kept up-to-date.

12.7   Terms of employment

A well-drafted contract of employment for an employee who is exposed to or creates confidential information in the course of their work will contain IP clauses, confidentiality clauses and restrictive covenants. The confidential information clause should be carefully defined and should be separated out into obligations applying during and after the period of employment respectively. IP provisions can require employees to report and document all inventions and processes to ensure that the employer has the benefit and can protect them accordingly.

Terms concerning garden leave and limited non-compete obligations may also offer practical protection for trade secrets. However, for restraint of trade reasons (see above) it is unlikely that a single form of confidentiality clause will be suitable for all employees at all levels. A restrictive covenant that is likely to be enforceable against a finance director with a minority interest in the company may not be enforceable against a more junior member of staff.

Contracts should be appropriate to the employee's role, seniority and exposure to sensitive material. Equally, where an employee is promoted over time to more senior roles and given access to more sensitive information, the HR manager should ensure that their contract is updated appropriately. Contracts should also be reviewed regularly to ensure effectiveness in light of developments in statute and case law.

12.8   Effective management of employees

Good oversight of employees will also have the effect of mitigating risks. If an employee with access to confidential information is known to be disaffected, management should be alert to any unusual activity such as taking copies of documents or removing portable devices from the premises.

12.9 Departing employees

As an employee leaves the office at the end of their employment contract, the ability of the employer to control their use of information is considerably weakened in both legal and practical terms. Employers should ensure that employees deliver up all documents, laptops and mobile devices on departure.

In particularly sensitive circumstances it may be worth ensuring that certain departing employees do not have access to any highly confidential material from the point that the company learns that they are leaving. In the most serious cases activating a garden leave clause (ie, a provision permitting the employer to prevent the employee coming onto the premises during a notice period, whilst still paying their salary) may be justified. It is obviously useful to include such a clause in contracts for this eventuality.

An exit interview with each departing employee has many benefits for the business, but in particular it presents a useful occasion on which to emphasise the continued confidential nature of certain information and obtain confirmation, perhaps in writing, that all relevant confidential materials have been delivered up or deleted.

12.10 Corporate transactions and NDAs

Businesses rarely find themselves in a position where they feel obliged to disclose their secrets to third parties and even their closest rivals, but that is often the situation during a due diligence process, where a business seeks outside investment or a share or business sale. It is tempting for rivals to show an interest in an acquisition with the aim of using the information disclosed in such a process for their own business. Alternatively, a company might be genuinely interested in acquiring or contracting with another because of its trade secrets, only to decide on inspection of such secrets that the confidential systems or processes can be replicated.

As well as seeking to protect the business's trade secrets, the sellers may want to ensure the confidentiality of the fact of the sale process itself. It is often advisable or necessary to avoid notifying employees, customers or the market of the possibility of a potential sale before the appropriate time.

As previously noted, in the absence of a written agreement a corporate due diligence process related to a potential acquisition will typically be one of those circumstances where the law will impose a duty of confidence. Nonetheless, it is expected, and preferable, to disclose confidential information only after the execution of a non-disclosure agreement (NDA), in which a potential bidder will provide assurances for the benefit of the seller and the target organisation.

NDAs may also include further specific protections for the disclosing party beyond confidentiality but defending similar interests, including undertakings by the recipient not to solicit key employees or customers for a limited period. Note, however, that overly onerous undertakings of this nature may be unenforceable as a restraint on trade or may offend competition law.

NDAs are commonplace when a seller discloses to a buyer, but are also advisable between potential joint venture partners or joint buyers. It may be particularly useful to clarify the parties' ability to use information created for their intended mutual benefit, such as a professional report on a target business.

Given problems of enforcement and proving breach, it is best to also take practical precautions. It may be possible to release information in stages: perhaps providing high-level information at an early stage and only disclosing the most confidential details later, when it is more certain that the buyer intends to complete the acquisition. This approach may also be adopted where the business is being marketed competitively to a number of bidders, so that the most confidential details are released only later when only the most committed potential buyers remain.

It is often the case that sellers have confidentiality at the forefront of their mind at the start of the process, but put such considerations aside once an NDA is signed, with the effect that they no longer consider it a priority when the deal stalls or collapses. In reality, this is the point at which there should be the keenest focus on ensuring compliance with the NDA, for example serving any required notices that all documents containing confidential information should be returned or destroyed. This is because the potential buyer will often be thinking about alternatives to the failed deal, such as setting up its own similar business from scratch, perhaps discretely using the information obtained during the aborted acquisition or poaching key employees from the target business.

13. Exploitation of trade secrets and confidential information

Technical trade secrets and confidential information can, like pure IP rights, be exploited by licensing. In many cases such information will be included in a definition of 'know-how' and may be provided to a licensee alongside IP rights in a technology transfer agreement. It may also form part of a technical assistance agreement where a licensor agrees to communicate and demonstrate technology to a licensee.

Many similar issues apply to know-how licences as to patent licences. However, there is a more fundamental need to ensure the confidentiality of any information provided both before, during and after the term of any licence as, unlike IP rights, the information will lose its value if it is no longer confidential. Where such information needs to be provided whilst the licence is being negotiated, this will require that an initial NDA is signed before such disclosure, containing many of the prescriptive terms discussed above in the context of an acquisition-related NDA regarding the use, distribution and copying of all such know-how.

As technology transfer agreements or licences are often cross-border, because of the significant variation in trade secrets law across jurisdictions there is an additional need to ensure that local law will protect the Licensor's know how adequately and that all necessary formalities and procedures are followed. This will require local law advice in the territories concerned.

14. Chapter summary

- Whilst certain forms of IP right, and particularly patents, are more tangible and in very many cases offer better protection, confidentiality and trade secrets play an invaluable role in protecting research and development work and in those matters where protection has not been applied for, or are not suitable for such protection. Confidentiality is an inexpensive, self-help form of protection which is relied upon heavily by small- and medium-sized businesses.

- The law has sought to protect trade secrets and confidential information in a commercial context, but there remains a constant risk of disclosure and practical difficulties in enforcement where there is a suspected breach. The criminal law may not address the theft of confidential information, whilst the risk of civil damages may not be sufficiently dissuasive. Legal proceedings must be carefully managed to maintain confidentiality and, where possible, confidential arbitration may be preferable.
- Businesses that wish to rely on confidentiality to protect valuable assets must always be mindful of it. The owners of trade secrets need to ensure that they are only disclosed in circumstances where the confidential information is clearly defined and the duty of confidentiality is reinforced.
- When dealing with contractors, licensees and potential parties to corporate transactions non-disclosure obligations should be contractual. However, additional steps can be taken to manage the disclosure and handling of information to ensure that contractual obligations are complied with.
- Employees are a key risk. For employees engaged in senior and technical roles, confidentiality should be an everyday feature of their interaction with their employer, from the contract they sign on day one, through the processes they follow every working day, until their exit interview before they leave the building for the last time. Managed correctly, the most valuable of those secrets will still be protected when the employee starts work the following morning with a competitor.

Freedom to operate

Alexander Korenberg
Kilburn & Strode LLP

1.   Introduction

Only the educated are free.
Epictetus (55AD–135AD)

So far, this text has focused on capturing, acquiring and managing your own IP rights. Of course, your competitors and other third parties will be seeking to do the same. IP rights held by third parties represent a risk to your freedom to operate. This chapter focuses on patents.

Just like your own patents enable you to stop or threaten to stop others from doing what is covered by your patents, others may do the same to you. What is more, the fact that you may have covered your own product with patent claims only means that you have a right to exclude others from practising within your claims. It does not entitle you to practise yourself what is within your claims, for example, if doing so would infringe somebody else's patent. Whether you patent yourself or not, patent rights held by third parties will represent a potential risk to your freedom to operate.

It is never possible to fully prove a negative: the absence of conflicting rights. This is the case even with the most comprehensive searching and analysing. There is therefore, strictly speaking, no such thing as freedom to operate. Rather, the task is one of managing the risks to your freedom to operate represented by conflicting third-party patents. This is likely to involve looking for such patents. A number of approaches and strategies are possible, depending on a variety of factors such as your acceptance of risk, your market position and strengths, and the resources you are able or willing to commit to managing freedom-to-operate risks. However, it is critical to understand the risks and issues involved in relation to third-party rights, and your freedom to operate must be understood to enable rational decisions to be made.

Thus, even the well-informed can never be sure to be fully free to operate. However, by being educated about third-party rights and freedom-to-operate issues, the risks to your freedom to exploit your innovations can be understood and acted upon.

2.   Reasons for engaging in freedom-to-operate risk management
If it is not possible to establish complete freedom to operate with full certainty, then the question is: why engage with this issue? While it is not possible ever to be certain

about your freedom to operate, it is only by engaging with the issue that rational decisions are possible. The level of engagement will very much depend on your specific circumstances, as will the possible actions taken as a result of any risks uncovered. How to arrive at a rational strategy, which factors to take account of, how to evaluate risks and how to mitigate them are discussed below.

While any amount of freedom-to-operate analysis cannot guarantee not being at the receiving end of a patent infringement suit – in particular, in technological areas where 'patent thickets' and non-practising entity (NPE) activity are prevalent – the downside risk of the expenditure of defending an infringement suit and potentially being unable to proceed with a given activity typically makes at least some investment in freedom-to-operate analysis worthwhile. Gaining information about freedom-to-operate risks allows mitigating actions to be taken or for a risky activity to be abandoned entirely before significant investment occurs.

3. Developing a freedom-to-operate strategy – decision factors

Developing a freedom-to-operate strategy requires a multi-factorial analysis specific to your business and the competitive and market environment in which you operate. Case studies illustrating how the factors discussed below may play out are provided at the end of this section.

Table 1 illustrates how internal and external factors may influence your strategy decisions about how much to do to assess your operating freedom.

Table 1: Factors affecting FTO strategy

	Do more	Do less
Internal	• Risk averse • High stakes • Long time to market • Blockbuster product	• Limited resources • Insurance • Strong patent portfolio • Portfolio of products
External	• Litigious environment • Target large market share • Many patents in space/market • Fragmented ownership	• Patent backwater • Have large market share • Few patents in space/market • Known patent ownership

3.1 Internal factors

A number of the relevant factors relate to your mindset, what you do and what resources are available.

(a) Approach to risk

At the outset, if your approach to risk is that even a high risk of being unable to proceed with a given activity is acceptable, or that the activity in question will be engaged in regardless of the outcome of any freedom-to-operate analysis, your strategy should be a simple one: to proceed with the activity without carrying out any freedom-to-operate analysis. This saves the potentially substantial cost of engaging in such an analysis, which in any case would not affect your actions. Nevertheless, it is a bold approach rarely followed if all issues are considered.

A risk-taking approach to freedom-to-operate may sometimes be appropriate in circumstances where this will affect only a limited number of consenting people. However, in most settings — in particular, if third-party investment is involved – a more fine-grained approach is likely to be more appropriate. Even then, there will always be a trade-off between any residual risk remaining after a freedom-to-operate analysis and the cost of the analysis. The more resources invested in the analysis, the more confidence can be gained about the level of risk associated with a given activity. Thus, a very cautious approach may be investing large funds in searching for competitive patents, further funding to analyse carefully all search results, obtaining legal opinions where any doubt remains and so on. By accepting an overall higher risk (less confidence in knowing the risks involved), the analysis can be curtailed to a level where the cost is acceptable and in line with a level of risk that you are comfortable with.

(b)　***Available resources***

Even if your acceptance level for risk dictates a highly thorough freedom-to-operate analysis, this simply may not be feasible given the amount of resources available to carry out the analysis. Any freedom-to-operate analysis strategy must not only fit with the derived risk profile, but also be realistic in terms of affordability. Some resources that need to be considered are:

- funds for engaging external advisers;
- internal capacity and knowledge to carry out at least some of the tasks involved;
- management time; and
- time of technical personnel that may be involved in analysing third-party patents.

The trade-off between risk and cost is illustrated in Figure 1 below.

Figure 1: Risk v Cost take-off (general)

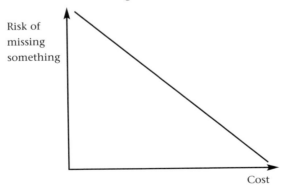

(c)   *Insurance*

There are several ways in which one can obtain 'insurance' against patent litigation. It is possible to underwrite patent litigation risks by taking out litigation insurance, but underwriters often require an amount of due diligence, which amounts to significant freedom-to-operate analysis. Other forms of non-traditional 'insurance' are also possible. New patent aggregator entities exist that aggregate patents to remove them as an infringement risk to their subscribers. Finally, having a significant patent portfolio covering some of a competitor's activities affords a certain degree of 'insurance' by providing negotiating chips if the competitor patent becomes a freedom-to-operate issue. In such circumstances, it can be possible to reach a settlement by cross-licensing or simply through the prospect of mutually assured destruction by patent infringement litigation. If a specific activity or product can be considered 'insured' to some extent, a strategy with higher risk levels may be acceptable.

(d)   *Other circumstances*

Many other factors will influence how the question of freedom to operate is approached. Much will depend on your circumstances, for example, whether you are an individual entrepreneur, in partnership with a few like-minded individuals, a privately held company, a publicly traded company or dependent on third-party investment. A more cautious approach may be dictated by responsibility to investors or shareholders; but on the other hand, if there is a one-way street situation in which any result of a freedom-to-operate analysis will not affect the course of action taken, a light-touch or no analysis at all may be more rational.

(e)   *The activity to be cleared*

The effort involved in clearing a product and elucidating freedom-to-operate risks will strongly depend on the complexity of the product and the number of features requiring analysis. For example, for a new drug the composition, excipient, medical use and dosage regime could individually infringe different patent claims. For a complex product, such as a car or a mobile phone, meanwhile, many components need to be considered (eg, software features, antennae, operating system, user interface features, engine, car body, suspension, control software, power steering). While the complexity of the task at hand is not in itself a reason to refrain from managing freedom-to-operate risks, in a universe of limited resources, the effort and cost involved in clearing a product will likely influence the degree and detail to which the product can be cleared.

Another important question involves the investment of resources and time in bringing a product or service to market. If a product takes years to develop and gain regulatory approval (as is typically the case in the pharma industry), the downside risk in potentially lost investment is relatively large. If a product can be developed and marketed in a comparatively short period of time, there is relatively less at stake. Thus, the downside of a freedom-to-operate problem blocking a development coming to market effectively is much higher in regulation and research-heavy industries than in industries where time to market is relatively short.

3.2 External factors

No enterprise operates in a vacuum and the environment in which you operate in will influence what freedom-to-operate strategy would be appropriate. In particular, it matters who your competitors are, the structure of the marketplace you operate in, how you are positioned in it and the nature of the patent landscape in which you operate.

(a) Competitors and marketplace

While there is a hypothetical freedom-to-operate risk based on the presence of a granted patent with an infringed claim, the risk is real only if there is also somebody who is willing to enforce the patent. Thus, if the marketplace you operate in is not active in patent litigation, the actual risk is likely to be lower than in circumstances where one or more competitors are actively enforcing patents in your field. Clearly, there is always the risk that a 'patent backwater' is suddenly hit by a storm, but a more relaxed approach may be justifiable if you know your competitors and patent litigation is not commonly engaged in your field. If, on the other hand, you operate in a territory where litigation is frequent and likely (eg, consumer electronics, in particular mobile phones; pharma), clearing the way for a new activity is more pressing. It all depends on the specific circumstances. For example, when a planned activity is likely to take significant market share from a competitor, taking a good look at the patents of that competitor would be prudent.

(b) Patent landscape

A related but separate factor is the landscape of patents in the field you operate in. For example, clearing a product in a field in which patenting activity is high and patents are held by numerous entities and not necessarily only by a manageable number of main competitors, locating relevant patents and then dealing with them will be relatively more difficult. Generally, where patenting activity is high and there are many incremental patents covering similar concepts, establishing freedom-to-operate risks with any degree of certainty will be more difficult. This is not to say that in such circumstances a freedom-to-operate analysis should not be engaged in, but such an analysis is likely to be more of a general risk management exercise rather than being capable of elucidating freedom-to-operate risks with a degree of certainty.

3.3 Case studies

The ways in which the factors thus far discussed interact to inform strategy will always depend on the details of each case. Nevertheless, how this may play out can be illustrated by the following hypothetical examples, which are inspired by real-life scenarios.

(a) Start-up 1: early stage

Company A has developed a new internet-delivered service. The company has very few employees other than its directors and at this stage requires very little capital investment to operate. The main focus is on developing its own intellectual property (IP), which is considered the main asset. Limited resources and a high tolerance for risk suggest a light-touch freedom-to-operate clearance. Working with its technical people and subject-matter experts, using an amount of in-house developed keyword searching and industry knowledge, a search is carried out and filtered to a shortlist of about 20 patents, in respect of which the company is not certain that they can be ruled out. A session is scheduled with the company's outside patent counsel to discuss potential issues connected to the identified families in an all-day meeting. The outcome finds at least one apparent differentiator for each considered patent, so that no immediate concerns are identified. A number of potential issues are identified that may become relevant with future developments and these are documented. A document detailing the findings and explaining the results in terms of risk management is produced for investors. Company A and its investors are aware that this outcome is based on a very limited amount of investigation, but they are happy with this in the context of the overall risk profile.

(b) Start-up 2: investor demands

Company B has been engaging in research and development (R&D) for some time and is in the process of arranging a further funding round to set up a proof of concept plant. Freedom to operate has not been considered a high priority, but investor demands for information on freedom-to-operate risk need to be addressed now. In an attempt to save costs, the company produces an in-house search using patent classifications, which retrieves a large number of documents. Discussing the approach with outside patent counsel, the potential pitfalls are explained and a search is commissioned. This search takes the in-house search as a starting point, but in reviewing the search strategy it becomes clear that important areas of classification have been missed. Working in collaboration with the searchers and patent counsel, a new strategy is developed with the searchers providing a retrieval-only search for manual filtering by technical experts in-house at the company. This results in a cost-effective update of the search, making use of technical resources available in-house. In the end, only a small number of documents are identified as potential concerns and passed to the patent counsel for further study, together with leads for potential invalidity attack. A report is produced that manages to classify all documents of concern as low risk based on a combination of infringement and validity analysis, but also consideration of the fact that the patentees in question are not competing in any field even vaguely related to the activities in which Company B is engaged.

(c) Small- to medium-sized company: tool manufacturing

Company C operates in a marketplace where there are a limited number of competitors well known to it. Patenting activity is mostly low, apart from one of the company's competitors. Historically, the company has not engaged in freedom-to-operate analysis, on the experience of operating in a market for decades without seeing any significant patent litigation activity by its competitors. However, in starting a new project, the company becomes concerned with a particular competitor having large market share in a field it would like to enter. The competitor's portfolio is analysed in detail and full legal opinions are obtained where issues are detected. After several rounds of design changes to avoid potential infringement problems, market entry can be cleared.

(d)   Multinational corporate: electronic communication devices

Company D is a large multinational corporation that manufactures and markets electronic devices. Increasingly, these devices are networked. While the company is actively developing its own patent portfolio, it is concerned that this is ineffective against patent threats in the communications area, in particular from NPEs. A process is put in place to consider freedom-to-operate issues early in the company's standardised development process, following proof of concept, with updates scheduled at all key process stages, with a final assessment and clearance prior to tooling. Freedom-to-operate analysis is focused on new features where there is no historical in-house experience of the patent landscape. For these features, the analysis is outsourced, but is managed by the company's in-house department.

4.   Evaluating freedom-to-operate risks

Having established a freedom-to-operate strategy, in particular regarding the trade-off between risk and cost, how should you go about establishing freedom-to-operate risks? The process can be broken down into four main components:

- searching for relevant third-party patents;
- analysing what is found;
- based on that analysis, evaluating risks; and
- deciding on any actions to be taken.

4.1   Clearance searching

The first step in evaluating freedom-to-operate risks is to search for third-party patents that may be relevant to the planned activity. Such a search is fundamentally different from the kind of prior art search that is carried out by patent offices when they search your own applications for patents (or when you search in advance of filing applications to establish whether a new idea may be patentable; or when you search for material to invalidate a competitor patent).

Table 2: Different types of search

Prior art search	Freedom to operate search
Looks for all documents published prior to a relevant date (today, the filing priority date of the application/patent in question)	Looks for granted patents that may yet be in force and, usually, pending applications
Looks for disclosures that may be relevant to the claims you wish to pursue	Looks for claims that may be relevant to the product that is subject of the freedom to operate search
Not necessarily only patents documents	Patents documents only

A frequent false assumption is that if you have a patent application covering the product to be cleared, a lack of relevant documents in a patent office search report indicates that there are no freedom-to-operate issues. While the patent office search may turn up a document which, on analysis, represents a freedom-to-operate risk, the converse is not true. For a thorough freedom-to-operate analysis, a separate search taking account of the above parameters must be carried out.

Patent searches (both prior art searches and freedom-to-operate searches) are best done by dedicated patent searchers or information experts with experience of searching for patents in the relevant field. This is because patent searches can be more complex than you might suppose. Keyword searches are rarely reliable enough for searching for certain subject matter and an experienced patent searcher will know how to navigate the subject-matter classification applied to patent applications and granted patents by patent office examiners (discussed below). Even when searching for identified competitor names, there are pitfalls. While it is important to use specialists with the right skill set to carry out the search, it is also important to understand the issues involved in order to be able to use the search in an informed way.

Engaging in a freedom-to-operate search is by definition a difficult proposition, as it sets out to prove a negative: the absence of relevant patents. It thus follows that a freedom-to-operate search will always be, to some extent, open-ended, as it is always possible to search more and in further detail. The right level of search, as a trade-off between the cost and comprehensiveness of the search, therefore needs to be developed in collaboration with the patents searcher and patent attorney involved.

What follows is intended to give a sense of the issues involved and how they affect the trade-off between cost and comprehensiveness. The following sections thus provide a brief summary of some detailed points about searching for freedom to operate.

(a)   *Subject-matter search*
The most comprehensive kind of search is a search that looks for patents related to the subject matter of the product or activity to be cleared. This is consequently also the costliest kind. There are various ways in which technical subject matter can be searched, but common to all is a necessary preliminary step to define what needs to be searched. If a product contains a single new feature that has not previously been cleared, defining the subject matter to be searched is easy. If several features or aspects of a product need to be cleared, the search correspondingly will be more complicated. In fact, where a product contains several independent features, a comprehensive clearance may require a corresponding number of independent searches and subsequent analysis.

As mentioned above, there are various ways in which technical subject matter can be searched in patent documents – in particular, searching by patent office subject-matter classification, for example, International Patent Classification (IPC) or Cooperative Patent Classification (CPC) codes, or keyword searches. These are briefly discussed in turn.

A classification search makes use of the subject-matter organisation applied to patent documents by patent offices around the world, which effectively provides a subject-matter tree that can be used to identify collections of potentially relevant patents. Since features of a product or activity may be classified in several classifications, and since the classifications are rarely perfect or can be inaccurate in places, expert knowledge of patent classifications in the relevant subject-matter field is essential. With expert knowledge, using the classification system, a body of patent documents can be identified for further analysis.

A keyword search does just what would be expected: the text of patents documents is scanned for search terms and it is designed to retrieve relevant documents. At first glance, this may seem a comprehensive approach, as it does not rely on (potentially false and misleading) classifications. In fact, designing keyword search strategies that are specific to a desired subject matter without risking excluding potentially relevant material is very difficult, if almost impossible. Therefore, searchers tend to employ keyword searches as a back-up strategy where a classification search would result in an unmanageable number of hits to be analysed.

Any search strategy – be it based on a classification search, a keyword search or a combination of the two – will involve an amount of manual searching through automatically retrieved hits. This is because any automatic search strategy that retrieves a sufficiently small number of documents to be analysed in detail would almost certainly miss potentially relevant results. In practice, then, the gold standard of a freedom-to-operate search employs a strategy that returns a broad collection of documents by retrieving results in classifications at a level of detail aimed to minimise the risk of missing relevant documents in related classifications. This should be followed by a manual search through the retrieved documents to narrow a typically large set of results to a manageable number of hits that can be analysed further. Given that the most time-intensive part of such a search is the manual review, this approach will be costly. Where the cost would be prohibitive or a manual search through the set of hits simply not practical, relatively broad keywords can be employed to reduce the amount of manual filtering required and therefore reduce costs.

(b)   *Name search*

As already discussed, a subject-matter search can be fairly open ended and possibly retrieve a large number of documents that need to be manually filtered. In situations where the competitive landscape is well known such that there are a limited number of possible competitors of concern, a less costly approach can often be to search for patents held by identified competitors. If a large number of patents is held by a competitor, this can be combined with a classification search, or an amount of competitor searching can be used to reduce the number of hits in a subject-matter search. As a further variation, where a particular field is associated with a number of limited inventors, a name search can be carried out by inventor names. This also has the advantage of capturing documents by the same inventor, irrespective of whether that inventor has moved jobs.

The clear risk associated with a name-limited search is that patents not associated with the searched names will be missed.

A name search can nevertheless provide a cost-effective alternative or addition to a subject-matter search. However, while searching by name seems straightforward, there are some subtleties in accounting for possible spellings and assignments of the patents in question, so it is advisable to engage the services of an information expert even for a seemingly simple name search.

(c)   *Geographical coverage*

As is discussed elsewhere in this book, patents are national rights and must be analysed jurisdiction by jurisdiction. This also means that if there are no activities to take place in a given jurisdiction; there is no need to search for and analyse patents in that jurisdiction. The number of search results retrieved can therefore be limited by focusing only on relevant jurisdictions. For example, if the main markets are, say, the United States and a selection of European countries, costs can be saved by limiting the search to these countries and not specifically searching in countries where activities are less significant.

The cost/risk graph is reprised here to illuminate how different approaches fit in with this from work.

Figure 2: Cost v Risk take-off (searching)

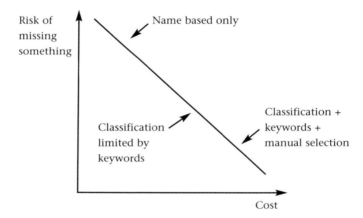

4.2   Understanding search results

Any professional searcher or information expert will provide a detailed outline of the search strategy employed together with the search results. While it is tempting to ignore this document, it is important to understand what has been done to be sure that the search is fit for purpose. Understanding how the search has been carried out is crucial to interpreting the results. Furthermore, there are a number of potential pitfalls to be wary of.

(a)   *Patent families and abstracts*

A patent is a national right. Patentees rarely file in only one jurisdiction. They usually use a first filing in a home jurisdiction to file patents for the same matter abroad. Such a collection of patents (and patent applications) is referred to as a patent family. To make the amount of information manageable, search results are typically presented family by family, with a representative family member providing headline information and reference information only being provided for the remaining family members. In this respect, it is crucial to remember that the claims can vary between family members, even if the general disclosure is the same. Since the variation of even one word can have a significant impact on infringement and validity, one cannot fully rely on the representative family member being presented to rule out a whole family. On the other hand, as a matter of practicality, it is typically not possible to review all documents in detail.

As a practical solution, it is therefore often expedient to review patent families using a representative member and consider the family further if this information indicates that there is a possibility that the family could be relevant.

Often, it is expedient to make this initial triage based on the abstract of a representative family member, on the basis that this is a summary of what the family relates to. This is not without risk, since the abstract does not necessarily reflect that which is claimed. However, as a tool for initial triage, a brief look through the abstract and drawings of the representative family member can provide an indication of whether the family could potentially be relevant or is so unrelated that the likelihood of one of the family members having a relevant claim is sufficiently small to be ignored. As with most issues discussed here, there is a trade-off between costs and risk in this review.

By way of illustration, a complex patent family is shown in Figure 3.

Figure 3: A (complex) patent family

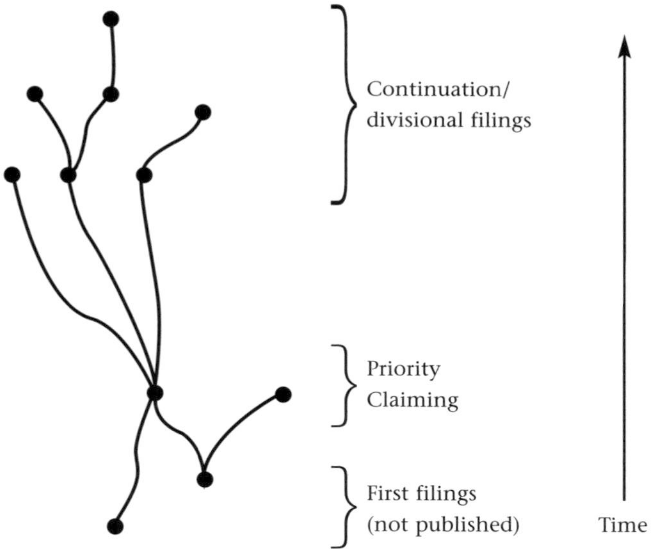

(b)   *Patent applications*
Because pending patent applications may one day mature into a granted patent, a comprehensive freedom-to-operate search should also retrieve relevant pending

applications, not only granted patents (although excluding pending applications may be one way to control budgets). This raises a number of issues: although a pending application may eventually grant, it may not, so assessing the risk it poses also requires an assessment of the likelihood of grant, which may not be straightforward. Even if the application eventually grants, the claims are relatively likely to change during prosecution from the version as filed/published, which would be the version retrieved. Keeping in mind the concept of a patent family illustrated above, there is also the possibility that further applications (divisionals, continuations) will yet be filed.

Pending patent applications therefore represent a moving target, requiring analysis not only of what the claims are now, but also where they may end up. Counter-intuitively, the analysis of pending applications is thus more involved than the analysis of granted patents in a freedom-to-operate search.

(c)   *Publication delay*

As discussed elsewhere in this book, a patent application typically does not publish until 18 months from when it is filed. This means that there will be 18 months' worth of patent applications pending when a search is carried out. Nothing can be done about this, but this is worthwhile bearing in mind. This is particularly so if you are aware of competitor activity and looking for competitive patenting activity that could, in time, become relevant to your freedom to operate. In this context, there will thus be an 18-month window of uncertainty.

(d)   *Status information*

Status information for patent applications and granted patents is, in our age of information, relatively easy to get from patent office online databases. Clearly, a patent application which is no longer pending or a granted patent no longer in force (eg, because renewal fees have not been paid or the patent term is up) pose no risk to your freedom to operate. At first glance, it therefore seems effective to limit any search retrieval to pending/in force patents or applications. However, in practice, this information is not reliably integrated in search databases and retrieving it therefore involves a significant amount of manual work. It is thus often more efficient to have a first pass of triage to filter out clearly irrelevant patent families and only obtain status information for patents in families that remain.

As an important caveat, the online status information mentioned may not always be reliable and it may be that seemingly lapsed applications or patents can still be revived under the respective local law. Therefore, relying on online databases is a useful tool, but it is not completely without risk. If a patent family of particular relevance is found, it would be advisable to confirm status information with local counsel.

4.3   Infringement analysis

Once a set of search results is obtained, it becomes necessary to investigate whether any of the patents and applications found pose a potential threat. Conceptually, this can be broken up into one or more rounds of triage, followed by further analysis where this may be necessary. What follows is not intended to be prescriptive, and different approaches may be appropriate or necessary depending on circumstances. However, approaches along the following limits have been found to work well in practice.

Figure 4: A FTO process

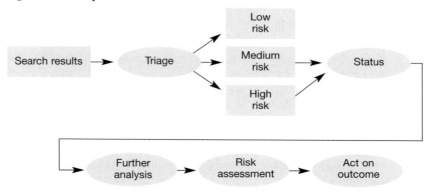

(a)   *Triage*

Since any freedom-to-operate analysis is an exercise in risk management, rather than finding certainties, a first pass through the search results could classify each patent family into one of three categories: low risk, medium risk or high risk. This could be done on the basis that, for example, if a patent family is clearly unrelated on the face of it, it is classified as low risk. If, looking only at the family information, it seems that it could be relevant, it is initially classified as medium risk. If it appears that the family is likely to be relevant, it can be classified as high risk.

In a second round, status information can be obtained from medium- and high-risk families and the risk level updated accordingly. Starting with any remaining high-risk families, live family members are then looked at individually to see whether the product or activity can be distinguished from the respective claims – that is, the claims recite at least one feature clearly not present in the product or activity. If the difference is significant, it may be possible to reclassify the document in question as low risk; if in doubt, it can be reclassified as medium risk and if no differences are found it remains as high risk. Medium-risk families can be reclassified document by document in a similar manner.

At the end of the triage, there will be one pile of low-risk documents, not to be analysed further; one pile of medium-risk documents that may need to be looked at further with a view to reclassifying as low or high risk, possibly with the aid of outside counsel; and a hopefully small or non-existent pile of high-risk documents.

In summary, the purpose of a triage along the lines described above is to identify those search results which are clearly unlikely to be of concern, those for which further clarification is necessary and those which are clearly of concern and need to be dealt with further.

(b)   *Further infringement analysis*

Given the number of results that are typically found in a freedom-to-operate search, a full legal opinion analysis of all search results is clearly neither practical nor appropriate in the context of a risk management exercise. However, where a patent application is perceived to represent a potential threat of significance following triage, further detailed legal analysis may be necessary, potentially including an investigation of the validity of the claims in question, in order to elucidate whether the risk perceived at first pass is real.

Whether a patent claim is held to be infringed depends on whether the adjudicating court believes that all elements of the claim are present in the alleged infringement. This is straightforward only in a few cases and is often a question with significant interpretative leeway. While some claims can be dismissed if a claimed feature clearly is not there, for others the analysis needs to assess whether a court would be more likely or not to hold a claim infringed. The closer an alleged infringement is to what is claimed, the less certain a finding of likely non-infringement.

As already established, patents are national rights. While patent systems around the world have much in common, there are significant differences. For increased certainty, again at increased cost, it may be advisable to consult local patent counsel for any high-risk patents found if the budget and commercial importance warrants this. Thus, the disparity between national patent systems is in effect another risk factor that can be reduced by spending resources to elucidate the infringement risk specific to the country in question. In practice, this may not need to take the form of a formal opinion, but an initial view from local counsel can often be helpful and provide some comfort without the expense of a fully worked-out legal opinion.

4.4   Risk analysis

The previous sections were concerned with infringement risks – that is, the legal question as to how likely a court in a relevant country would find a patent to be infringed by the proposed activity or product. Without suggesting that a patent that is clearly infringed should be wilfully ignored, the business risk is also clearly determined by the commercial context. A higher risk of an infringement finding might be acceptable where the likelihood of patentee bringing an action is low, for example, where the patentee is not a competitor and is operating in a completely different field. For instance, a white goods manufacturer is more likely to enforce (and not accept a licence) against another white goods manufacturer than against a company making refrigeration units for scientific research only.

If the risk is found to be real and significant at the end of this stage, a decision as to how to deal with this situation is needed, the extreme outcomes being to knowingly take the risk or to abandon the product or activity at risk. Between these positions there are ways in which freedom-to-operate risks can be mitigated and these are discussed below.

5.   When to evaluate risks

To state the obvious, it makes sense to engage in a freedom-to-operate analysis only if the outcome can still affect future actions. It is therefore imperative that if you to decide that a freedom-to-operate analysis to manage third-party rights risks is appropriate, the analysis be carried out at a point in time where you are not yet fully committed to the product or activity in question, so that if the worst comes to the worst, all options can be considered. Thus, it makes sense to consider freedom-to-operate analysis at a stage where the project is not yet fully engaged. On the other hand, the project must have progressed sufficiently far so that reliable information about what the product or activity will end up like is available, since the freedom-to-operate analysis would otherwise chase a moving target. Therefore, an appropriate time to engage in freedom-to-operate analysis could be subsequent to design freeze, before significant tooling and production resources are invested in the case of a manufacturing business. Other milestones may be appropriate triggers for a freedom-to-operate analysis, depending on the circumstances. Perhaps an amount of freedom-to-operate risk analysis may have to be carried out in order to complete an investment round.

The initial timing when to carry out freedom-to-operate analysis is clearly important. Further, neither the patent landscape nor, usually, the product or activity in question will stay the same forever. Therefore, the best freedom-to-operate analysis will eventually become outdated and it is good practice to schedule a periodic update of any freedom-to-operate analysis, depending on the speed with which changes are anticipated. Of course, there may be freedom-to-operate projects that are one-off, such as in the context of due diligence for a potential acquisition. However, if one is concerned with freedom to operate over a longer timeframe, periodically updating the analysis will ensure that changes can be managed.

6. How to mitigate risks

Between the two extremes of ignoring any risks and seizing all activity in question, a number of measures can be taken to mitigate freedom-to-operate risks. The presence of possible mitigation strategies effectively lowers the risk profile. Even if not engaged proactively now, they may be available later on in the event that any risks materialise.

6.1 Design around

A patent represents a potential freedom-to-operate risk if there is a threat that a court would find that all features of at least one claim of the patent are all present in the product or activity in question. Should such a risk be present, if the product or activity can be changed so as to be clearly outside the scope of the claim, the risk has been mitigated. This may be relatively easy where the feature in question is not central to the commercial value or can be replaced or changed without significantly affecting the value, and when the change can be carried out relatively easily. For example, a smartphone app that can be changed simply by issuing an updated version may readily be changed if a threat materialises. On the other hand, a design around may be more consequential – for example, if there is a need to change tooling or manufacturing processes.

6.2   Negotiate

If the patentee is not a direct competitor with a vital interest of excluding you from the market, the option of obtaining a licence can be a risk-mitigating strategy. This may be applicable in particular where the patent in question is a standards-related patent for which a licence on fair, reasonable and non-discriminatory terms is available. Whether the licence should be sought proactively or whether the potential availability of a licence is taken into account in evaluating risk will depend on the commercial circumstances and the perceived magnitude of the infringement risk.

6.3   Attack (or be prepared to attack)

A granted patent will represent a freedom-to-operate threat only if it has a claim which is not only infringed, but also valid. Therefore, one way to mitigate a freedom-to-operate risk is to attack the patent or prepare for such an attack. This can be done by researching potential prior art that can be used to invalidate the patent – for example, using a combination of in-house technical expertise and third-party searchers. If prior art is found which clearly invalidates the patent in question, the risk is to a large extent mitigated (however, see further on this below). Even if prior art is found on the basis of which the validity case is more balanced, this changes the balance of power.

The question of what then to do with any uncovered attack or attacks does not have a straightforward answer. On the one hand, clearing the way proactively, if successful, provides certainty, even if it brings legal costs forward, by definition. On the other hand, being well prepared also has advantages. Legal costs are deferred or possibly not incurred if the validity attack can be used successfully as leverage in future negotiations. Further, a patent that is judged as low risk due to its vulnerability will still look like an obstacle to competitors. Being fully prepared for any eventuality by not immediately acting on the identified attacks keeps the benefit of the information gained to yourself. Actively clearing the way, while possibly giving you legal certainty, benefits everybody but the patentee in question and therefore shares the benefit of investing in an invalidity attack with your competitors.

The answer to the question of when information gained should be used thus involves a trade-off between legal certainty (including for other competitors) and competitive advantage. Many specific factors will determine the answer to the question to defer or not to defer, but a universal factor will be how the relevant patent systems concerned treat infringement and validity questions. Where the courts hear validity and infringement together (eg, in the US and the UK), the case for being fully prepared is stronger because no effective decision on infringement will be reached by a court before a validity defence has been considered. In other jurisdictions, notably Germany, infringement and validity are heard by separate tribunals and it is common for defendants to be faced with an enforceable decision on infringement long before a decision on validity is reached. Such circumstances mitigate in favour of clearing the way.

While at first glance it seems advantageous to keep the investment in developing invalidity attacks to oneself rather than to clear the way (not only for oneself, but for everybody), detailed tactical considerations, in particular regarding the constraints imposed by how patent disputes are dealt with in a particular jurisdiction, will have to be taken into account.

6.4 Stockpile

Inspired by cold-war doctrine, the threat of attack can often be an effective defence. Thus, building an effective patent portfolio that can be used against competitors if needed will provide negotiating chips in case of attack. Having an effective patent portfolio can thus also mitigate for freedom-to-operate risks where competitors are concerned. However, the threat of counterattack is ineffective if the patentee in question does not engage in significant activities that can be covered by your portfolio, *in extremis* if the patentee is an NPE which engages in no other activity besides monetisation of a patent portfolio.

7. Chapter summary

- Others enforcing their patent rights against you is a risk to your freedom to operate – just as you may seek to enforce your patents against others, so may they.
- You can take measures to understand and manage this risk, but never fully exclude it – proving a negative is always hard.
- There is no one right approach to dealing with this risk – the more resources invested in clearing risks, the higher the likelihood that any problem will be uncovered. Depending on your circumstances, there will be a level that is right for you.
- The key is to understand the risks associated with any problem found, as well as the risk of missing something relevant. The right strategy will enable informed decision making based on an understanding of the risk.
- Having defined a strategy and understood the risk, you should act on the results: if all is clear, go forth. If problems are found, be prepared to deal with them – or you will need to make an informed decision to take the risk.
- Timing is important: it only makes sense to clear risks if you can/will still act on the results. Again, risk management needs to be an ongoing process as part of your IP strategy.
- Investigating risks not only allows you to plan and allow for any risks uncovered but also to take mitigating action.

Risks associated with patent rights of others cannot be eliminated; but they can be managed. Understanding of these risks enables decision-making and, if necessary, mitigation.

IP policing

Mike McLean
TechInsights

1.   Introduction

Recent years have provided significant examples of the benefits of policing and enforcement of patents' rights. Carnegie Mellon received US$750 million from Marvell Technology over the infringement of two patents; Microsoft struck a long-term partnership deal with Xiaomi that included the sale of 1,500 patents, a patent cross-licence and Xiaomi installing Microsoft software on its phones and tablets; and Swiss company Kudelski, a provider of digital TV security, agreed to a comprehensive patent licence with Apple that settled all pending patent litigation between the two companies.

You spend millions of dollars developing a new technology or product. How are you protecting that investment? Are you ensuring that others are not taking advantage of your patented technology?

A common business scenario is that a company adds a new asset class to their balance sheet with the filing of its first patent application. The value of this asset class builds as the number of patents in its portfolio increases. Maximising the impact and value of patent assets is often neglected when compared to efforts to ensure sufficient return from physical assets like real estate, equipment or product inventory. Patents differ from these assets in providing an exclusionary property right and therefore those rights require active policing in order to extract maximum value through direct royalty payments, expanded market share or lowering capital and supply costs.

Obtaining issued patents is certainly a big step for any company, but it is only the beginning. The rights afforded by a patent are not automatic. There is no central agency or government body that asserts patent rights and ensures that others are not implementing your patented technology. It is up to the patent owner to enforce the rights afforded to them by their patents. In other words, the patent holder has to be aware of the scope of coverage provided by their patents, what is occurring in 'the field' in terms of potential infringement, and implement a policing operation to detect unauthorised use of the protected technology and to assert those rights.

Extracting value from a patent portfolio requires identifying parties that are using the patented technology in a current product or that have interest in using it in a future product, linking that use to a commercial outcome, and articulating to the party or parties the need to compensate the patent holder for this use in a fashion commensurate with the commercial outcome. Communicating this need for compensation is greatly aided by clear 'evidence of use' (EoU) that can only be gathered through an active policing programme. Implementing a policing programme requires an understanding of the rights granted by individual patents or portfolios of patents, developing a strategy to direct the investigation of potential uses of those rights by identifying potential infringement of those rights through specific investigation techniques and establishing credible evidence to support an enforcement action or monetisation programme.

Several notable large firms have developed extremely successful patent monetisation programmes. For example, telecommunications giant, Nokia, is forecast to generate more than US$1 billion in 2016 from licensing primarily cellphone handset patents. Other members of the 'billion dollar club' include Ericsson, Qualcomm and Microsoft. The foundation of these licensing efforts is an effective policing programme.

2.   Patent protection

Patent protection should be thought of as occurring on two levels. At the finest level are individual patents; at a broader level is a portfolio of patents developed from the aggregation of the individual patents. This portfolio creates a landscape of patent coverage.

2.1   Individual patents and claims

The legal protection afforded by a patent is generally misunderstood and is frequently presented incorrectly in the media and by the general public. A patent's legal coverage is not defined by its title. If this were the case there would be two million patents protecting a 'Semiconductor Device'. Legal protection is also not defined by the abstract. It is also rarely defined by the product that may incorporate the patented technology. The legal coverage afforded by a patent is defined by the claims. The claims are those awkwardly worded sentences at the end of a patent. Claim language can be very dense and is written in a very particular format that often employs a very precise interpretation of a good fraction of the words therein. The claims are often much narrower in scope than the title, abstract or a simple summary.

So, what does a claim look like and how is it read? Probably the most instructive way to consider this is with an example. The next section presents a fictitious invention and claim by way of illustration of this.

2.2   Background to a fictitious invention and sample claim

Aluminum foam is an interesting material. It is as simple as it sounds; foam is formed during the solidification of molten aluminum. The trick, though, is maintaining bubble integrity during solidification. The foam can be fabricated with varying bubble sizes and is generally between 80% to 90% air; it is very light. This material provides very interesting, and impressive, energy absorption characteristics, with each bubble wall dissipating energy. Because of its rather unique appearance it has been used as a cladding material in architectural applications. Here rectangular panels are attached to interior or exterior walls. One obstacle for exterior applications though is likely waterproofing the edges of the panel. The panel edges will be irregular and rough because they cut through the bubbles of the foam, resulting in poor sealing characteristics. Thus, a system is needed that can both affix the panels to the surface on which they are being mounted and, at the same time, waterproof the edges; forming a seal between panels.

Foamify is a manufacturer of aluminum foam, and has invented a system that overcomes this sealing obstacle, allowing broader use of their panels for exterior cladding applications. US Patent X,000,007 was issued for the invention. Elements of the claimed structure are presented in Figures, 1, 2a and 2b. The '007 patent has a single claim, which reads as follows:

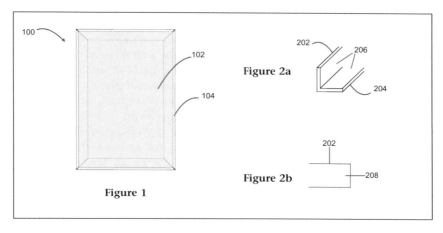

Figure 2a

Figure 2b

Figure 1

1. A system (100) for affixing a metal foam panel (102) to a surface, the system comprising:

a first, second, third and fourth segment, the segments being attached to one another at ends thereof forming a rectangular frame (104), each segment having a first (202) and second (204) arm, the first and second arms being at an angle to one another;

a first sealant applied to a first surface of the first and second arm, the first sealant appropriate for sealingly affixing a portion of the panel to the first surface of the first and second arm; and

a second sealant (208) applied to a second surface of the first (202) and second arm, the second sealant appropriate for sealingly affixing the second surface of the second arm to the surface and the second surface of the first arm to an adjacent frame,

wherein the panel (102) is rigidly fixed to the surface and to adjacent panels.

A claim has basically two sections: the preamble and the body. The preamble sets the environment and provides structure or functionality that will allow the elements to operate. The second part is the body; it contains the elements of the claim, which are the basis for legal protection.

The legal protection of the claim can be 'ballparked' with a plain language reading such that additional information or interpretation of the terms are not needed. The claim of '007 describes a 'system' having a particular structure and arrangement of a frame, having segments and arms, and two sealants. The frame is rectangular in shape, but the material is undefined. Each of the four segments has two arms and these arms form an angle between them. Finally, there are sealants, not necessarily the same, on both sides of the arms. The nature of these sealants is not specified. The advance over the prior art might be the combination of the structure and the use of sealants on both sides of the arms.

When thinking about Claim 1 in terms of policing, we need to determine whether evidence can be gathered demonstrating that each and every claim element is being used in an unlicensed product (that is without agreement from Foamify). The claim does not specify the frame material, which is a good thing. In this case, the claim could encompass or 'cover' either an aluminum or a steel frame. The claim states that the frame is 'rectangular'. In a plain language reading this may create problems as a competing manufacturer may market a square frame or a frame of a different shape altogether and be outside the claim's legal coverage.

A strict, legal reading of the claims can be a bit more involved than the above ballpark. A strict reading would require a qualified attorney in the patent's jurisdiction. In the case of the '007 patent, a US patent attorney would be able to give an accurate reading of the terms that considers how such terms have been interpreted in previous case law and what arguments were made to the US Patent Office during the prosecution of the '007's application, ie, what arguments were made when obtaining the patent. Two terms in the claim that may require such an interpretation are 'rigidly' and 'sealingly'. Case law or communications with the Patent Office may indicate how rigid something has to be to be 'rigid' and how good a seal is provided by 'sealingly'.

In the end, the ballpark read suggests the '007 provides legal coverage for a system for affixing a metal foam panel having a certain configuration of a frame, segments, arms and sealants.

3. Portfolio coverage

With the issuance of its first patent a company has started to develop a portfolio. With the issuance of additional patents the portfolio grows and a landscape of patent coverage is created. Systematically categorizing the portfolio in relation to a company's technology and products is key to understanding the coverage provided by the portfolio and to identifying specific patents for use in policing the organisation's patent rights.

A portfolio of patents seems to be a simple enough concept. Patent applications are filed and as more patents are issued the portfolio grows, creating a landscape of coverage. Probably the easiest way to explore the concept is to work with the '007 patent example. Again the '007 patent may be the first patent issued to the company. It may have been determined that the use of a sealant on the surfaces of the two arms does not provide the desired mechanical stability in some situations, and a new frame structure is developed. This structure has ridges along the length of the valley, corresponding to notches on the panel. There may in fact be two or three patents here. One relating the new frame structure, one related to the panel structure and one related to a method of manufacturing the panel. Additionally, a method of fabricating flat surfaces on the panel, in regions that contact the arms, may be developed. This new panel structure is found to both improve the seal, and the flat regions are thick enough that the panels can be affixed to a frame with screws, or the like. Again one could envision a patent for the panel and one for the method of manufacturing this new structure. Of course there could be other areas of use of the panels or their method of manufacture, or supporting systems that may well provide material for future patents.

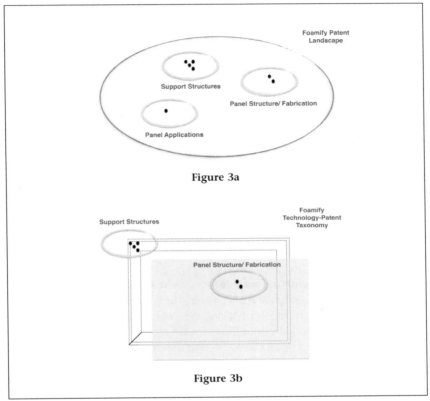

Figure 3a

Figure 3b

Figure 3a presents the Foamify patent landscape based on the above discussion. There are three areas of technology in which the seven patents have been grouped. At the moment the 'densest' area of coverage appears to be in support structures. On the other hand, this may be the most specific of the three areas. For example, the panel fabrication area may present patents with broader application as the panels could be used in a number of applications or have number of support structures. With similar arguments, the panel application area would have a scope between the other two.

It is now time to return to policing of patent rights. Policing becomes more effective when there is a portfolio of patents. For example, the four patents within the support structures area could provide more chances of finding infringement in a product. Having a number of patents here would also limit the avenues of 'working around' any individual patent. A portfolio therefore adds weight or substance to a company's IP position, which in turn will improve the chances of deterring potential infringers. It is worth noting that these arguments hold in particular when the patents are strategically placed around important areas of technology. If the seven patents were simply randomly scattered in isolated segments of the portfolio it would not carry the same weight.

An organisation with a larger portfolio will need a more sophisticated approach to organising its portfolio to get a clear view of the protection that it provides. Grouping the patents into two orthogonal taxonomies often provides the most useful results. One taxonomy contains product related categories. The second taxonomy contains technology related categories. The granularity of the categories should be targeted at creating groups of 20–200 patents to allow for efficient triaging when identifying patents for a given policing initiative. The count of patents in each category provides a quantified view of strength in a particular space. Identifying the strongest patents in each area is an important next step. This involves assessing the patent claims as described earlier and understanding if the claimed technology is being currently used by third parties and if that use can be detected. Assessing patents in this manner requires individuals skilled in the art (ie, people knowledgeable of the subject matter) with an understanding of how technology is being implemented by multiple parties in a given field and how to interpret claim language. It also requires a defined process to ensure consistency across a group of practitioners and a knowledge management tool to allow for ongoing use and management of the assessments.

4. Developing a policing and enforcement strategy

Knowing what is and what is not protected by your patents is a big step forward. From here a business strategy for policing the patent rights needs to be considered and developed to unlock the value therein. A key piece of this strategy will be determining the scope of the policing effort. Focusing the effort on direct competitors will defend the company's market share and price points. Expanding the policing effort upstream or downstream in the supply chain can provide opportunities to lower capital or supply costs and to expand market share. Further expanding the policing effort into adjacent or alternative markets can provide significant opportunities to monetise the patents through licensing royalties or asset sales.

4.1 Determine your strategic patents

A policing effort focused on direct competitors requires an identification of the patents that best protect the products in question. You need to ask a number of questions. Are there strategic or 'blocking' patents within your portfolio? Such patents are fundamental to the products of interest and would be used by almost any competitor. Are there other patents that may be relevant but whose use will depend on design or implementation choices made by a given competitor? Identifying both types of patents requires understanding key aspects of technology that will define or differentiate a product within the market space and alternative design approaches that may provide the same or similar results.

It is time to go back to the example of the '007 patent. The patent claims a system for affixing panels of metal foam and Foamify is in the business of making such foam panels. Potential targets would include those companies that also make metal foam cladding systems including the frame or companies making the support structure (frame) for this application.

A recent real-life example of the use of a 'blocking' patent to protect market share involves Blackberry and Typo. Blackberry has long been known for the physical keyboards on its handsets, a key differentiating factor that kept a core group of users from switching to Apple or Samsung products. Typo launched an iPhone case that included a physical keyboard – directly addressing this major point of differentiation that is a primary part of the Blackberry brand identity. To protect its products in this market space Blackberry filed suit and was granted a preliminary injunction in March, 2014.

4.2   Understand the technology landscape

Expanding a policing effort beyond companies that are your direct competitors requires a broad understanding of the technology landscape. Questions to be asked here include: are there patents that claim a variety of applications for component or building block technologies? What other products would benefit from the innovations protected by the patents? Again, you need to understand if the relevant patents are fundamental 'blocking' patents or whose use will depend on design or implementation choices.

Returning to the '007 patent, we might look at a ceramic filter between two fermentation tanks in say a brewing process. Here, the edges of the filter must be sealed to ensure liquid does not pass outside the filter. Now though, there is a problem because of the breadth of claim on one of the '007 patents. The preamble recites a 'metal foam' panel. We might further speculate that a legal opinion that determined this language is restrictive because it cannot be applied to other panel materials. In this case we would be limited in the policing and subsequent monetisation of the patent. Broader monetisation of the '007 patent would have required language that simply recites a 'foam' panel.

Organisations looking to expand their policing efforts need to make a key strategic decision: should the policing effort be focused to a particular product or market segment or be structured to investigate all products from companies of interest? Philips is a great example of a company pursuing the first strategic option – its website lists over 50 technology or product areas that it describes as functionalities which are the focus of individual licensing programmes. The alternative choice of policing on a company-by-company basis is common in industries like computers or semiconductors where there are dense patent thickets associated with a given product area due to the cumulative nature of the technologies required to develop and manufacture products in those fields.

5.   Identifying infringement

Whether your goal is the protection of a market space or the monetisation of assets it is important to develop an approach to identify potential infringement and gather evidence to support that contention. Strictly speaking, infringement is a very particular legal term whose determination can be quite involved and is the realm of IP counsel. However, there are many steps along the path to such a determination that can be undertaken by a corporation or specialised technical consultants.

The goal of identifying infringement is to access the value of the company's intellectual property to further the strategic objectives of the business. For the purposes of this chapter, the focus is on patents. However, management, policing assertion of other IP rights such as trademark, copyright and design rights is also important. In some industries, such as food and beverage, the valuable IP lies less in patents and more in trade secrets protecting recipes and in brand attributes such as trademarked name, logos and packaging.

As mentioned earlier in the chapter, the key to extracting the value from patents is through clear demonstration that another entity is practising the invention described in a valid patent and linking the use of the claimed technology to a financial outcome. Building a systematic policing programme to deliver the evidence needed to demonstrate unauthorised use is an important step to delivering value to the business. A two-staged approach is advised:

- gathering intelligence to identify potential areas where the patents are in use by competitors; and
- gathering evidence: the creation of the evidence of use that is required to engage with the third party who is practising the same patented technology.

A sound policing strategy will allow you to prioritise your areas of interest according to strategic priority, which will allow for the most effective use of available resources. The first stage will involve creating a monitoring process and usually some preliminary investigation of the areas of interest to gather easily obtained data that may provide indications of unauthorised use of the patented technology. Decisions can then be made on where to perform the more in-depth investigations of the second stage which are needed to develop conclusive evidence of use.

Frequently, robust evidence of use will require reverse engineering of a product. Reverse engineering may generally be considered as the analysis of a product to determine its structure, method of manufacture, functionality and how that functionality is being implemented. Reverse engineering is a commonly used procedure for performing competitive analysis, to develop interoperable products or to assess patent infringement. To perform reverse engineering will require you to acquire the product of interest and systematically evaluate it through such example techniques as teardown (disassembling the product to understand what components it is made from), functional testing of the product (evaluating the behaviour of the product when it is operating) or compositional analysis (to understand what a product is made from). The type of reverse engineering analysis required will depend on both the product under evaluation and the patent claims you are wishing to support.

5.1 Stage 1: gathering intelligence

The initial stage of a preliminary investigation is an exercise in listening to the areas of interest by keeping your eyes and ears open. This should be a routine activity whose scope is dictated by the strategic decision regarding the extent of the policing activity – direct competitors, adjacent/related markets, or casting your policing net as wide as possible so that is not limited to a subset of technologies, markets or competitors. Deciding scope will dictate the companies and products that are of interest to the investigation and will, of course, determine the degree of effort and expense of your programme.

How does an organisation begin to gather relevant information? An initial step is to set up automated searches and alerts related to key corporate names or terms associated with aspects of the technology that monitor product announcements, technical publications, conference proceedings, white papers, data sheets, user guides, repair manuals, other product literature, patenting activity, financial results, financial analyst reports and market analysis reports. Research may also include the monitoring of social media. In the end you should be aware of information coming from or related to the companies and products of interest. The organisation should also gather observations from its field staff: what information is sales and marketing collecting from the field and what have technical staff seen or heard at conferences or from discussions with peers at other companies?

What types of information indicate a policing opportunity? For example, are there marketing claims that sound like advantages associated with the technology? Do these marketing claims suggest a feature or advance that sounds related to technology disclosed in the patent(s) of interest? Marketing claims can be found in a variety of places such as media interviews, advertisements, videos, product demonstrations, website copy and product brochures. When considering social media monitoring, do research or manufacturing staff indicate that they are practising technologies in their role that are related to the technology? Are there online discussion forums where there are posts hinting at new product features that are relevant?

Looking again at the example of metal foam and the '007 patent. Assume an early intelligence gathering caught a competitor's press release indicating that their panelling system now provides "a mounting system providing an improved seal around and between panels". This would certainly be of interest. Further, they show a photograph (Figure 4) of their system. It shows a portion of four frames with panels, where the frames are adjacent to one another. The structure looks similar to Foamify's when frames are placed side by side, eg, Figures 1 and 2a.

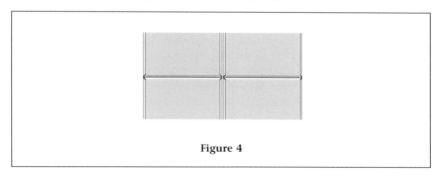

Figure 4

5.2   Stage 2: gathering evidence – sourcing and reverse engineering
Assuming at this point that the intelligence gathering stage has proved fruitful and you have decided to begin a more detailed investigation to develop evidence of use. The first step from here is to rank the potential targets. Is there one company of interest that, at this point, appears to be of more strategic interest to you – perhaps you wish to block their entry into your market, or has seen a large increase in revenue. Ranking of potential targets is important because at each stage going forward there will be an increasing amount of time and resources required to further the investigation.

(a)   Evidence of Use
The gathering of evidence can take many forms. It has already started in the intelligence gathering phase, and in some cases the collected documents including, datasheets, marketing documents, white papers or photographs may provide the required evidence of use. This is the exception as companies will generally be cautious in providing technical details in support of their marketing literature. In the vast majority of cases you will have to begin collecting evidence of use from actual products to support any patent claims.

Gathering Evidence of Use (EoU) information begins with the acquisition or sourcing of the suspect product. In the '007 patent example we would need to acquire a frame system. Assuming that the use of metal foam panels has become very popular and the mounting systems can be bought from any home improvement store. In such a case you would purchase a frame system, which in this example will be considered to have all of the necessary parts, including the sealant. Once in hand, the reverse engineering begins.

(b)   Reverse engineering
Again, it is important to do some planning before deconstructing the acquired product. You need to consider the claims in terms of what needs to be illustrated to indicate use of the claimed technology. This is known as preparing a claim chart. In such a chart you would highlight each and every element that collectively demonstrates use or presence of the claimed technology. A partial claim chart of claim one of the '007 patent is shown in Figure 5. In support of the selected claim elements presented in this chart you want to identify the presence of a frame, the four segments, first and second arms and first and second sealants. The relationship between elements and possible operation may also be of interest. A detailed plan for testing or reverse engineering the product is developed to determine if each and every claim element can be found in the product of interest.

As in every process of evidence gathering, having an accurate chain of custody (a paper trail) is important. Records of the purchase and receipt of the product should be kept as well as detailed records of any investigative work performed. It is a good practice to capture images of the intact packaged product, showing how the product looks at the time it was purchased to illustrate how it is marketed and, or sold. When considering the foam metal panels in the '007 case, initial photographs may show the whole structure and the basic relationship between elements. A cross-section

1. A system for affixing a metal foam panel to a surface, the system comprising:

   a first, second, third and fourth segment, the segments being attached to one another at ends thereof forming a rectangular frame, each segment having a first and second arm, the first and second arms being at an angle to one another;

   a first sealant applied to a first surface of the first and second arm, the first sealant appropriate for sealingly affixing a portion of the panel to the first surface of the first and second arm; and

   a second sealant applied to a second surface of the first and second arm, the second sealant appropriate for sealingly affixing the second surface of the second arm to the surface and the second surface of the first arm to an adjacent frame,

   wherein the panel is rigidly fixed to the surface and to adjacent panels.

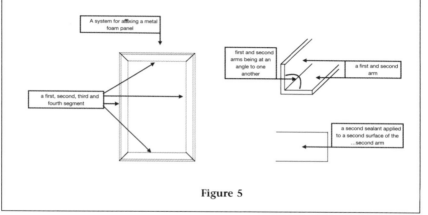

Figure 5

through a segment might show the arms and the relationship there between. Evidence around the first and second sealants may take more work. You might look for plastic to protect these features before use, or you might perform a simple test to show how any films that are present may operate as sealants. Finally, you may embark on a chemical analysis to identify the chemistry of the sealants. This may either provide circumstantial, or indirect evidence such as the presence of chemical elements. It may, on the other hand, provide a 'signature' of a known sealant. At the end of this process you want to have very particular physical evidence of the selected elements of the claim. The evidence of use is in hand.

6. Policing in various industries

Companies in different industries will need to have different approaches to policing IP. Differences in technology, in the availability of products and information, and the number of products or technologies to be investigated can vary widely.

6.1 Mechanical

The '007 patent is an example of a 'mechanical' patent. Mechanical patents are often simpler in the sense that they often refer to a relation of macroscopic structures or the function that such structures perform. As such, gathering evidence for this type of patent may often be more straightforward than that carried out in the other industries. Techniques used to gather EoU might include basic optical photography, measurements or deconstruction of the device to show a relation between parts. Specific tests may need to be undertaken to show the movement or operation of the machine or structure.

6.2   Electronics and semiconductors

It is probably fair to say that the electronics and semiconductor industries are very mature in terms of patent policing. There is a long history of evidence gathering, reverse engineering and patent enforcement in those industries. The nature of the patented technology will dictate the policing techniques used to investigate the product of interest. Patents claiming manufacturing processes or the resulting structures require materials analysis techniques and high magnification imaging offered by a variety of electron microscopes. The images of the structures found in the product and the materials used in those structures can reveal the process used in manufacturing to an engineer or scientist with experience in this particular field. Patents claiming circuit arrangements will require that the circuit be extracted from the semiconductor device or circuit board. This involves identifying the connections between specific circuit elements to develop the schematic for the circuit – a simple process at the board level, but one that requires electron microscopes and image processing software for state of the art semiconductor devices. Circuits can be quite simple, like a flip-flip, a logic configuration, or a simple analog block or they can be very extensive such as a semiconductor memory, a microprocessor core or a complete radio. Patents claiming function or performance features may be investigated using circuit reverse engineering if the function is implemented by a circuit. Moreover, software is being used to implement significant amounts of device functionality so software reverse engineering has become an important investigative technique. This may involve extracting code from a semiconductor memory or accessing the code through other means. Static analysis is then performed to disassemble the code (break it into its constituent parts by separating instructions from data) and decompile it to a level that will provide functional understanding. Typically the most significant challenge is isolating the segment of code performing the operation of interest. Dynamic analysis techniques such as code tracing and debugging can be very helpful in that regard. If the investigators are lucky, the code may contain comments in a readable format that may also be very helpful. Alternatively, the investigation may turn to functional testing of an operating device to understand how it performs under specific situations. This requires the ability to access specific points of interest within the system and to control the stimulus or operating parameters of the system in a way that allows the cause and effect of the system response to be accurately determined. All to say, each investigation is different in terms of difficulty and cost. Customised analysis programmes with phased analysis are best practice in managing large analysis projects. It also makes sense, wherever possible, for companies to enforce across multiple products or companies to leverage the expense of developing the analysis techniques.

The convergence of technologies in this space into a single product can make policing more difficult in terms of detection, but with a greater number of opportunities in terms of relevant patents. A mobile phone uses telephony, computing, imaging, displays, batteries, gaming and a myriad of other technologies much of which are being integrated onto fewer semiconductor components. This makes testing and reverse engineering more challenging. Such an investigation may require several months of effort, costing US$200,000 to US$500,000. These numbers are small when compared to the potential licensing or litigation returns, which may run to hundreds of millions of dollars. Preparing a licensing campaign is a significant undertaking. Companies will often perform a detailed analysis of the return on investment and the consequence of not taking action. However, the benefits of successfully executing licensing programmes can be very large as evidenced by the billion dollar licensing club members mentioned earlier in this chapter.

6.3 Chemical and energy

This represents an immense group of technologies that are likely to become increasingly important. The chemical group spans the gamut of industrial and household chemicals. This may traditionally include petroleum-based industries, creating an overlap with traditional oil and gas-based energy. Alternative energy presents an interesting example within this group. Consider solar energy, here the fundamental silicon-based photovoltaic technologies used to make the solar cells are quite old. However, the recent move toward alternative energy has brought about a considerable wave in patents because of the increase in potential market size. This may include new material and structures for the photovoltaic cells, to the electronics that brings the generated energy to the grid, to energy storage systems designed to balance the output to the grid. It is anticipated that the field will continue to grow over time. Further, the economic and societal impact of an energy technology can be immense, making the need to police and enforce important.

If we continue with the solar example, the techniques for collecting evidence of use can be similar to those of the electronics space. Namely, we could look to techniques for determining physical structures and chemistries, and for determining the circuits and electrical components required to harvest the energy from the solar cells.

6.4 Medical devices

The field of medical devices is another area of significant technology convergence with chemical and biological technologies coming together with mechanical structures and electronics and communications devices. One example would be a smart blood glucose monitor that has wireless connectivity and communicates the patient's test results directly to a smartphone, these results may also be automatically shared with the patient's doctor and there may be remote cloud-based storage of the archived data and a web interface for patient and doctor to review the data. Another example is point of care diagnostics leveraging 'lab-on-a-chip' technologies which are now performing real time *in situ* chemical analysis without the need to send samples off to remote test laboratories. Advances in miniaturisation place analysis capabilities in a medical professional's hand or permit the use of remote care at a patient's home. Interesting challenges arise when a medical equipment manufacturer integrates medical functionality into a device like a smartphone. Consider a heart rate monitor in a mobile phone, for example. This device may use different technology to collect a person's heart rate, when compared to a traditional hospital or office monitoring system. There may be algorithms for the manipulation of data that is the same as for the larger systems. Thus, manufacturers have to be cognisant of existing technologies, even if the form factor is very different. We can generally look to similar techniques used in the electronics industry for the determination of basic structure, chemistry or signals. For example, there may be patented algorithms around the daily collection of heart rate data. Trends or variations in this data may be indicative of X or Y condition. So you could determine, via monitoring the electronic signals within the functioning device, what data is stored in the device's memory. It may also be possible to determine what calculations are performed on the data and even detect the use of a particular algorithm. There will also be a host of techniques particular to medical systems. These might include the use of reagents or antibodies to determine specific 'medical' chemistry. Chemists experienced in techniques for detecting particular types of reagents are useful here.

7.   **Conclusion**

Active policing of patent rights is a key activity in deriving value from a patent portfolio. The evidence gathered by a policing programme plays a significant role in demonstrating the value of the patents and can be a major driver of success in the use of the patents to defend market share, generate income streams, secure investments or provide access to needed technology or markets. Establishing a systematic policing programme requires understanding the scope of coverage provided by the patent portfolio, identifying products using technology that overlaps with that coverage and gathering evidence that confirms the use of the claimed technology and creates leverage for the patent holder in a given situation. Organisations with such a programme can obtain significant advantages for their business. The investment often required to build an effective policing programme can be significant but the returns can be 10–100 times that investment in simple financial outcomes.

8.   **Chapter summary**
   - Know the protection provided by a patent claim or a portfolio of patents.
   - Implement a process to gather information from a range of sources that identify possible uses of protected technology.
   - Develop the investigative techniques needed to demonstrate evidence of use and link this use to a financial impact.

IP licensing

Richard Buttrick
RBIP Ltd

1. Introduction

Intellectual Property (IP) licensing is an optional, but important, enabling element of IP strategy. This chapter explores how the building blocks of IP licensing work, with examples of the tactical and strategic choices they offer. Together these building blocks present a broad range of options and choices for IP owners. While these tend to make IP licensing complex and technical, it also becomes a subtle and creative art, capable of driving remuneration, often cash revenue, from IP.

IP strategies have both passive and active elements, and IP licensing is an active commitment by an IP owner that will transform their IP strategy. IP licensing is a proactive way of realising value created in IP, and carries with it both risk and reward. Although a great deal of attention and focus is given to monetisation of IP through licensing, IP licensing has many strategic uses, for example, cross-licensing of one IP portfolio with another to reduce IP infringement risk enables freedom of use of a competitor's technology.

When establishing an IP strategy that includes IP licensing, the ultimate goal of the strategy and the licensing needs to be clearly established, because that goal must underpin and drive the licensing process as well as the licences generated. Lack of clarity in a shared, agreed outcome can cause not only disruption to the licensing process but also affect the quality and effectiveness of the licences ultimately generated. Take, for example, the simple notion of monetising a patent by licensing. Is the goal to maximise the revenue returned, which may involve licensing for a modest royalty for a longer period, or to seek higher, likely short-term, revenues?

It is quite common for companies to come into IP licensing with a hope, even an expectation, of quick and high returns. Such an approach may not only sub-optimise revenue generation, but these expectations can readily become unrealistic and undermine the licensing process itself. The mantras of successful monetisation through IP licensing centre on slicing and dicing market opportunities over extended periods to create sustained revenues. Whichever outcome is desired, clarity and shared communication of the desired outcome are necessary prerequisites to successful IP licensing.

While the focus of this chapter is on how the building blocks of IP licensing can offer tactical and strategic opportunities for an IP owner, a fundamental basis for success must be the quality of the IP being licensed. If the mantra for value in property is "location, location, location", then for IP it is "quality, quality, quality". Typically, the higher the quality of an IP asset, the higher its value, and also the easier and more straightforward the IP asset is to license. This reflects a potential licensee's desire to have access to IP assets of higher quality. Quality will – or will at least tend to – sell itself. Determining and understanding the quality of any IP that is to be licensed is thus an important prerequisite in framing both a realistic, desired outcome and the most appropriate route to licensing. Taking another simple patent example, it is common to cluster patents into bundles or portfolios so that potential deficiencies, like weak or narrow patents, will be offset. For the potential licensee an aggregate risk or opportunity is created with a portfolio of patents. Avoiding or eliminating all of a bundle of patents is less likely for the potential licensee, so even if the individual patents might not be the best, 'grade-A' quality, the need to take or usefulness of a licence must be justifiable.

When forming the framework of an IP licensing programme, an IP owner needs to address a range of choices and options. A licensing programme will have at its core a set of common licensing terms, which will define the permissions given under licences in that programme. Equally significantly, they will define the limitations that form part of the licences. The core terms will also set out goals for remuneration, including royalties and other cash payments. Another important component of a licensing framework is an appreciation of the risks and threats that a licensing programme may generate. These can range from a loss of financial investment in a licensing programme if it is not successful, to reputational issues that can arise from some forms of assertive licensing.

The history of IP licensing goes back to the earliest days of IP, and it was famously part of Thomas Watt's chosen method of exploiting his patents on the steam engine at the end of the 18th century, which helped kick-start the industrial revolution. Since then, a body of precedent and standard forms for licences has been built up over the generations, and there are a many schemes for licensing with specific application, such as for Standards Essential Patent (SEP) licensing, software licensing and many more. Even so, while each situation will benefit from and build on these established forms and approaches, each will be unique and have its own challenges and opportunities.

2.   Understanding the outcome

This section aims to help answer a number of important questions. First, what is being licensed? Secondly, why is it being licensed? And finally, what is wanted from the process?

Before starting IP licensing, clarity on the desired outcome is essential. It is all too easy to focus on an element of an outcome, such as cash revenue, and miss the overall picture.

The first thing to get a clear grasp on is what is being licensed. This may seem obvious, as there will likely be a package of one or more pieces of IP intended to form the basis of a licensing programme, but not all IP is equal. Indeed, even seemingly similar pieces of IP like patents can be very different in quality and hence in value. IP owners, particularly those who have been involved in the generation of their own IP, are unlikely to have pragmatic view of quality. Therefore an independent evaluation of the quality and value of the IP to be licensed is needed, and a range of assessment services is available through independent IP advisory companies and individuals with IP licensing expertise. In addition, the emergence over the last decade of IP valuation as an independent professional activity has added an alternative option to the established and equally professional but more empirical, pragmatic view of licensing experts. These differing perspectives can help prepare IP owners for the acid test of putting their IP into the marketplace. Once in that marketplace, one of the by-products of IP licensing is the insight that can be gained from third-party evaluation of the IP package being licensed. It can come as a salutary experience to be told by potential licensee after potential licensee that your much loved IP is in fact not worth the paper it is written on or more likely that it is only worth a fraction of what is hoped for. So, a realistic evaluation of the IP to be offered for is an essential starting point for any IP licensing programme before going to market.

Having had the quality of IP to be licensed assessed, the next step is to establish the purpose for licensing and the circumstances in which the licensing is taking place. For example, the most likely and common situation is where an IP owner is not exploiting the IP commercially themselves and wants to derive value from it by having someone else use it. In some IP-based business models such third-party exploitation is inherent and essential, and IP licensing structures become business norms. One such form of IP is copyright in literary works where licensing is the standard form of business exploitation, and where associated rights – like film and TV rights – are licensed to create additional channels of income. Some forms of brand licensing, like franchising, are built around a similar economic model, where the IP is generated with the intention of exploitation through licensing others. In other cases, an IP owner may have tried and failed to exploit the IP, or not have the resources to fully exploit it. This is common with patents, particularly where a family of patents covers a broad range of geographic markets. Few companies can expect to exploit IP fully across the majority of markets let alone all markets around the world, so IP licensing may be a way of addressing untapped opportunities. In some situations, particularly with complex technologies in consumer markets, an IP owner can be exploiting their own IP, but be using the IP of others too, and vice versa, and IP cross-licensing can be a way of reducing or eliminating risk and creating 'freedom to operate'. Each situation will be both unique and commonplace, and clarity in understanding the fundamentals of the situation will set the boundaries for an IP licensing framework.

One of the most important elements that will be a cornerstone of IP licensing is the question of what is wanted from the IP licensing – the remuneration for the licence – whether it is access to third-party IP or a business opportunity or revenue, or something else. The answer to that fundamental question – what is wanted – needs to be cemented in realistic analysis. To be successful this question needs to be framed in the context of what the IP to be licensed actually is and why it is being licensed.

It is important to see the overall outcome from IP licensing not simply in terms of the remuneration, for example, revenue, generated from it. That remuneration will stem from a third party's successful exploitation of the IP, and that third-party exploitation will change the markets being exploited. In some situations, for example, where a brand is being licensed, the IP owner's own presence in that market will be raised. The consequences from IP licensing go beyond the revenues that are derived, and those consequences – part of the outcome – need to be evaluated, understood and accepted before an IP licensing programme proceeds. There will almost inevitably be unintended consequences from licensing programmes – part of the risk and threats that need to be evaluated – so the outcome may not be what is expected, and a continual assessment of the overall outcome of a licensing programme is needed as the programme evolves.

With an initial view on the desired outcome for a licensing programme captured as the basis of an IP licensing framework, the development of a programme can begin. This will involve choosing the building blocks of an IP licensing programme, and how they will be deployed.

3. Quick licence overview

At the core of an IP licence, an IP owner gives permission to someone to do something that would otherwise not be possible without access to the owner's IP. That this sounds vague and general is the point. Although IP licences tend towards certain types or common forms, there are practically limitless alternatives to the way a licence may be defined. There are common or at least recurring elements in IP licences, which can conveniently be thought of as the 'dimensions' of the licence. These also define its scope.

The 'dimensions' of a licence can be summarised as the what, where, who, how and when. These five dimensions recur in the granting of IP licences. It's in the choosing of how to use these dimensions that lies the art and science of licensing. Steered by the rest of a company's IP strategy and implemented through an IP licensing framework, the aim is to devise the best, or most productive, licence to achieve the chosen outcome, including revenue generation. This is where the 'slicing and dicing' happens.

Looking more closely:

- what is the IP being licensed?;
- where is its territory?;
- who are the IP owner and the licensee?;
- how are the activities being licensed?; and
- what is the life of the licence?

Some of these become specific to the IP being licensed, so for example 'how' under a patent might include manufacture of a product, while under copyright it might be the publication of a literary work. Thus the IP being licensed will constrain the dimensions of a licence, but there is always room to develop ways of realising value.

Value realisation may be enhanced by dividing territory or markets, and granting parallel licences to optimise revenue generation from an existing market, or providing licences with limited life spans, which encourage a licensee to a make a maximum effort for a limited time. Conversely, a licence may be simplified – giving a licensee more latitude – by making a licence worldwide and for the life of the IP, to give them time and opportunity to develop a market. The appropriate licence to be granted will not only be dependent on the IP owner's aspirations and a potential licensee's needs, but also more general business circumstances, such as the developmental state of a market. In this sense an IP owner's aspirations need to be tempered by the reality of the circumstances.

In summary, the scope of an IP licence can be considered in terms of five basic dimensions of the scope of the licence, which can be adapted – sliced and diced – to develop ways of realising value.

3.1 What: the IP being licensed

A wide variety of IP can be licensed, including:

- know-how;
- trade secrets;
- patents;
- copyright;
- design rights; and
- brand, including trademarks.

Some of these forms of IP such as know-how and brand also embrace other forms of intangible assets, such as the collective knowledge, experience and skills that employees have, the value inherent in the business' relationships and so forth, which may, usually by necessity, be drawn in under the umbrella of an IP licence.

It is possible to license IP to its fullest scope, for example, it is possible to license a patent without restriction on the product (or process) covered by the licence. The licensee is then given permission to produce any product within the scope of the patent. It is however more common to limit the product in some way, either to a specified, defined product – the licensed product – or through a product within a particular technical field – the field of use. The 'what' of the licence grant is thus commonly expressed as a combination of the IP and a licensed product or a field of use.

Taking a hypothetical but real world example, a patent covering a wireless technology such a Bluetooth could be applicable to a range of products, for example, mobile phones, tablet computers, remote controls, health sensors and headphones. A licence to such a patent could cover all these products, a selection, only one, or a field of use, for example, remote controls for industrial use.

The IP to be licensed will usually be given or fixed, but 'what' is licensed under that IP can and often needs to be chosen and defined. This represents an important tactical, even strategic tool for the IP owner. It can be an important part of the process of 'slicing and dicing' of IP to maximise value return for an IP owner. It becomes particularly important when dealing in sole or exclusive licences (this is discussed further below) where an IP licensee is given a special position.

In some circumstances licensing one form of IP may lead to the need or at least the expectation of access to other IP. Know-how licensing is often complemented by show-how licensing, perhaps in the form of paid for consultancy, because the capture and transfer of know-how is often difficult.

3.2   Where: the territory

The territory of licence defines and limits where a licensee can use the licensed IP. IP arising under national law is inherently territorially limited in its effect, and usually, in practice, IP to be included in a particular licence will not extend to every country in the world.

At first sight then the IP owner has the option of setting the territory for a licence to be all or a sub-set of those countries where the licensed IP has effect. Indeed, it is quite usual to be licensing patents and trademarks that cover only the major industrialised nations, or even particular markets, because IP protection strategies will tend to target these. Nevertheless, it is common to give worldwide licenses for simplicity, and certainty for the licensee. The alternative, to give territorially limited, for example, country specific licences, is also common, particularly to achieve a particular purpose, such as market segmentation.

The choice of territory for an IP licence is thus dependent on three things: the IP to be licensed, the intended markets – existing or expected – and the preferred approach to licensing, based on the desired outcome, as captured in the IP licensing framework. Territory becomes a significant facet of a licence when one or more of these factors limits the selection of territorial coverage for a licensee. A 'worldwide' territory can be seen as a 'neutral' selection, implying that territorial limitation is not significant for the licence. In some cases territorial limitation is part of the essence of a licence, for example, in the territorial limited licensing of literary copyright allowing publication of a book in United States but not Europe, or in the case of trademark/brand licensing where a licence can even be for part of a country.

A natural case of a territorially limited licence is where the IP only exists in one country. Take a situation where an IP owner has a registered design for the United Kingdom. Assuming for simplicity that there are no other related registered rights to be licensed, then a licence under this registered design would only be for the UK, whether or not this was made explicit in the licence. Making the territory explicitly the UK would help transparence and mutual understanding of the licence, and would also create clarity in case – as there might well be with designs – there are other unregistered IP rights which exist. It is usual to specify the territory of a licence even if it may seem to be inherent in the IP being licensed.

Between the extremes of country-by-country and worldwide licensing there are also important regional issues to consider, particularly concerning regional trade blocs, such as the European Union and the North American Free Trade Agreement (NAFTA). The EU trade bloc, for example, is built on the free movement of goods and free competition. EU law and regulations can impact some forms of licences – particularly those involving exclusivity – and licences should not attempt to supervene such law and regulations. Such limitations make it more straightforward to license trade blocs such as the EU as single territory. However some IP strategies – including brand licensing – aimed at maximising remuneration may well have country-by-country licensing as an essential element. Whenever country-by-country licensing within a trade bloc is a key part of an IP strategy, the issues of trade bloc law and regulation become of central importance and specialist advice is needed.

Worldwide licensing has the benefit of simplicity and may avoid potential issues arising from laws and regulations relating to trade blocs. However, worldwide licensing is not without its pitfalls, notably concerning royalties, and particularly where products are made and sold in territories not covered by the licensed IP. Take the case of patented products manufactured in China and sold in major markets around the world. Where patent protection exists in China all of the patent products can legitimately be subject to a licensing fee, typically a royalty. If on the other hand patent protection only exists in some of the major markets, then only some of the patented products will attract a licensing fee. In many situations manufacturing is distributed across countries with and without patent protection, and there is a similar situation for markets. In such situations the practicalities of determining which product was produced and/or sold in a patent protected country can be enormous, and a pragmatic approach to accounting and royalty setting is needed. So, where there is a mix of manufacturing and sale under or outside patent protection one practical solution is to use global sales of a product but apply a discounted licensing fee. The simplification of the territory to 'worldwide' can thus create complications with determining remuneration that themselves need to be simplified to achieve a practical and pragmatic outcome.

3.3 Who: the IP owner and the licensee

The most common and simple form of licence is between two entities, commonly two companies. Many variations are possible, for example the IP owner and licensor may be a non-practising entity such as a sole inventor or a university. All entities will be making choices based on their personal situation or circumstances. At a more complex level, the nature of some entities can impact the choices available for licensing and even the structure of a licence.

The identity of an IP owner can limit the range of preferred options for a licence. Typically universities license technical innovation through patent licences, often without know-how because university generated research know-how is early stage. So, a common form of licensing for universities is what is known as 'naked' patent licensing. Entities such as universities and individuals will rarely have brand and related IP to license. The identity and nature of the IP owner can dictate the range of IP to be licensed and also the terms on which it is licensed.

In some cases complexity can be inherent in the corporate structure of the IP owner and/or IP licensee, which can affect the nature or structure of a licence. Often large corporations have a complex structure, for example, a hierarchy of parent and subsidiaries, a suite of national entities or a structure where IP is held in an IP holding company. Any of the structures can directly affect 'who' is licensed and 'how'. Where a large company is an IP licensee, to enable effectively a corporation which has a hierarchy of parent and subsidiaries, a choice will need to be made regarding 'who' within the hierarchy should be a party to the licence and 'how' they should benefit. The parent may be the named licensee and the licences granted extended to 'subsidiaries', but this will inevitably lead to a series of important questions about what a 'subsidiary' is, and which 'subsidiaries' are to be covered by a licence. For example, is any subsidiary of the parent at any time, or only those 'subsidiaries' existing at the date of the licence agreement? All these subtle, seemingly technical decisions can impact the overall outcome and the successful implementation of an IP strategy.

An important potential conditioning of an IP licence is to make it exclusive or sole. A licence is sole when only the IP owner and the one licensee can use the IP, while under an exclusive licence only the licensee can use the IP and even the IP owner is precluded from exercising the IP. An exclusive licence puts a licensee close to being 'in the shoes' of the IP owner, though national laws may not give an exclusive licensee all the rights of an IP owner, for example, the ability to litigate registered IP, such as patents for infringement. More commonly IP licences are non-exclusive, with an IP owner seeking remuneration from multiple-licensees for access to its IP.

It is an economic benefit for a licensee to have an exclusive licence, as the licensee can seek 'monopoly' profits, and the IP owner can expect correspondingly higher remuneration (this is discussed further below). Whether exclusive licensing is an overall benefit to an IP owner is a much more complex question, which may not readily be answerable, despite its importance to IP owners. Comparative prediction of remuneration from 'one' licensee versus 'many' licensees can give a theoretical, economic view of the options, but within these different models the varying risks will likely make useful comparison difficult. This is particularly the case when a new market is to be created, rather than an existing market exploited. Whether a single, 'driven' licensee is better than multiple equally incentivised licensees will often be down to individual perspective. This sort of choice is particularly important for non-practising entities such as universities who create early stage IP ahead of market-led demand, and whose IP strategy will likely be focused on direct financial remuneration.

Two important sub-elements of 'who' is being licensed are 'have-made' rights and sub-licensing. Where an entity does not have the capability to manufacture one, some or all of the products, a licence may include rights allowing a licensee to have a product or products made for subsequent sale by the licensee. A typical situation for this is where the licensee wants to sell a product under its own brand using supply from OEMs or ODMs, with retail-brand consumer electronics being a good example. For the IP owner inclusion of 'have-made' rights complicates the practicalities of licensing, for example, auditing of manufacture, and consequently the risk of unregulated use of the IP licensed. However, this may allow for higher royalties by licensing higher up the value chain. 'Have-made' rights are quite common, unlike sub-licensing rights, which put the licensee in the position of being able to licence the IP with limited approval, if any, from the IP owner. Though sub-licensing can be controlled, for example, by limiting it to approved pro forma licences, there are comparatively few situations where an IP owner will not want to do such licensing themselves, so sub-licensing rights are uncommon.

3.4   How: the activities being licensed

While IP licences will often give permission for a licensee to 'use' the IP, some forms of IP including registered rights such as patents and trademarks, and unregistered rights like copyright, have particular rights which the IP owner is able to control and therefore to licence. With patents, typical rights include manufacture, use, sale, lease and importation of products, with have-made being an important additional element, as discussed above.

In many situations all of these 'reserved rights' of the IP owner will be licensed, so that the licensee is fully able to make use of its licence. More sophisticated arrangements can be used as a means to seek to increase remuneration – another way of 'slicing and dicing', but these arrangements inevitably lead to more complexity in the licensing structure, which will need to be justified by greater added value to the licensing programme. An example of this is where a licensee is not given a general licence to sell but is only allowed to sell to specifically licensed entities who themselves are licensed to sell on, perhaps under a related IP licence, for example, a brand licence. Another similar arrangement can be made where having licensed one entity in the middle of a value chain, the IP gives 'non-assertion' undertakings to that licensed entity's suppliers, but only for supply to that licensed entity.

This parsing or separation of rights can find particular uses or applications. In software licensing the various 'reserved rights' associated with copyright can be used to control what a licensee can do with the software. A licensee may be given the right to copy and use the software, but not the right to modify or translate the software. Open source software licensing makes use of these controls to impose strict rules on those adapting open source software, while literary copyright licences, for example for books, may permit a translator to translate a work and have rights in the translation, but not give the translator a licence to sell the translation without paying a share of revenues to the owner of the copyright in the original work.

These sorts of sophisticated uses of specific forms of authorisation under a licence have developed in particular fields and sectors of IP licensing. It is likely that whatever the IP for whatever outcome, there has been a similar licence for the same scenario before. The IP licensing industry relies a lot on an established precedent both in the structuring of licences and – as discussed below – in terms of remunerations. These standard types of licences form a useful starting, and often end, point for users.

3.5   When: the life of the licence

The final dimension of an IP licence is its life. Here it is important to distinguish between three things: the life of the licence, the life of the licence agreement and the life of the IP being licensed. These can be different or the same depending on the tactical and strategic choices made.

Each form of IP has its own lifetime. A well-known example is copyright – typically the author's life plus 70 years. Patents usually have a 20-year term, and know-how has an unlimited life, provided that it is kept confidential. These are important to bear in mind when framing the life of the licence given under the IP, and also the life of the agreement.

It is quite common to make the term of the licence and the term of the agreement the same. However, it is possible to make arrangements where the term of licence is less than the term of the agreement. One typical example of this is where the licence grant has the potential to change during the life of the agreement. So a licence agreement may initially give an exclusive licence for a certain term, and that exclusive licence may be extended on some conditions, for example, revenue levels being met. The agreement may revert to a non-exclusive licence if they are not met.

More conventionally, the choice is often between a fixed term, say five or 10 years, and the life of the IP, as long as that lifetime is consistent with business planning. Extra care needs to be taken for cases where the IP has unlimited life such as brand or know-how. Know-how licensing can be coupled to the life of a related patent in combined patent and know-how licences.

The choice in selecting licence and licensing agreement lifetime comes down to a case of balancing stability for the parties, the effort in renegotiating and, most importantly, changes in the commercial basis for the licence. When licensing deals are struck it will be on the basis of predictive assumptions of both the parties, which are clearly likely to become less reliable with time. Common lifetimes of five and 10 years allow for a reasonable period of exploitation, with some market development and other changes, while allowing the parties to revisit their original assumptions in case there have been disruptive developments or changes, such as a failed market or a superseded technology.

4. Remuneration

The main reason for IP licensing is usually the pay-off – what the IP owner gets in return for giving the IP licence. This 'remuneration' is a balance to the licence granted, the scope of which is defined by the five dimensions discussed above, ie, the remuneration of the IP owner should match what the IP licensee gets in the licence grant.

What determines the level of remuneration for the IP owner is a combination of the value of the IP and the IP licensee's ability to realise that value. Another way to look at this is that the IP owner and IP licensee will each have their own view of the value of the licensed IP, and having determined the scope of a licence the two can usually reach a deal on the level of remuneration if there is an overlap in the perceived value.

In the context of product or service sales, the remuneration should be within the added value for the IP licensee of the licence. So, if the IP licensee can charge US$1 more for a product because of an IP licence, then the IP owner can get a share of that US$1. The inevitable negotiation will be on the size of the opportunity and the relative shares of the pie.

One well-known concept in IP licensing is the '25% Rule', which suggests that an IP owner should get 25% of the added value brought by the licence. This is not so much a rule as a guideline, and not so much a guideline as practical place to start. More bullish negotiators may start at 50% while circumstances such as market and price uncertainty may make a smaller percentage pragmatically sensible. Clearly the art is not taking too much and killing the goose that lays the golden eggs, while milking a healthy return.

Remuneration through monetisation, routinely for cash, is of course very common, and though much rarer it has been known to accept other forms of remuneration than cash when monetising IP, with commodities such as oil and grain being rare but known examples. There are other forms of remuneration, for example, where the desired outcome is the inward licensing of IP, for example, to reduce risk for freedom of use or to inwardly licence enabling IP, the remuneration for the outward IP licence can be the inward IP licence. A portfolio cross-licence is a simple example of this form of arrangement.

Usually the desired outcome from IP licensing will dictate the form of remuneration chosen, but circumstances may change this, as in the case of taking non-cash remuneration, for example, inward licence to counter-asserted IP, when monetising IP through assertive licensing.

The two most common mechanisms for cash remuneration are lump sums – commonly upfront or fixed annual fees – and running royalties. Setting these forms of cash remuneration requires an understanding, including a calculation, of the value to be extracted by means of the licence. Fixed fees or running royalties are simply alternative but common methods of levying cash remuneration, and whichever is chosen it is important to understand where the money to pay for it is coming from, and how much, realistically, is available.

A running royalty on a product or service will need to come from the margin – gross or net – on the licensee's product. Whether it is perceived to be gross or net will depend on the licensee's perspective of seeing the royalty as part of the bill of materials for the product or as a tax on net profit. Either way there needs to be sufficient margin to bear the royalty, so the product or service and the market to which the IP is applicable become important factors for determining the scale of a royalty. For such practical reasons it is most common to assess royalties as a percentage of a sales price, often the ex-factory price for products. Determining the royalty base is as important as setting the royalty percentage. It is also known to have fixed royalties, for example, US$1 per product, and such fixed royalties have distinct advantages when it comes to accounting for royalties as it is easier to count products sold then revenue received by a licensee.

Royalty setting can be realised in a variety of ways. Most industries have norms for royalties, or at least a distribution around a norm, which have been sampled and tallied by confidential studies. So, norming figures of 5%, 10% and 15% of sales price recur in studies across ranges of industries, with a spread around the norm. However, whatever the industry norms, understanding the business model, and consequently the likely margin or margins of a potential licensee, is key to being able to establish a realistic royalty. Simplistically, trying to argue that the royalty should 'only' be 1% is likely to be futile if the net margin on a product is only 2%–3% and the IP licence only adds 0.5% to the margin.

Another common way of establishing royalties is by precedent, ie, an established royalty for the same or similar IP. As already mentioned, the IP licensing industry favours precedent for the form of licences, and this preference extends to already established royalty rates, particularly for similar IP. In some circumstances, notably Standards Essential Patent (SEP) licensing, its known to publicise or at least share such royalties, or at least a figure that is a common starting point for negotiation.

SEP licensing is a special, and recently important, subset of patent assertion licensing. In return for having a technology incorporated into a national or international standard, the IP owner commits to licensing the IP, usually patents, on that technology on Fair, Reasonable and Non-Discriminatory (FRAND) terms and conditions. What is a FRAND royalty is determined by a good faith negotiation, which the IP owner and licensee commit to as part of the process of working with standards. For some standards, such as mobile phone standards, whole industries have emerged with many patents being asserted as 'essential' to the implement a standard. The licences usually have the same scope, ie, to allow implementation of a standard, so the primary issues are to determine whether the patents are 'essential' to implementing a standard and to determine what the appropriate royalty should be.

Special circumstances may affect the level of remuneration under a licence. Remuneration for an exclusive licence would be expected to be higher than for a non-exclusive licence. A running royalty might well be at a higher rate for an exclusive licence, but where exclusive licences tend to be attractive for an IP owner is having a combination of running royalties and up-front fees, or more especially fixed annual minimum royalties, particularly in the early years of a licence. Such fixed minima are intended to encourage an exclusive licensee to accelerate sales of a product, because it may well be paying more royalties than it is actually earning.

5.   Risks and threats

Risk and threat management is an important aspect of IP strategy. It usually centres on threats posed by third-party IP; it is not usual to focus on the potential risks or threats around one's own IP. When doing IP licensing, however, such attention is needed, particularly to avoid unforeseen and undesirable consequences which might adversely affect the reputation of the IP owner.

Reputational risk is inherent in some forms of IP licensing. One significant area of reputational risk arises in brand licensing, where a third party is putting products or services into the marketplace. The quality of those third-party products or services will impact the brand being licensed. In brand licensing, therefore, quality control plays an important, even central role.

Another risk is that an IP licensing programme might fail, with loss of the investment of effort and time in that programme as well as potential reputational damage. Whilst this risk may not be avoidable, it is prudent to understand and actively manage the costs associated with IP licensing. A suitable method for this is to do a rolling discounted cash-flow analysis for the programme, including costs, in conjunction with analysis of the value of the remuneration from the programme.

The profile of a licensing programme, and the manner of its execution can affect the reputational risk associated with the failure or even the success of a licensing programme. Some forms of IP licensing are more assertive than others. IP licensing associated with existing IP infringement is one area that often requires strongly assertive programmes, even involving litigation in some circumstances. Patent and copyright infringement licensing fall in to this category. The more assertive a licensing programme, the more likely there may be adverse reputational spin-offs. The more complex a company's business, the more likely there may be an adverse impact from IP licensing on some other part of the company's business.

A small range of IP licensing models exist which use highly assertive, litigation-centric tactics in association with IP acquired solely for such use. These models, where the IP owner is sometimes associated with the term 'troll', carry with them levels of reputational risk of an even higher order of magnitude.

6. Working with licence agreements

Getting a licence negotiated and transformed into a licensing agreement is a significant undertaking. Getting the deal done and the agreement signed is just the beginning of the life of the agreement. Some features, such as accounting and auditing, routinely appear in licensing agreements and are part of the day-to-day life of an agreement, while other features, such as technical support, or show-how, will be included when and where needed.

6.1 Accounting and auditing

All cash bearing IP licence agreements will have some form of accounting provisions, and usually auditing provisions as well. The accounting provisions will cover the practical mechanisms for getting remuneration due, for example, running royalties, from the IP licensee to the IP owner, while the auditing provisions are there so that the IP owner can check that everything is working as it should be.

The accounting provisions will typically set out the IP licensee's duties in reporting on sales of the product or service in question, and then payment of the royalties due. So, quarterly or semi-annual reporting is common, with payment lagging further behind.

Auditing is important because the accounting processes of licensees seldom live up to expectations. This is not necessarily down to sharp practice. Few companies will have a routine mechanism for checking for each new product or service what IP licences are being exploited, though for smaller companies with only a few licences this should be easier. Feedback from auditing suggests that a significant part of accounting failures arise from unintended breakdowns in internal communication within an IP licensee.

6.2 Technical support and show-how

For some technology based licences ongoing support may be required by an IP licensee, which may take the form of a package of or on-demand consultancy. Show-how may be a specific part of the package of a licence, with successful demonstration of a technology being linked to payment of remuneration.

6.3 Legal aspects

Like all legal agreements there will be a deal of 'boiler plate' in a licence agreement, usually to cover potential problems or failures, such as bankruptcy of an IP licensee.

Among these provisions restrictions are commonly place on an IP licensee's freedom to transfer a licence agreement to another company, including through acquisition. IP owners commonly want to protect themselves from their IP being inadvertently licensed to a competitor, so restrictions on transfer of licences and licence agreements are common, for example, by giving the IP owner the option of terminating the licence agreement in the event of the licensee being taken over.

7. **Conclusion**

This chapter has introduced the field of IP licensing in a broad and general way to help highlight the strategic and tactical opportunities that IP licensing brings. The building blocks of IP licensing provide a broad range of options and choices to allow IP owners to implement their chosen approach to IP licensing, and this chapter has laid out what will be the ground work for IP owners to make those choices and begin to create a framework for IP licensing. The detailed choices of any particular, practical situation are best addressed with the help of expert advice and a worldwide network of IP licensing experts exists to provide both global and local knowledge, and help IP owners navigate the complex world of IP licensing.

8. **Chapter summary**

- IP licensing is an important optional element of IP strategy. The realistic goal of IP licensing needs to be captured and forms the basis an executable licensing framework. A good licensing framework will capture the expectations for and key terms of a licensing programme, including desired remuneration, as well addressing risks and threats.

- Sound licensing programmes are based on a clear, independently assessed view of the quality and value of the IP being licensed, and an equally clear assessment of what is wanted from licensing the IP. There are many established IP licensing business models, which can give insights and understanding of the potential overall outcome of IP licensing. Risk and threats in an outcome need to be evaluated alongside desired outputs like revenue.

- The scope of an IP licence can be considered in terms of five basic dimensions of the scope of the licence, which can be adapted – sliced and diced – to develop ways of realising value.

- A wide variety of IP can be licensed, either completely or for specific products or fields of use. The selection and definition of licensed product or field of use is an important tool for maximizing value return for an IP owner.

- The territory of a licence is dependent on the IP being licensed, the markets being addressed and the chosen approach to licensing. Territory can range from 'worldwide' to country specific. 'Worldwide' licences can cause complications for determining licence fees when the licensed IP does not match the countries of manufacture or markets.

- Typically, IP licences are between two entities, usually companies, and the nature of those entities will affect the structure of licence, with more complex company structures causing more complications for licensing. Sole and exclusive licences put a licensee in a beneficial preferred position by limiting competition, but need to be used carefully as benefit for the IP owner is not certain. Have-made rights and sub-licensing rights can be used to further distribute rights under licensed IP where the primary licensee does not personally have all the necessary capabilities to exploit the licensed IP.

- The 'reserved rights' of an IP owner can be licensed together or selectively. Selective licensing of the 'reserved rights' can be used to extract more of the embedded value in the IP. The IP licensing industry uses established licensing structures and agreements for recurring licensing situations.

- The life of the licence, the life of the licence agreement and the lifetime of the IP are distinct, and can be aligned or distinguished. It is common for licences and licence agreements to be set for fixed terms or for the lifetime of the IP. The length of the term is determined on the basis of the prevailing and foreseen business, particularly market conditions, at the time of licensing.
- The remuneration for an IP owner is the counterbalance to the licence granted to the IP licensee, and can be cash or non-cash, eg, a return IP licence. Cash remuneration is often on the basis of a running royalty – a percentage of price or a fee per unit – with upfront and annual fixed fees as an addition or alternative. Royalties reflect the IP licensee's opportunity to realise value from the licensed IP, and often follow industry specific norms.
- Understanding the consequences of IP licensing and managing risks and threats is an important aspect of a successful IP licensing programme. Risks such as reputational risks and financial, investment risks should be addressed throughout the life of licensing programme. Some forms of licensing, such as highly assertive, litigation-based licensing carry higher levels of risk.
- Licensing agreements address the running of a licence once a deal has been done. Accounting and auditing, and technical support are important additional aspects of IP licensing agreements. These secure value for an IP owner and successful licensing for both parties.
- IP licensing can augment an IP strategy by realising value from IP. The remuneration can be directly monetary or can flow in other ways, such as in-licensing of third-party IP. A range of models of IP licensing have built up over time, which offer a variety of starting points for new IP licensing programmes. These models are built around a set of common parameters or dimensions that collectively define the programme. These basic dimensions of a licensing programme can be used to create an endless variety of models and the science and art of IP licensing is to use these to form a licensing programme to achieve the outcome wanted by an IP owner.

Non-practising entities

Colin Hunsley
Josue Ortiz
ClearViewIP Limited

1. Introduction

Dealing with non-practising entities (NPEs) – whether this means defending against approaches from them, attempting to mitigate the risks associated with their activities or working with them to generate patent licensing income – has been an inevitable strand of work for many intellectual property (IP) teams over the last several years, particularly in specific jurisdictions and certain industries.

Arguably, NPEs have existed for as long as the patent system has, and will continue to exist for a long time to come. However, from the mid-1990s onwards an unprecedented NPE ecosystem emerged, which brought about a relatively fluid market for patents, a variety of NPE models and a range of initiatives conceived to counter NPE activities. In that context, a complete and robust IP strategy would necessarily have to consider NPE activities.

The recent legislative changes in the United States[1] have led to a somewhat generalised perception that NPEs have been significantly hampered in their ability to succeed, with their subsequent demise, or at least much diminished influence, inevitable. Undoubtedly there are facts and data that support this perception to a certain extent; but this chapter suggests that a more accurate description of the current situation is that NPEs are going through a period of change. NPEs are likely to adapt to the new realities, their activities may become more focused but overall new patterns of activity are expected to emerge. More likely than not, NPEs will continue to require inclusion in a complete corporate IP strategy.

---

[1] First, the Leahy-Smith America Invents Act (AIA) enacted on 16 September 2011 stops the practice of cost saving via litigating against all accused infringers of the same patent in a single case, and only allows the case to be filed against multiple defendants if the right to relief comes from the same infringement, ie, if they jointly infringed in the same action. This had the effect of limiting the number of defendants NPEs could file cases against at once (www.sgrlaw.com/ttl-articles/1779/). Secondly, Section 6 of the AIA, with an effective date of 16 September 2012, expanded *inter partes* review (IPR) so that any person other than the patent owner may petition the United States Patent and Trademark Office (USPTO) for *inter partes* review of a patent requesting to cancel at least one claim as unpatentable; and introduced a new 'all-issues' post-grant review proceeding in which parties may seek cancellation of patents on validity grounds nine months after the patent is issued (www.aipla.org/advocacy/congress/aia/Pages/summary.aspx and www.uspto.gov/patents-application-process/appealing-patent-decisions/trials/inter-partes-review). Thirdly, the 2014 Supreme Court ruling from the case *Alice Corporation v CLS Bank International* 573 US, 134 S Ct 2347 (www.supremecourt.gov/opinions/13pdf/13-298_7lh8.pdf) stated that abstract ideas require an inventive implementation in order to be patentable. This has had a huge impact on the validity of many software patents: according to some sources IPRs that cited the Alice verdict have had a 70% success rate (www.lexology.com/library/detail.aspx?g=300e6862-012d-49dd-bed4-ba8ae4477397).

2. Definition of an NPE

In the most general sense an NPE is a holder of a patent right (eg, ownership, an exclusive licence, right to exploit etc) that does not intend to deploy the patented technology in a product or service. Such a patent right holder could be completely passive, without any intent to derive a direct economic benefit from those rights. For example, there are financial institutions that will take patents as collateral for a loan, often actually having the patents assigned to them, so they hold patents they do not practice, but have no intent to derive any direct economic benefit from them aside from possibly selling the assets should the borrower default. An individual inventor could equally be entirely passive in respect of a granted patent in his name. Generally, the distinction made between passive patent owners and those given the NPE designation is that NPEs are entities that have taken steps to, or at least are assumed to intend to, derive a direct economic benefit from patent rights without making use of the technology.

Multiple types of organisations fall within this broad definition, even if we allow for the requirement of extracting a direct economic benefit from the patent or patents. For example, universities fit this definition, as well as companies that make and sell products underpinned by their patents but that also run licensing programmes in respect of patents they do not otherwise use.

In an attempt to either legitimise or oppose certain types of NPEs, they are often defined or classified by describing a specific type of entity or behaviour. For instance, most would argue that there is a fundamental difference, by virtue of their relative contribution to innovation and society in general, between a research institute seeking to license its patents and a company specifically created to buy patents, litigate them and derive income from settlements, damages awards and/or ongoing licence fees. So, to refer to the latter, the term Patent Assertion Entity (PAE) is often used, either as a specific type of NPE or to define NPEs narrowly. The derogatory term 'Patent Troll' is used by some interchangeably with the term NPE, though most would restrict this to NPEs who threaten or initiate litigation. However, there are some that take the view that a Patent Troll is any entity that assertively licenses any patent that it does not practice, regardless of whether the entity has a range of products or services that do implement other patents it owns. Others would argue that the term 'Patent Troll' is appropriate only in respect of entities that exhibit certain licensing behaviours, such as: seeking multiple settlements which are of an order of magnitude lower than the cost of defending an action, so coercing early settlement; attempting to license without properly investigating the infringement case and the validity of the patent or patents; targeting end users of a product or service, as opposed to the manufacturer or seller of the product, or the service provider; issuing aggressive and unclear demand letters; and/or operating through a series of shell companies to make it difficult to trace their assets and the full extent of their activities, as well as to limit their risk and liabilities.

The debate around these distinctions and therefore the actual definition of what constitutes an NPE is certainly interesting from an economics and business ethics point of view. However, this chapter looks at NPEs from a pragmatic corporate strategy perspective. From this perspective, it is important to differentiate the various types of NPE, not to arrive at a definition of what is an NPE or to propose a taxonomy of NPEs but in order to assess their respective relevance to a particular company and to formulate an appropriate engagement strategy for each of type of NPE. Engagement here means either defending against NPEs or working with NPEs, as indeed many well-known companies have done.

Table 1: Historical snapshot of the NPE world

2000	Acacia Research[2], founded in 1993, refocused its corporate strategy on patent exploitation
2000	Intellectual Ventures founded[3]
2001	IPValue[4] founded
2003	Acacia Research listed on NASDAQ
2005	Open Invention Network launched by IBM, Google, Novell, Philips, Red Hat and Sony to safeguard Linux against licensing demands and litigation
2006	RIM settles with NTP for US$612.5 million
2006	WiLAN[5] focuses its business on protecting and monetising patented technologies
2007	MOSAID (now ConversantIP)[6] expands its focus to license patents acquired from third parties
2008	Allied Security Trust[7] founded, set up by Google, Verizon, HP, Cisco and Ericsson

continued on next page

---

2   Acacia Research describes itself as an intermediary in the patent market and the industry leader in patent licensing. It partners with patent owners to unlock financial value, available at www.acaciaresearch.com/about-us.

3   Intellectual Ventures is a privately-held invention capital company, claiming over 40,000 IP assets in active monetisation programmes, US$6 billion of committed capital and US$3 billion cumulative licensing revenue, available at www.intellectualventures.com.

4   IPValue have partnered with companies to commercialise their patent assets since 2001, available at www.ipvalue.com.

5   WiLAN helps inventors monetise their patented technologies, their patent licences cover a variety of markets and relate to diverse technologies, claiming over 30 partnerships and almost 300 licensees, available at www.wilan.com.

6   ConversantIP offer IP management services including patent licensing and litigation management. They claim over 12,000 patent assets, available at www.conversantip.com.

7   Allied Security Trust is a defensive patent holding company that acquires patents of interest on behalf of its members. It provides its members a licence to the acquired patents and the opportunity to own the patents outright. If none of its members is interested in acquiring the patents, they are offered back to the market for sale, available at www.alliedsecuritytrust.com.

2008	RPX Corporation[8] founded, backed by Kleiner Perkins and Charles River Ventures
2009	Australia's CSIRO settles with 14 companies for A$205 million
2009	Innovation Network Corporation of Japan set up by the Japanese government
2010	Intellectual Ventures launched its first ever patent lawsuits against nine companies
2010	Vringo[9] listed on NASDAQ
2011	France Brevets[10] set up by the French government
2011	America Invents Act signed into law
2011	MOSAID acquired by Private Equity Fund Sterling Partners for US$590 million and is renamed ConversantIP
2012	CSIRO settles with nine companies including AT&T, Verizon and T-Mobile for A$220 million
2012	Marathon Patent Group[11] goes public
2012	Acacia Research buys 4G pioneer Adaptix for US$160 million
2012	Rockstar Consortium formed by Apple, Blackberry, Ericsson, Microsoft and Sony to purchase Nortel portfolio
2013	Intellectual Ventures publishes a list of approximately 75% of their 40,000 patent assets
2013	Rockstar initiates action against eight companies, including Google and prominent handset manufacturers

continued on next page

---

8   RPX Corporation offer the defensive acquisition of patent assets, among other services, for its members to reduce litigation risk from NPEs, available at www.rpxcorp.com.

9   Vringo develop and monetise telecoms related technologies. They advertise a portfolio of over 600 patent assets, available at www.vringoip.com.

10   France Brevets is a French sovereign investment fund fully dedicated to patents with a worldwide perspective. Funding is deployed to build strategic patent positions and monetise them through effective and focused licensing efforts, available www.francebrevets.com/en.

11   Marathon Patent Group is a patent acquisition and licensing company with a diverse portfolio of over 300 patent assets, available at www.marathonpg.com.

2014	Rockstar and Google settle
2014	Inventergy[12] take out US$11 million loan from Fortress Investments Group, secured against their IP
2014	*Alice Corporation v CLS Bank International* decision by US Supreme Court
2015	RPX purchases assets of Rockstar and the company folds
2015	Google launches License on Transfer (LOT)[13] as an NPE defensive strategy
2015	Apple ordered to pay US$234 million to Wisconsin Alumni Research Foundation
2015	Apple ordered to pay US$532.9 million to Smartflash LLC
2016	Carnegie Mellon University settles with Marvell Technology Group for US$750 million

3. A classification of NPEs for IP strategy

A number of dimensions are useful when trying to differentiate NPEs from an IP strategy perspective. This section considers those that in the authors' experience are the most important to take into account in any engagement with an NPE. When faced with an NPE demanding licence fees, a good understanding of its profile is essential to formulate a robust defensive strategy. Equally, when considering NPEs to work with, the characteristics of each NPE are an important factor in the selection decision. The chapter discusses why understanding these factors is important in the following two sections.

3.1 Range of commercial interests

NPEs vary in terms of the breadth of their commercial objectives. Perhaps the simplest case is that of entities that exist solely to extract financial gain from patents they do not practice. However, even such entities often have more than one commercial objective. Some will want to continue to acquire patents, others will at times be particularly interested in reaching a publicised settlement irrespective of the financial return. As the complexity of the entity increases so does the range of commercial interests. Intellectual Ventures operates a portfolio of funds which

---

12   Inventergy acquire and license patented technology. They advertise over 700 patent assets relating to Telecoms, available at www.inventergy.com.
13   Licensing on Transfer is a cooperative patent-licensing agreement to reduce NPE litigation. It assures patent licences to all members of LoT when a patent asset is transferred to an external entity, available at www.lotnet.com.

demands cyclical fund raising activity if the organisation is to continue to exist beyond the life of the newest fund. Universities are generally more interested in industry collaborations – in the form of spin-outs or funded research than in licence fees. When engaging with an NPE it is essential to understand its particular range of commercial interests, in general and in respect of that particular engagement.

3.2 Patent origin

Some commentators incorporate into their definition of NPE the fact that the patents exploited by the entity were sourced externally. However, there are NPEs that own home grown patents arising from legacy or ongoing investment in innovation. InterDigital[14] is a good example of an entity that owns patents that arise from ongoing research and development (R&D). ConversantIP built its reputation from licensing internally developed memory patents. Intellectual Ventures aspires to a hybrid model, claiming significant investment into ground-breaking research in addition to their more obvious massive patent acquisition activity since inception. A further model is that used by Acacia Research, where they have, on occasion, bought innovative companies such as Adaptix Inc[15] in order to exploit their patents. The patent origin distinction is important for a variety of reasons. Defensively, it is useful to know who the original patent owner was, what level of influence the original owner has in NPE decisions, whether it is likely to benefit from the patent exploitation proceeds, and if it is likely to be particularly sensitive about reputational or relationship damage. In terms of selecting an NPE to work with, it is important to know whether the patents will be bundled with other third-party patents and fundamentally whether the NPE generally sources IP externally in the first place.

3.3 Rights held

In respect of NPEs that source IP externally, it is critical to understand from a defensive strategy perspective whether they have assignment of the patents or only a licence or rights to exploit. Patent pools are not generally perceived as NPEs, but they certainly do not practice the patented technologies themselves (although generally most contributors to the pool do), and by definition source patents externally and seek to extract a direct economic benefit from those patents. Interestingly many patent pools not only do not take assignment of the patents but also do not have rights to litigate the patents. For example, IPValue generally does not own outright the patents it licenses on behalf of its clients. While it is difficult, and not always possible, to actually know what specific rights an NPE holds from public records, largely because of their extensive use of shell companies, it is certainly viable to develop a sufficient level of understanding to inform discussions with NPEs.

3.4 Patent revenue model

While NPEs have the common objective to generate patent income, there are

---

14   InterDigital have developed mobile communication technologies since 1972 and are believed to hold about 20,000 patent assets which they license to other companies, available at www.interdigital.com.
15   www.wsj.com/articles/SB10001424052970204409004577157470455118362.

significant variations in their pursuit of this objective. ArrivalStar gained notoriety by securing early and inexpensive settlements from litigations filed against hundreds of targets, including small businesses. This is very different from Intellectual Ventures' approach, which revolves around large portfolio licences and a comparatively low level of litigation activity. WiLAN follows yet another path, engaging in litigation much more frequently than Intellectual Ventures and generally not settling for nuisance value. There has been some debate amongst commentators as to whether defensive patent aggregators, such as Allied Security Trust (AST) and RPX Corporation, are NPEs. AST being a non-profit organisation is less prone to debate. RPX was set-up as a defensive mechanism against NPEs; their patent purchasing and aggregation activity targeted at cutting the supply of new patents to NPEs. Yet some argue that it is just a benign NPE because the company buys patents that it does not intend to practice and – even if it will never assert the acquired patents – it effectively licenses its members to the patents it owns. Again, rather than debate whether or not RPX is an NPE, the point made here is that their revenue model, which is based on their ability to acquire patents and membership fees, is very different to other patent holders.

3.5 Financial structure

NPEs include publicly listed companies, often referred to as Publicly Listed IP Companies (PIPCOs), private equity backed entities (eg, ConversantIP), small privately-held organisations and sovereign patent funds set up with substantial investments from national governments such as Korea, Japan and France. It is useful to understand the financial structure of a particular NPE when dealing with it, including who are their shareholders (see Table 2 below). Clearly this is considerably more difficult for privately held entities, but even a general understanding of the financial position of the NPE will be extremely useful.

3.6 Reach

It cannot be emphasised enough that not all NPEs are created equal. Misconceptions about the reach of NPEs are not uncommon and these often originate from broad generalisations of NPEs. It is often assumed that NPEs are small outfits with limited human resource capabilities. This will be true of some NPEs but many have very capable and experienced licensing executives, often having more people than their targets have devoted to the defensive effort. In fact, many NPEs have senior employees that have come out of very well-known and respected operating companies. It is also sometimes assumed that NPEs deal only with software patents. Until the recent legislative changes in the US, there was indeed a large volume of NPE litigations related to software, but this has not been by any means the only industry in which NPEs have operated (see Figure 3 below). On the other hand, sometimes it is assumed that NPEs have a geographic reach broader than that which they actually do. Even large and prominent NPEs have had a very US-centric focus, not only in respect of their litigation activity (many NPEs have targeted far east companies first but have sued them in the US) but also in terms of not purchasing foreign counterparts and abandoning many of the ones they did buy at the next renewal

Table 2: A financial perspective of NPEs

Below is an overview of shareholders in PIPCOs.

Vringo	Interdigital	Acacia	Research	Marathon	Inventergy	Unwired Planet	Pendrell
Shares held by insiders	9%	1%	2%	29%	36%	23%	25%
Shares held by owners	5%	5%	5%	5%	5%	5%	5%
Shares held by institutional investors and mutual funds	11%	72%	101%	8%	9%	40%	54%
Float held by institutional investors and mutual funds	12%	73%	103%	11%	14%	52%	71%
Number of institutions holding shares	59	251	136	19	16	76	71
Sample blue chip investors	Vanguard, BlackRock, Goldman Sachs	Vanguard, Black Rock, JP Morgan	Vanguard, Fidelity, Oppenheimer Funds	Vanguard, Fortress, Goldman Sachs, Fidelity	Fortress, BlackRock, UBS, Vanguard	Vanguard, BlackRock	Vanguard, BlackRock, Farallon Capital

Source: S&P Capital IQ, data as of 31/12/2015.

point. As a result, their patent holdings outside the US are significantly smaller. This is changing, with an identifiable increase in the number of European patents bought by prominent NPEs over the last couple of years. Overall, the European holdings of most NPEs remain a tractable problem from a defensive perspective. Clearly, in engaging with an NPE, it can only be beneficial to have a proper understanding of its reach and capabilities.

4.   NPE trends

As mentioned previously, NPEs are generally perceived to be going through a period of transformation, largely as a consequence of legislative changes in the US and, to a lesser degree, due to a perception of a potentially favourable environment in

Europe once the proposed Unified Patent Court comes into force.[16] NPEs have taken a number of tentative steps to adapt to the current environment, however, it is as yet unclear how successful these changes will be and whether these steps will be accelerated any time soon.

In terms of litigation, it is clear that NPEs are increasingly active in Europe whereas their activity was practically non-existent before 2012 (see Figures 1 and 2 below). In contrast with the slow decline in the number of defendants in the US since 2011 (although it should be noted that the total number defendants in 2015 was roughly on par with the number in 2010), Europe has seen a sharp increase in actions filed by NPEs. Nevertheless, more than one order of magnitude difference remains between the total number of cases filed in these two jurisdictions. The expansion from the US as a jurisdiction of choice is perhaps best exemplified by the global litigation between Vringo and ZTE. Germany is now often seen as a viable jurisdiction for NPEs, and more generally for all patent infringement litigants, for a variety of reasons, including cost, the efficiency of the courts and the fact that the possibility of an injunction is a significant incentive for companies to settle.

Figure 1: Slow shift in geographic focus

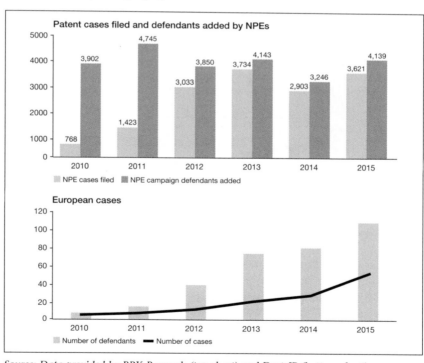

Source: Data provided by RPX Research (top chart) and DartsIP (bottom chart).

---

16   Information about the Unified Patent Court and the latest news, roadmap and timescales available at www.unified-patent-court.org/.

The chart at the top of Figure 1 shows the total count of NPE cases filed in the US per year, in terms of lawsuits filed and the number of defendants involved. This shows a slow decline, or at least a lack of growth, depending on the time period considered, in US NPE litigation. The chart at the bottom of Figure 1 shows the level of activity of 11 NPEs known to be active in Europe, again in terms of number of lawsuits and number of defendants. Information on European NPE litigation is not as readily available as it is for the US, nevertheless the data below is believed to be sufficiently representative of the state of affairs. Despite the growing European litigation trend, note the order of magnitude difference in scale.

From an industry perspective, a shift in the last few years towards automotive and med-tech industries has been noticeable. This is exemplified by Intellectual Ventures' licence to Ford Motor Company,[17] but there has been a string of automotive and med-tech related announcements from NPEs in recent months. Acacia Research in particular has a longer history of activity in these two sectors. Nevertheless, as seen in Figure 3 below, from 2012–2015 the bulk of US NPE patent litigation remained within the technology, media and telecommunications (TMT) sector.

Figure 2: NPEs industry focus: number of individual NPE litigations filed in the US per technology sector from 2012–2015.

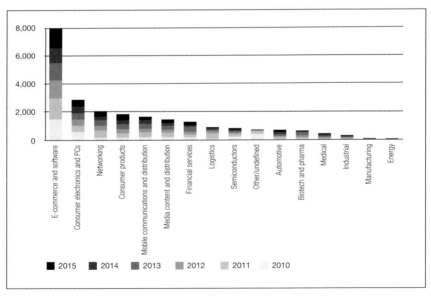

Source: RPX Research.

There is a general perception that NPEs have substantially reduced their patent acquisition activity, which has had a knock-on effect on the patent brokerage

---

17   www.iam-media.com/blog/Detail.aspx?g=d1e0c649-ef6f-4959-ae49-79d65aa59830.

market, with several brokers exiting the market altogether. There is an apparent trend of increased selectivity from NPEs to acquire portfolios that they believe can still be successfully licensed in the new environment.

Shifts in business model have also emerged. The general tune is a gradual shift from pure patent licensing activities towards combined technology and patent licensing; more in tune with a positioning around innovation and working with early stage companies. Examples of these include Dominion Harbor Group's IP Bank for Startups,[18] and Vringo's various strategic initiatives since 2013 to diversify its business model by investing in various technology development initiatives.

The more difficult environment in which NPEs are having to operate and the gradual shift in their strategies suggest that consolidation in the NPE space may well occur. Indeed, Uniloc Luxembourg and Marathon Patent Corporation announced an intention to merge in August 2015 (the merger was not completed),[19] and Uniloc continued its mergers and acquisitions (M&A) initiatives with an offer to buy Acacia Research for US$189 million in cash in March 2016.[20]

It is indeed possible that NPE activity has been successfully and irreversibly curtailed in the US, so that overall, in time, there will be less litigation, fewer patent acquisitions and a reduced number of NPEs. Current data does not really support this view, at least not yet. It only points to the growth in NPE activity having been curtailed. Undoubtedly strong portfolios will continue to be bought, licensed and litigated. But it is true that new realities and recent trends point to a need to revisit engagement parameters with NPEs, both on the defensive side as well as when intending to work with them.

The next section considers possible strategies to engage with NPEs on the defensive side.

5. Defending against NPEs

Companies defending against approaches from NPEs generally have two general objectives in mind: minimising, or if possible eliminating altogether, any out-payments to the NPE; and avoiding being seen as a soft target, thus minimising subsequent approaches by the same or other NPEs. In practice these objectives must be balanced against the cost of defending the NPE approach, which is the fundamental factor leading to settlements with NPEs. It is important to recognise that whether litigation has been initiated or not there are costs associated with responding to NPE advances. Often these are internal costs in the form of time and attention devoted by the in-house legal team; as a result, these initial expenditures are not always seen in the same light as the external costs associated with defending an actual lawsuit, in a sense they are more easily tolerated. Nevertheless, the costs prior to a lawsuit can be substantial. Of course, there are other factors that inform

---

18   Dominion Harbor Group provide a Patent Value Optimization platform that includes IP auditing and licensing services, available at www.dominionharbor.com.
19   www.streetinsider.com/Corporate+News/Marathon+Patent+Group+(MARA),+Uniloc+Terminate+Proposed +Merger/11352105.html.
20   www.marketwired.com/press-release/uniloc-announces-189-million-cash-offer-to-acquire-acacia-research -corporation-nasdaq-actg-2105454.htm.

the settlement decision. For example, the degree of management distraction caused by the NPE, the risk of an injunction and timing in relationship to other business activities, eg, fund raising, initial public offering (IPO) or M&A activity.

More often than not defending against NPEs is seen as a reactive endeavour. In general companies tend to see working with defensive patent aggregators, referred to above, as the only viable exception to the reactive mode of operation. It could be argued from experience that proactive preparation is also possible in many instances and, furthermore, that preparedness leads to the delivery of the two general objectives of minimising cost and preventing subsequent approaches.

In the past, defending from NPEs has been difficult because of an asymmetry in the engagement. A well-known asymmetry stems from the fact that the operating company cannot counter-sue or cross-license, as it would in a dispute with another operating company, because the NPE does not sell products or services. There are other asymmetries: at the outset, the NPE will control the timing of the engagement, opaqueness about the extent of the NPE's patent holdings will create information asymmetry (some NPEs deliberately obfuscate their patent holdings by assigning them to a large number of shell companies), and the NPE will have dedicated resources to this activity while the operating company's executives and legal team will have multiple other projects and problems on their plate.

To a large extent, an integrated defence strategy will be aimed at breaking down this asymmetry. It may not be possible to balance fully the engagement but it is possible to have a much more level playing field with a well-developed response plan and access to the right information, which takes us back to the importance of understanding the NPE one is dealing with.

A robust response plan can enable the operating company to take control of the timing of negotiations very early on, eliminate the threat of the unknown by identifying NPE patents in the relevant technical areas, then evaluate the systematic attack of the NPE's patent portfolio (for example, through the US *inter partes* and post-grant review proceedings, European oppositions or German nullity actions), and potentially pursue the beneficiaries of the NPE licensing proceeds. Ideally a robust response plan would let the NPE perceive early on that it will be very difficult, time consuming and costly to pursue their licensing demands as well as deliver to the operating company substantial negotiation levers for immediate disposal. This is very difficult to achieve in a purely reactive mode, making some degree of proactive preparation very valuable. But even without proactive effort it is possible to reduce the asymmetry of engagement which NPEs have exploited (see Table 3 below).

Note that certain NPEs are often referred to as Patent Assertion Entities (PAE). It is essential to recognise however that there is not a single entity that has litigation as its end goal. Litigation is a mechanism that NPEs use to reach their financial objectives. Income, either in the form of damages, settlement or ongoing royalties, is their end goal. This distinction is important because in the end dealing with an NPE is a commercial matter, and the decision to fight or settle at each juncture of the engagement has to be a strategic and business decision. Of course, this decision will be informed by legal considerations and the legal team will provide essential input. But a successful and pragmatic defence will recognise that this is not, at its core, a legal matter.

Table 3: Defensive engagement checklist

Information that is crucial to formulating a robust response plan is presented below.

NPE profile	• Reach and degree of sophistication of the NPE • Key NPE relationships: shareholders, executives and other stakeholders, original patent owners – particularly those that have an ongoing interest in the licensing proceeds • Current range of commercial interests of the NPE
NPE business intelligence	• Current financial position of the NPE • Recent licensing and acquisition deals by the NPE • The NPE's revenue model: low/nuisance settlement, portfolio licence, one-off deals or regular licence renewals
NPE portfolio intelligence	• Extent of the NPE patent holdings in relevant technical areas • Geographic footprint of the NPE's portfolio • Patents underpinning existing royalty-bearing licences • Patents that could be invalidated, whether part of this engagement or otherwise
Operating company ammunition	• Library of prior art in the relevant subject matter • Patent held by the operating company that could be of significant value to the NPE

This point is closely linked to the range of commercial objectives that each NPE has. While income generation will always be a primary objective, often there will be other objectives, which can be leveraged to achieve the two chief defensive objectives mentioned previously.

While many operating companies will think of engagement with NPEs as purely a defensive activity, it is of course possible to work with NPEs, either selling patents to them or licensing patents through them. The next section considers this facet of the IP strategy as related to NPEs.

6.   **Collaborating with NPEs**

Despite the vilification of NPEs, it remains an undisputable fact that to operate, NPEs must source assets from other entities, and have indeed sourced assets from prominent operating companies that continue to operate as product-based companies (see Table 4 below); ie, NPEs do not always procure assets from operating companies in distress although that has clearly been a significant source of patents. Of course, an exception to the external sourcing of patents are NPEs that have home grown patents. It appears very few companies manage to continue to invent once they set course on a patent-centric, as opposed to a product-centric, strategy. Often NPEs either migrate to a patent acquisition model, or fold once they either run out of licensing targets or when the patents come to the end of their life (either through expiry or invalidation). On the other hand, it is also clear that a broad range of companies have made the decision not to sell patents to NPEs nor to rely on NPEs to run licensing programmes on their behalf.

So, there will be many companies that at some point will make the decision whether to work with NPEs or not. Often the decision will be in the context of wanting to exploit their portfolio or because an NPE has approached them to pitch for their business. It is clear that each company will have to make its own decision in its specific context, so this chapter offers only some of the arguments companies have made for and against working with NPEs.

Arguments in favour of working with NPEs:

- the NPE model is seen as a valid mechanism to extract value from patent rights, or at least the approach taken by NPEs is perceived as more professional;
- once the decision to generate patent income has been made, NPEs are a significant market participant (for both patent sales and privateering[21] deals);
- as a corollary to the above point, excluding NPEs from the list of potential acquirers or licensing partners will significantly reduce the prospects of achieving the patent income generation objectives;
- excluding deals with NPEs creates a disadvantage versus competitors that do work with NPEs;
- working with NPEs gives access to expert and dedicated resources (this argument is often mentioned in the context of patent privateering, as is the case for the remaining arguments on this list);
- there is a lower risk of counter-assertion;
- working with NPEs allow executives to continue to focus on the core business;
- there is a perception of higher income potential from licensing than from patent sales, but it is difficult for an operating company to run a licensing programme by itself; and
- there is an attractiveness of a fully contingent arrangement that may be hard to get from a law firm directly.

Arguments against working with NPEs:

- the NPE model is seen as fundamentally unethical and detrimental to the industry as a whole, therefore working with an NPE can create negative publicity;
- even if it could be shown that some NPEs conduct business in an ethical and professional manner, selling to NPEs is to feed the larger problem of unethical NPEs;
- since the company has opposed the NPE model, it would be inconsistent to deal with NPEs;

---

21 'Patent privateering' is a term used to describe an arrangement between a patent owner, usually an operating company, which extends rights to an NPE, often ownership, to license certain patents with a proportion of the licensing proceeds being shared back with the operating company.

- opening the door to an NPE, on a sale or privateering deal, increases the risk of subsequent approaches by that NPE with licensing demands;
- the company has the resources and expertise to run a licensing programme on its own, so sharing the revenues with a third party, NPE or otherwise, should be questioned; and
- it is better to be in control of the licensing programme (targets, litigation and settlement decisions) which may not be possible working with an NPE – their activity could cause some negative reaction from targets including counter suit activity.

Once a company has decided to work with an NPE it becomes necessary to convince the NPE that the patents the company wants to sell, or to license through the NPE, can deliver a suitable return on investment. The NPE's investment will comprise the purchase price (although there is anecdotal evidence that more and more deals are fully back-ended) and the costs of running the licensing programme, including litigation in many instances. To calculate its return on investment the NPE will apply a significant risk discount factor. Therefore, it is essential that the operating company demonstrates that the patents are in use by third parties and that the products or services that practice the patented technology are of sufficient economic scale. Validity is usually something that the patent owner will not look into, in terms of additional prior art searches to those performed in prosecution, but it can be useful to highlight any data points that demonstrate a particularly good vintage. NPEs will of course perform their own due diligence with regards to infringement, validity and financial potential, but it is down to the seller to put forward a compelling case at the outset. It is important to know what sort of assets NPEs are seeking to buy at a particular moment in time. This may include specific technical or market areas, or certain profiles in terms of age, jurisdictions and number of assets.

The next step is selecting an NPE to work with. This could be seen as a simpler decision from a patent sales perspective than from a privateering perspective: essentially sell to the highest bidder and hence approach as many NPEs as is practically possible with a patent sale offer. However, there are important factors to be taken into account. Some companies will sell to a patent aggregator or to a patent pool, but not to patent licensing entities. Whereas others will consider a wider range of NPEs but will still want to exclude those with a revenue model based on nuisance value settlements. Behind these decisions is the potential downstream effect of the patent sale, often preserving the good reputation of the company is a chief consideration in establishing to which NPEs companies will sell to.

It is true that the decision is more complex in privateering settings. The track record, patent revenue model and downstream licensing revenue share model of the prospective NPE are very important. Some companies will not sell to NPEs that have pursued them in the past with licensing demands, whereas other companies take exactly the opposite view and will want to work with NPEs that have created a good impression when licensing patents to them. The technical areas of expertise of the NPE are also of significance as is whether they have ongoing licensing programmes in similar areas which could create a conflict or at least be a distraction for the NPE. Some NPEs will bundle assets together, which is something the operating company may or may not welcome. If this is done the revenue sharing model could be complex and become contentious, which again is something to consider.

Table 4: Sources of IP and client base

Prominent companies have sold patents to NPEs or use their services to license third parties (often referred to as 'privateering').

Sample companies that have sold patents to NPEs			
Nokia	Siemens	Alcatel Lucent	Micron Technologies
Philips	Sony	Raytheon	Daimler AG
France Telecom	Mitsubishi	Huawei	Freescale Semiconductor
Bosch	Panasonic	Lenovo	AT&T
Citrix	Hynix Semiconductor	Samsung Electronics	IBM
Fujitsu	Matsushita	RAI	Hitachi
Sample companies that have used NPEs to license their patents			
Renesas Electronics	Panasonic	BT	PARC
NXP Semiconductors	Mitel	Ericsson	Huawei
Nokia	Apple	Sony	

Source data: ClearViewIP Limited.

7. Conclusion

NPEs are a fact of life and most successful organisations will encounter them at some stage either seeking to use their services or as a result of an approach from them. How these relationships develop can be managed by the non-NPE party and using carefully considered strategies will allow the best way forward to be reached. Those that simply ignore the concept can expect to be less well placed when they are in the NPE's sights. This chapter recommends taking NPEs seriously and developing appropriate strategies to prepare for an approach or carrying out reasonable research before engaging with them.

8. Chapter summary

- Keep an overview of your business from the perspective of the patents that matter in protecting your business together with those that could present a freedom to operate threat.
- Use this overview to monitor patents that are offered for sale and where possible take particular note of which companies are buying, this could be traditional operating competitors as well as NPEs.
- Monitor NPE trends by asking: are they moving into geographic or technology sectors that are becoming relevant to your business? Of particular note is the growth of activity in Europe together with a shift into automotive and medical technologies. The automotive sector is likely to become a particular hotspot given the telecoms technologies being adopted for the connected and driverless vehicles of the future.
- New product offerings or new market entries can be attractive to NPEs where they have already established a patent thicket so careful review of the threats should be considered at these times.
- Once it is apparent there may be a realistic threat to your business focus on the practical steps that can be taken. Determine the vigour and persistence the potential NPE threat has adopted historically. Use this to help plan your tactical response. Consider their patent portfolio and determine those of relevance to your business so that you can respond to the typical high volume, too expensive to defend approach.
- Build a knowledge bank focused on your own expertise and history in your business area to identify a prior art library that can be unleashed. Consider all the challenges you can make including the opposition procedure in Europe and the Inter Partes Review in the US. Remember the NPE's main asset is its patent portfolio so any challenge is particularly damaging.
- While it may seem rather overwhelming to action and manage the above there are a range of organisations that can help and will be very familiar with the tasks involved saving you having to reinvent the wheel.

The authors would like to acknowledge Tim Butler, Andrew Killeen and Tim Higgs for their research.

IP and tax strategy

Richard Turner
FTI Consulting LLP

---

1.   Introduction

The aim of this chapter is to provide an overview of the increasing importance of intellectual property (IP) to the corporate tax strategy, its policies and the attractive tax incentives available for innovation. A safe starting assumption is that IP – its development, maintenance and exploitation – is core to tax strategy and that IP strategy is likely to be incomplete without understanding the tax implications. Tax planning, particularly where it involves IP, carries unfavourable connotations that have come to the fore in recent years. It is widely understood that many multinationals create or move their IP and other intangible assets to companies in tax havens. These companies then charge affiliates in countries with higher rates of tax for the use of these assets. The charge attracts tax relief and the income is taxed at a much lower rate, if taxed at all.

This type of arrangement is not as prevalent as many suspect and, as the discussion on transfer pricing below suggests, has become much more difficult to implement with the desired effect. This aspect of tax strategy will be put aside for the remainder of this chapter. Tax strategy and planning remains essential for all compliant businesses, particularly those operating across borders. When it comes to IP, this necessitates understanding:

- *the spectrum of IP assets used in the business* – the full scope of IP and intangible assets in the business, who owns them, how they are used and their economic contribution;
- *their economic ownership as distinguished from their legal ownership* – when IP is created and used throughout a group of companies economic and legal ownership is often blurred;
- *transfer pricing requirements* – the difficulties in understanding economic ownership can present challenges in understanding the taxing rights; and
- *the availability of innovation incentives* – often countries offer incentives for multinationals to develop and monetise their IP within their jurisdiction, therefore choosing where to develop and hold IP requires careful consideration.

For many businesses, it is sufficient to endeavour to centralise all IP in a single company or country. This is not always possible where new companies are acquired or IP rights are developed by teams spanning more than one country.

Case study

If a multinational chooses to transfer rights from Company A in Country A to Company B in Country B, there is a likelihood that a tax liability will arise in Company A calculated on the market value of those rights. Certain reliefs may be available to defer or eliminate the tax charge but these are unlikely to be available if one of the principal motivations for the transaction is to reduce tax. Alternatively, Company A might be able to utilise certain tax attributes such as tax losses. If there is no possibility of mitigating the tax cost, the remaining option may be to licence existing IP rights allowing the new rights to be created in Company B. Over time the licence fees will reduce as the value of the old IP decreases.

This chapter reviews two key influences on tax strategy as applied to IP. The first part discusses innovation incentives. The most prevalent of which are:

- research and development (R&D) tax incentives – used to stimulate and support innovation so that new value-generating IP rights are created; and
- innovation boxes (IP boxes) – provide tax incentives to exploit the rights from the country in which they were created.

The second influence is transfer pricing. The principal objective of which is to establish an appropriate allocation of taxing rights where IP is created and used across national borders.

2. Innovation incentives

2.1 Overview of the general international landscape

In recent years, governments have started to react to the mobile nature of income streams from IP by introducing 'innovation incentives' designed to retain the IP within their jurisdiction. These IP box regimes are designed to reduce the corporate tax on profits derived from the exploitation of IP rights. Following on from R&D incentives, which give relief on input expenditure, IP box regimes are designed to give tax relief on the output. The combination of the two can provide significant fiscal support for innovation.

2.2 IP box regimes

IP box regimes are government provided incentives designed to promote the development and retention of IP in the country of origin.

While there are currently a limited number of countries who have adopted these regimes, much lower than the incidence of R&D tax incentives, over the last decade they have become increasingly popular. In 2004 only France and Hungary operated IP box regimes. However, there are now many more.

The regimes offered by these countries lower the effective tax rate on qualifying IP from somewhere between 5% and 15%. The majority of the countries offering forms of IP box regimes limit qualifying IP to patents, although this can be extended to include other rights that are functionally equivalent to patents. Broadly speaking, these are rights that are both legally protected and subject to similar approval and registration processes. The Organisation for Economic Co-operation and Development (OECD) definition covers:

- patents – defined broadly to include utility models, IP assets that grant protection to plants and genetic material, orphan drug designations and extensions of patent protection;
- copyrighted software; and
- other IP assets that are non-obvious, useful and novel.

Qualifying income generally includes the sale of patented items and royalties. This can be extended to the sale of patent rights themselves or the use of patented processes in income generating activities.

Some of the initial IP box regimes were not considered to have included sufficient restrictions on acquired IP in an effort to attract mobile IP. These regimes came under scrutiny of both the European Union (EU) and also the OECD's project on base erosion and profit shifting (BEPS). As a consequence, the connection between the original development and subsequent exploitation has become a mandatory requirement for any regime of this nature to operate effectively. This is covered in more detail in the next section.

2.3 OECD Review of Harmful Tax Practices

The OECD has implemented a series of initiatives to resolve the issue of tax BEPS. One area where there was perceived to be reason for concern was in IP boxes which allowed multinationals to move profit in order to access lower tax rates.

Recent research results show that firms' intangible assets are more likely to be held in low-tax subsidiaries than tangible assets and that the location of patents is responsive to corporate income tax. Reports estimate that profit shifting leads to significant revenue loss for high-tax countries. There are concerns that the tax treatment of the returns from exploiting IP may distort the intended outcome from the location and organisation of firms' real activities and may lead to the erosion of government revenues.

After 2013, the OECD and the G20 countries initiated a collaboration to address the issue of tax BEPS. The goal of the collaboration was to address the growing concern over aggressive cross border tax planning in the 'race to the bottom' and to create a fair and equitable international tax environment.

The OECD and G20 adopted a 15-point Action Plan to resolve the issue of BEPS. Action 5 in the 2013 BEPS programme looked to address the matter of harmful tax practices which offered low tax incentives. The key themes were transparency around how incentives were offered and substance requirements for a potential claimant. The OECD raised the issue of preferential regimes in relation to intangible property, a source of mobile income, including IP, as a potential base-eroding concern. At the same time, it was acknowledged that providing tax incentives to promote R&D and consequently innovation are often necessary in promoting the continued growth of an economy. This was aligned with the second pillar of the BEPS project as a whole, which was to draw taxation more tightly to substance by ensuring that taxable profits could no longer be artificially shifted away from the countries where value is created.

To address this concern, the Forum on Harmful Tax Practices (FHTP) considered a number of methodologies for ensuring that sufficient activity is required for IP box regimes, ultimately settling on the nexus approach.

This approach permitted benefit only if there was a "direct nexus between the income receiving benefits and the expenditures contributing to that income". Expenditure would therefore act as a proxy for substantial activities. The purpose of the nexus approach was to grant benefits only to income that arises from IP where the actual R&D activity was undertaken by the taxpayer itself. This goal is achieved by defining 'qualifying expenditures' in such a way that they effectively prevent mere capital contribution or expenditure for substantial R&D activity by parties other than the taxpayer from being eligible. As a consequence, claimants who acquire IP that has already been largely developed or who contract research out to affiliates will have any benefits limited by the relative proportion of this non-qualifying expenditure to the overall cost of developing the underlying IP asset.

In late 2014 the UK and German governments published a joint proposal to advance negotiations on the new rules of preferential IP regimes. The recommendations used the nexus approach but included transitional arrangements so that legacy regimes could remain open for existing IP and be grandfathered until 2021.

2.4   Impact of IP boxes

The recent expansion in the use of IP boxes has given rise to greater scrutiny as to whether they do actually provide a benefit to the country offering them.

An issue for governments is understanding the extent to which an IP regime might create a positive impact on their economy.

There are at least three reasons that a government might introduce an IP box:

- to encourage firms to increase investment in innovative activities;
- to attract (or retain) mobile investments that may be associated with high-skilled jobs and knowledge creation; and
- to raise revenue more efficiently by differentiating tax rates on more mobile income streams.

Long-term growth is often the consequence of innovation and retaining investment domestically, and therefore countries are inclined to believe that reduced tax revenue is a fair price to pay for this. There is evidence to suggest that countries that offer an IP regime do experience a positive effect on levels of investment in innovation although at the same time the IP regime could result in a significant cost as a consequence of funding the reduced tax base.

It is certainly the case that many companies base investment decisions on qualitative tax measures rather than detailed economic modelling. In fact, the modelling of the cost of taxation remains remarkably unsophisticated with many groups using a flat percentage based on the statutory tax rate in the country in which they are headquartered. The mere fact that a country has an IP regime with a low headline rate can often be enough to influence an investment decision. There was a noticeable decline in the number of companies migrating from the UK as a consequence of the government's commitment to introduce an IP box regime before the rules were drafted and fully understood.

As more countries introduce regimes, their relative impact is likely to be reduced. At the same time, limitations imposed under the review for harmful tax practices may result in fewer countries opting to adopt this type of regime instead of opting to reduce their headline rate of corporate income tax.

3. R&D incentives

3.1 Overview of the general international landscape of R&D incentives

R&D incentives have long been a tool used by many governments to encourage innovation within their economy. This section provides an overview of recent trends around the globe in the provision of R&D incentives.

It is widely held that high levels of R&D can improve economic prosperity through promoting innovation and the sharing of knowledge. However, as the benefits of privately funded R&D will extend the enterprises undertaking the research, companies can be deterred from R&D investment as they will be unable to enjoy the fruits of the entire economic return. Therefore, countries use fiscal incentives to encourage levels of R&D internally and bridge the gap where the market fails to provide optimal levels of R&D.

Fiscal tax incentives are a more indirect way of supporting R&D. However, some governments instead opt to use grants and contracts. R&D tax incentives are prevalent across OECD countries and often match and sometimes exceed government spending on more direct methods of funding.

The number of countries offering either or both to businesses has increased over recent years. This growing popularity has been spurred by increased international competition and the rise in multinationals fostering internationally mobile R&D. It is therefore important for governments to keep their fiscal policy globally competitive. The appeal of indirect incentives arises from the fact that they are more simple to implement and administrate through the existing infrastructure of the corporate taxation system. They do not impact the budget of research ministries and they can more easily be adjusted as the tax system tends to be updated on an annual basis.

Over the last decade, the number of OECD nations that have incorporated R&D incentives into their tax law has doubled. Non-OECD countries also offering forms of an R&D incentive include Brazil, China, India, Russia, Singapore and South Africa. Exceptions are countries such as Germany and Mexico that offer cash based grants directly to the company.

These fiscal incentives can vary considerably from country to country, although the concept of qualifying R&D activity is relatively consistent. The most commonly adopted form of R&D incentive is a repayable tax credit which can amount to 30%–50% of qualifying expenditure. Other countries use super deductions which result in additional tax relief.

3.2   Salient features of R&D regimes

R&D incentives can vary country-by-country; this part outlines the principal components of the regimes.

The definition of qualifying R&D is comparable across the various countries offering incentives. Some regimes require a pre-approval from the taxing body or research department. This can be costly to administer and the lead time in obtaining approval prohibitive.

Claims for R&D tax incentives are often only considered at the time that the tax return is prepared. As a consequence, qualifying activities are often overlooked particularly where a line of research or project is terminated at an early stage. Companies who adopt procedures for evaluating R&D for tax purposes on a real time basis are likely to improve the level of incentive that they receive. There is often considerable overlap between the requirements for tax purposes and innovation capture systems leading to a case for the two to be integrated.

In many countries, the taxpayer can self-assess what activities qualify with the tax authorities then critically reviewing claims on a selected basis. Disproving qualifying R&D is difficult, costly and time consuming for tax authorities. As a consequence, there is an increasing trend in more aggressive claims. This will inevitably lead to a tipping point when authorities will then have to become much more stringent.

Many advisers prefer to work on a contingent basis and this often suits the company where they do not have a clear perspective of the level of benefit available. This encourages both parties to include projects on or just over the boundary of qualifying activities. This has led to an increasing volume of claims for softer innovation where the available pot might otherwise be allocated to innovation capable of more objective validation such as registrable IP.

There is a broad range of options deployed for stimulating R&D, such as the quantum of the incentive, the nature (ie, tax based or direct grant) and the specific activity it targets. According to a recent OECD report, the most common form of R&D incentive is a tax credit which is offset against the tax bill or repaid. In recent years over half of the OECD countries that had adopted R&D incentives used this approach. R&D tax credits are broadly categorised into three groups: a volume based credit, an incremental credit and a hybrid credit which is a combination of the two.

A volume-based credit applies to all qualifying R&D expenditure regardless of any historic comparator. An incremental tax credit is based on additional amounts of R&D expenditure exceeding a certain threshold which are usually based on an historical average. Incremental credits are typically less beneficial in aggregate than a volume based credit. To manage the level of commitment to the regimes, they may often be capped. In recent years the emphasis has changed from complicated incremental or hybrid schemes to simplified volume-based alternatives.

Some countries offer additional tax relief in the form of a super deduction. This is where qualifying R&D expenses can be increased by a certain rate to achieve an even lower tax liability. This rate is ordinarily around 150%–200% but in a few countries sometimes subject to conditions this can be much higher, between 200% and 400%.

Other types of incentive include social security and payroll withholding tax credits on the wages of R&D employees. This type of R&D incentive is unlikely to be used on its own and will generally form the part of a multi-faceted scheme.

Some territories link the incentive to activity undertaken in the territory whereas others include R&D undertaken overseas as long as the ultimate cost is borne by the claimant. These broader regimes have allowed multinationals to organise their affairs to access a single incentive. As a consequence, all or substantially all of the IP arising from the research is then beneficially owned by a company operating within the territory providing the incentive.

Several countries attempt to stimulate growth in smaller companies by offering additional incentives depending on the company size. Supporting small and medium enterprises (SMEs) in this way can often enhance investor sentiment and allow companies to enhance fundraising. Under the same principle some countries offer more generous incentives to preferential industries for example environmental, biological or high technology industries.

3.3   The impact of R&D incentives

While the use of R&D incentives is more established than IP boxes their level of effectiveness in terms of behavioural impact and productivity is less well understood.

An increasing number of detailed studies on the impact of R&D tax incentives have been undertaken yet still the understanding around the effectiveness of R&D tax incentives and how a scheme should be designed to maximise its impact remains limited. There is little evidence around the behavioural influences of these regimes and the output in terms of productivity and growth. This is borne out by recent changes to R&D regimes where there has been little or no trend in either enhancing or reducing the relative level of benefits.

The motivation behind R&D incentives is based on the hypothesis that a high level of R&D within an economy can inspire growth as it encourages knowledge spillovers which consequently lead to innovation. Innovation is essential to ensure an economy does not stagnate, however, as there is an element of public good within R&D knowledge, governments use R&D incentives to encourage companies that might otherwise be deterred from investing in R&D.

A substantial amount of R&D expenditure is uncertain in its outcome and as to whether it will actually deliver a return. It is also irreversible in that it is much less likely that investors can recoup their investment in the event of failure. For this reason access to funding can be more challenging. In the current globally competitive environment, fiscal policies aimed at mitigating the effects of market failure must be substantial in order to be effective in achieving their goal. R&D tax incentives have become popular as they are simple to implement through corporate tax systems and they can be altered with existing policies making it less expensive for the government to administrate.

As a consequence of the potentially high costs for government, there is a disadvantage with indirect R&D incentives. With a grant, the amount is determined beforehand whereas with a tax incentive it can be difficult to discern what the future cost will be, which is especially relevant in the case of volume-based incentives.

Governments do, however, have the option to limit the incentives by offering incremental tax incentives or by applying a cap to the credit amount.

There is evidence to suggest that, from a company perspective, compliance with R&D tax regimes can be time consuming and costly. A recent survey among UK manufacturers concluded that compliance with the tax credit system was difficult and unreliable. This can discourage companies from making a claim on expenditure as the costs of making the claim are too high. In turn, this reduces the impact of R&D incentives.

It does appear, however, that calls to simplify the tax system are being answered with the shift in recent years to moving from complex incremental and hybrid schemes to volume-based ones. This raises again the question of cost to the government. However, there is evidence to suggest that with increased government expenditure through generous incentives, there is an increased amount of R&D expenditure incurred by business. This suggests that the objective of these fiscal incentives is being addressed.

4.   Transfer pricing

4.1   Overview
The global commercial landscape has changed dramatically over the last few decades. Many businesses have substantially expanded their international trade and established multiple branches and subsidiaries overseas. Some of these groups of companies have become large multinational groups, dominating the industry and comprising a network of multiple companies spread around the globe. The businesses themselves have also changed: intangible assets including IP rights are now accountable for most of the corporate value. According to an independent research, while intangibles represented 15% of corporate value in 1975, this figure had risen to nearly 85% in 2015.

Sophisticated corporate structures have evolved, often with subsidiaries in low tax jurisdictions, for the purpose of minimising and sometimes avoiding paying a 'fair share' of tax in the countries where they earn most of their profits. As international trade has increased both in volume and value, transfer pricing has come to the top of the agenda for all tax authorities. Furthermore, concerns over the amount of tax payable by multinationals have more recently been expressed by a number of politicians and the media.

4.2   Definition of transfer pricing
Transfer pricing could be described as a set of rules analysing the terms of transactions between companies within the same multinational group (including, but not limited to, price) and seeking to bring these conditions in line with those that would be expected to exist between the unrelated companies, contracting under market forces.

Essentially, transfer pricing rules are designed to ensure that profits of multinational groups are taxed in those countries where the economic activity generating those profits has been performed (ie, where the value has been created).

Although there are some exceptions from the application of the transfer pricing legislation, such as an SME exemption in the United Kingdom and Denmark, most businesses should ensure that they are fully compliant with transfer pricing requirements, especially where two or more taxing jurisdictions are involved.

The cross-border transactions between the group companies often involve intangible assets, with transfer pricing rules coming into play in the cases of royalty payments, R&D services, assignment of an intangible asset or determination of ownership. It is generally accepted that transfer pricing issues concerning intangible property are the most complex for both the tax authorities and taxpayers.

4.3   OECD and BEPS

The OECD is looking to resolve the issue of BEPS; this section describes the development of recent BEPS actions in relation to transfer pricing.

The transfer pricing legislation of most countries, with the most notable exception being Brazil, is largely based on the OECD Transfer Pricing Guidelines for Multinational Enterprises and Tax Administrations (the OECD Guidelines), first published in 1979 and revised recently following the completion of most of the BEPS project in October 2015. One of the most important areas of change was transfer pricing of intangibles.

Since the publication of the BEPS reports in 2015, there have been multiple developments implementing changes in domestic legislation. Although one of the goals of BEPS was to align the transfer pricing rules globally, differences in legislation can be expected. In order to strengthen the transfer pricing compliance and exchange of information amongst the EU member countries, the European Commission is working on an EU-wide action to establish the outputs of BEPS projects on a statutory footing.

As the recommendations under BEPS are being gradually implemented in domestic legislation, greater scrutiny by all tax authorities is expected, especially in relation to intangibles.

4.4   OECD definition of intangibles

The OECD is looking to adopt a broad definition of intangibles, this section provides a definition of 'intangible' and examines its intended scope.

Tax authorities regard intangible assets with particular caution. An intangible asset for these purposes is defined as follows: "something which is not a physical asset or a financial asset, which is capable of being owned or controlled for use in commercial activities, and whose use or transfer would be compensated had it occurred in a transaction between independent parties in comparable circumstances".

The OECD Guidelines' definition of intangibles is broad, and, potentially, capable of including a wide variety of intangible assets, including IP rights. The adoption of a "broad and clearly delineated definition of intangibles" was one of the goals of the OECD BEPS project. The importance of a clear definition cannot be overstated. A definition which is too narrow could result in many intangible assets falling out of scope and could, for example, be easily transferred cross-border without attracting a tax charge. Adopting a definition which is too broad could lead to valuable tax incentives being claimed outside the intended scope.

The definition would generally include an intangible asset recognised and protected by law (for example, a patent or a trademark), although the existence of such protection is not a necessary prerequisite for the asset to be recognised as an intangible. On the other hand, intangibles which are important for transfer pricing purposes are not always recognised for accounting or legal purposes For example, certain types of marketing intangibles, such as client lists and data, would not commonly be capitalised on a company's balance sheet.

4.5   Ownership of intangibles

The classification ownership of any asset is important for discerning where the economic benefit lies, this is especially important for intangibles from a transfer pricing perspective. This section outlines the importance of ownership of intangibles when determining transfer pricing.

Understanding the ownership of intangible assets is important and not necessarily straightforward. Generally, the starting point, although not decisive, is legal ownership. For example, a UK company developing a novel drug and patenting it in the UK, will be the legal owner of the drug formula. However, it may often be the case that two or more companies belonging to the same group collaborate in the pre-clinical and clinical development. It may then be more complicated to establish who the ultimate legal owner of the asset is, particularly in the absence of a contract.

As noted above, the principal objective of transfer pricing is to recognise the profits of a multinational group in the country or countries where the economic value is created as opposed to the country where the legal owner of the intangible assets resides. Thus, the OECD Guidelines adopt a distinction between economic and legal ownership of intangible assets, and these two do not always align.

It is the economic ownership of the intangible asset that entitles a company to profit from its exploitation, whether through sale or licensing. In contrast, the legal owner might not be entitled to any share in profit arising from the transaction. This will most obviously be the case where the legal owner acts solely as the title holder of the intangible asset in question, having little or no personnel capable of understanding or controlling the functions necessary to develop, maintain or manage the asset.

In the example above, the UK company which developed and patented the drug will be both its legal and the economic owner. Under the transfer pricing principles, the UK company will be entitled to receive all the profits generated from licensing of the formula to another company, whether part of the group or unrelated, or from the manufacture and sale of the drug.

In contrast, in a second example where two companies one in France and the other in Spain collaborate to develop a drug the position may be less clear. The companies could have agreed in advance which one of them is to own the resulting formula to the drug (ie, legal ownership) and set out their decision in a legally binding contract. The economic ownership, however, would have to be established following extensive transfer pricing analysis. This analysis would generally involve what is referred to as 'functional analysis', with the decisive factors being the functions each company performed, assets they used and, importantly, risks assumed in the development of the drug.

The transfer pricing analysis in the second example could lead to a conclusion that, from a tax perspective, the economic ownership of the drug formula should be allocated between the French and the Spanish companies, for example, in the proportion of 30%/70%. The French and/or the Spanish tax authorities, following their own analysis, could arrive at a different conclusion and often do. The second example is based on two jurisdictions, but it is often the case that several companies across the globe contribute to the development and exploitation of the same underlying asset.

The potential complications in relation to economic ownership could be partially or wholly mitigated through a carefully drafted contract. This contract would define the respective roles and responsibilities of the companies involved in the development of the intangible asset, their financial contributions and nominate the future legal owner of the asset. In addition, it could be possible to agree an Advance Pricing Agreement (APA) with the tax authorities, which could involve multiple jurisdictions, if required. Although an APA could help to secure peace of mind and certainty for the multinational group, it can often take several years to agree and the application process is typically costly.

4.6 The arm's length principle

The arm's length principle is fundamental to transfer pricing and, in essence, requires related companies to transact with each other as though they were independent.

The arm's length principle is fundamental to the OECD Guidelines and transfer pricing. The full definition is contained in Articles 9(1) of the OECD and UN Model Tax Conventions and, in essence, requires related companies to transact with each other as though they were independent, thus seeking to replicate market forces influencing contractual negotiations between the unrelated companies. The arm's length principle would apply to all the contractual terms of the transaction in question.

Tax authorities have the power to make adjustments in cases where they conclude that the arrangements between the related parties are different from comparable independent companies. This could result in additional tax payable by the group and, often, penalties.

4.7 Functional analysis

The starting point is to understand the transaction in question and analyse functions each company performs, assets they use and risks they assume in relation to that transaction (the 'functional analysis').

The application of the arm's length principle to an intercompany transaction involving intangible assets comprises a number of steps. In addition to analysing the contractual terms governing the transaction, it is essential to understand the nature of the intangible asset in question and, most crucially, perform a functional analysis. As described above, a functional analysis involves analysing the contributions of the parties. In relation to intangibles, these functions could involve R&D, management and maintenance of the intangible asset, its legal protection and so forth.

Functional analysis helps to identify intangible assets utilised in the intercompany transaction and determine how these assets contribute to the creation of value within the group. From a transfer pricing perspective, it is not the performance of the actual function that is most important (although even routine functions should be remunerated), but which company actually exercises control over that function.

In the context of the example above, the most significant functions in the development a novel drug would involve: the design and control of the research programme, the control over strategic decisions and understanding and addressing regulatory requirements. A company is only capable of exercising control of a function through its employees. Therefore, having skilled and experienced staff capable of performing those tasks is essential.

However, the OECD Guidelines stress that entitlement of a group company to profit would depend on the risks it assumes (both financial and commercial), and its ability to control and manage those risks. The relevant risks may be those related to the development of the intangible asset, risk of product obsolescence, infringement risk, product liability, financial uncertainty from the exploitation of the asset upon its development, and so on.

These concepts can be illustrated by the following example. A UK company funds the R&D process of a novel drug in Germany, but does not employ any staff capable of understanding and directing the development process. The employees of the UK company are not managing the R&D budget and assuming no financial or other responsibility over the commercial risks. All the functions of 'special significance' are performed by the employees of the German company. Following the development of the drug, the UK company is registered as its legal owner.

In accordance with transfer pricing principles, the UK company would only be entitled to a risk-free return on the funding that it provided. However, the German company, although not a legal owner, would most likely be deemed to be the asset's economic owner. Accordingly, the German company would be entitled to all the profits resulting from the sale of the drug.

4.8   Transfer pricing methods

Following the functional analysis, the appropriate arm's length price could be determined by the application of one of the transfer pricing methods: Comparable Uncontrolled Price (CUP), Resale Price, Cost Plus, Transactional Net Margin (TNMM) or Profit Split methods.

There are many recognised difficulties in the application of these transfer pricing methods to transactions involving intangibles. As noted above, the arm's length principle involves a thorough analysis of the terms of the transaction between the connected companies comparing them to those between unrelated parties. A high degree of comparability is required in order to arrive at a reliable result. However, due to the fact that intangible assets are inherently unique by their nature, sufficiently comparable data is rarely available.

In addition, as in the example with the French and Spanish companies above, more than one party to the transaction could make a valuable contribution to the creation of the intangible asset, leading to the conclusion that all the profits from its exploitation should be split in proportion to those contributions. For this reason, the Profit Split method which allows for profits to be allocated, would often be the most appropriate for transactions involving intangibles.

5. Chapter summary

- Over the last decade, the number of OECD nations that have incorporated R&D incentives into their tax law has doubled.
- These fiscal incentives can vary considerably from country to country, although the concept of qualifying R&D activity is relatively consistent. The most commonly adopted form of R&D incentive is a repayable tax credit which can amount to 30%–50% of qualifying expenditure. Other countries use super deductions which result in additional tax relief.
- In addition to incentives for R&D, IP box regimes have been introduced by governments in an attempt to promote the development and retention of IP by offering a lower effective tax rate on qualifying IP. Most countries that offer a form of IP box have restrictions on what constitutes qualifying IP; this is often patents but can sometimes be extended to other rights.
- There needs to be sufficient activity in order to qualify for IP box regimes. The nexus approach ensures there is only a benefit if there is a 'direct nexus between the income receiving benefits and the expenditures contributing to that income'.
- It is often perceived by media and public that large multinational businesses have been increasingly implementing sophisticated group structures for the sole purpose of avoiding paying their 'fair share' of tax. As a result, the OECD's BEPS project recommends a number of updates to domestic tax legislation in order to counter harmful tax practices. Many of these updates are in the field of transfer pricing, with an increased emphasis on IP and other intangible assets.
- Transfer pricing rules require that all the transactions taking place within the same multinational group be at arm's length; ie, as would be expected to exist between the unrelated companies, contracted under market forces. Transfer pricing rules ensure that profits of the multinational groups are taxed in those countries where the economic activity generating those profits has been performed. In relation to an intangible asset, profits from its commercial exploitation should be recognised in the hands of its economic owner (which might not necessarily be its legal owner).
- Overall, managing transfer pricing for intangible assets can carry considerable complexity. Tax authorities across the world are becoming increasingly more sophisticated in their approach and international conventions are now facilitating the exchange of timely information.

About the authors

Lorna Brazell

Partner, Osborne Clarke

Lorna.Brazell@osborneclarke.com

Lorna joined the intellectual property disputes team in Osborne Clarke's London office in 2013 to head up the intellectual property litigation practice, following 12 years as a partner at Bird & Bird.

She graduated in geophysics from the University of Edinburgh *summa cum laude* and went on to research in geomagnetism at Cambridge. She then obtained an LLM with merit in corporate and commercial law from King's College London and qualified as a solicitor-advocate in England and Wales. She is recognised in national and international directories including *Who's Who Legal: Patents, Chambers*, and *Legal 500*.

Her work focuses on patents, designs and copyright and includes litigation in the English courts, oppositions and appeals at the European Patent Office and the management of parallel actions across Europe and beyond, as well as intellectual property diligence reviews, freedom to operate opinions, international portfolio management and patent licensing. Lorna has worked in fields from semiconductors, mobile telephony and computer architecture to DNA microarrays, multi-phase fluid dynamics, monoclonal antibodies and nanomaterials, and is engaging with the intellectual property issues of emerging technologies such as cryptocurrencies and artificial intelligence.

Richard Buttrick

Independent consultant, RBIP Ltd

rbuttrick@richardbuttrickip.com

Richard Buttrick is an independent consultant working with a diverse range of clients, including large multinational companies such as Koninklijke Philips, British Telecommunications plc, BAE Systems plc, global organisations such as the International Electrotechnical Commission (IEC), and small, growing companies like Design Blue Ltd ("D3O", UK) and Miortech (NL) to help them create and deliver value from intellectual property. He has extensive knowledge and experience of the creation and exploitation of intellectual property to maximise value, acquired through over 30 years in many different sectors, technologies and situations, including time with Philips, British Telecom and British Technology Group, an intellectual property licensing company. His expertise in Standard-Essential Patent (FRAND) licensing has lead to him being sought after as an expert witness both in dispute resolution and in litigation worldwide. He is a qualified UK and European patent attorney, and member of LES. He is a member of the *IAM Strategy 300*, which captures the world's leading IP strategists.

Peter Cowan

Principal consultant, Northworks IP

peter@ipstrategy.ca

Peter Cowan is the founder and principal consultant at Northworks IP, an intellectual property strategy advisory firm that was founded to help companies maximise value of their intellectual property assets through a business-focused approach to intellectual property. He holds BEng and MBA degrees and is currently pursuing his LLM degree.

He has created and led the growth of technology innovation and intellectual property programmes in companies from new start-ups to large multinational companies. He has worked with executives, inventors and technical teams across eight countries to help identify and protect their breakthrough innovations, across both mature and emerging markets. In his previous role at Schneider Electric, a Global Fortune 400 company, he lead strategic planning of the patent portfolio at several levels in the organisation, and developed and lead innovation programmes for new businesses. Within this, he educated and engaged teams to generate business-relevant patents by shifting the organizational culture to be intellectual property-centric within their projects and processes.

Colin Hunsley

Director, ClearViewIP Limited

colin_hunsley@clearviewip.com

Colin is a founder director at ClearViewIP, a UK-based intellectual property strategy consultancy. He has a degree in mechanical engineering from Imperial College, London. He is president of the Licensing Executive Society Britain and Ireland (LES Britain & Ireland), past chairman of the Institution of Mechanical Engineers Medical Engineering division and a former IAM 300 leading IP strategists member. Clients across a wide range of technology sectors use ClearViewIP to develop their innovative edge, build business value, identify and manage risk and unlock additional income streams from IP assets.

Colin's experience spans all stages of the intellectual property process from identifying and capturing intellectual property, filing patents, licensing patents and technology to initiating and settling patent litigation. Prior to forming ClearViewIP, he worked for BTG where he managed litigations relating to patent infringement against Microsoft, Apple and Zimmer with very successful outcomes.

Gareth Jones

Head of intellectual property, SwiftKey

contact@garethj.com

Gareth Jones is head of intellectual property for SwiftKey, a technology start-up at the intersection of artificial intelligence and natural language. SwiftKey was acquired by Microsoft in March 2016 and Gareth is currently responsible for managing the transfer of intellectual property operations.

Following a successful technical leadership career in software, and an appointment to master inventor at IBM, Gareth transitioned into a career in intellectual property. He has since coordinated global invention capture for Vodafone, managed all strategic and operational intellectual property matters for SwiftKey and is now part of the intellectual property team at Microsoft. He has defined intellectual property strategy, developed asset portfolios, reduced risk, defended patent litigation, managed due diligence and achieved a successful exit for a high-profile start-up.

Paul Kallmes

Co-founder, Metis Partners Inc

paul@metispartners.com

Paul Kallmes has two decades of IP management experience in a wide variety of industries. He has built and managed patent portfolios, negotiated complex licenses, performed valuation and due diligence exercises on IP portfolios, provided guidance to venture capital and private equity firms, and advised numerous young and established companies on IP strategies. He has worked with universities in commercialising their IP and is presently involved in spinning out two IP-based university technologies. He has taught IP management and licensing in North America,

Europe and Asia, and has presented many seminars on IP strategy. Currently he is working with a leading technology incubator in San Francisco to develop IP-centric education programs for entrepreneurs and investors.

Alexander Korenberg
Partner, Kilburn & Strode LLP
akorenberg@kilburnstrode.com

Alexander is a patent attorney and partner at leading European IP firm Kilburn & Strode. Alexander specialises in high-tech, medical technology and physics and has been described by his clients as an "exceptional attorney who we trust to handle our IP matters" (Chambers and Partners, 2014) and as "very competent and easy to deal with" (*MIP Handbook*, 2012). He is appreciated for his "in-depth understanding of clients' portfolios and true technical expertise" (*IAM Patent 1000*, 2016). Alexander read Physics at Imperial College London and was awarded a PhD from University College London for his research in computational neuroscience.

Mike McLean
Senior vice-president of intellectual property services, TechInsights
mmclean@techinsights.com

Mike McLean is a recognised leader in the intellectual property and patent strategy market. He is respected and sought after for his ability to assess complex situations and apply technical intelligence to ensure fact-based IP decisions related to patent licensing, patent portfolio management and IP monetisation. He works closely with the technology practices of major law firms, the in-house corporate counsel teams of key technology companies, and external licensing agencies where he helps develop, support and execute high-return patent strategies.

Nicholas Mitchell
Head of contentious IT, White & Black Limited
Nicholas.Mitchell@wablegal.com

Nicholas Mitchell is head of contentious IT at White & Black, based between the firm's London and Oxfordshire offices. He specialises in intellectual property and IT disputes for technology sector clients.

Nick advises on intellectual property litigation, cyber security, data protection and defamation matters for a range of international corporate clients with a particular focus on Japan and the United States. He acted for a number of years on disputes and contract management issues arising from major government IT projects.

He has written practice notes on cyber security crisis management and IT contract disputes for a leading online legal research service and regularly blogs on intellectual property and technology law issues at www.wablegal.com.

Josue Ortiz
Director, ClearViewIP Limited
josue_ortiz@clearviewip.com

Josue Ortiz is a director at ClearViewIP, a UK-based intellectual property strategy firm where he advises clients primarily in the technology, media and telecommunications sector. He holds degrees in telecommunications engineering and business and has specialised in intellectual property strategy and transactions for over 15 years while based in London, Philadelphia and Mexico City.

In particular, he has provided strategic advice to a number of companies dealing with non-practising entities. In addition, he has been heavily involved in a number of patent related litigations in the United Kingdom and the United States.

Josue has also led interdisciplinary and cross-border teams on the completion of a variety of sell side and buy side intellectual property deals, including on behalf of private equity firms. He is a regular speaker at intellectual property conferences and is listed in the *IAM Strategy 300* list of the world's leading intellectual property strategists.

Ryan Pixton
Partner, Kilburn & Strode LLP
rpixton@kilburnstrode.com

Ryan Pixton is a partner with Kilburn & Strode LLP. His trademark practice includes clearance searches, the filing and prosecution of applications, oppositions and cancellation actions and advising on licences and assignments. He works for clients ranging from start-ups to multinational corporations. His clients are drawn from fields including telecommunications, food and drink, gaming, fashion and music, whilst he has a growing 'greentech' practice.

Ryan also handles European Registered Design applications and advises clients on copyright issues and domain name disputes. He is listed as one of the world's leading trademark professionals by *World Trade Mark Review*, and is a contributor to a leading handbook for practitioners.

Stephen Robertson
DIrector and founder, Metis Partners Ltd
stephen@metispartners.com

Acknowledged as one of the "World's 300 Leading IP Strategists" by *IAM* magazine, Stephen founded Metis Partners in 2003 to assist businesses with the maximisation of value from their IP assets. He has advised a range of corporates and professional firms, including FTSE quoted companies, SMEs, global banks, insolvency practitioners, trustees and public sector organisations. Stephen's experience includes monetising IP assets, providing IP due diligence, developing IP strategies, IP asset brokerage and IP asset valuation. He also provides expertise with IP commercialisation, IP infringement and invalidity as well as using IP assets as security to restructure debt. He drove two major IP market initiatives: the IP Valuation Society, addressing issues

pertinent to professional IP valuers; and IP100, the United Kingdom's first IP league table, profiling and ranking innovative companies based on their investment and track record in IP creation, management and commercialisation.

Stephen graduated with a degree in law before qualifying as a chartered accountant with Deloitte & Touche, and has 20 years' experience in corporate finance.

He is currently the chair of the Licensing Executives Society (LES) Scotland and an active member of the LES Council Britain and Ireland.

He has contributed to European initiatives focused on national policy change – specifically IP-related finance and IP recognition among SMEs. Stephen has written and contributed to books and articles on IP strategy and valuation and he speaks on IP monetisation and valuation at global events, including World Intellectual Property Organisation, IPBC and BIP Asia.

Alex Tame
Director, Tame IP Ltd
alex@tameIP.com

Alex Tame is director of Tame IP Ltd, a newly formed company that was established to assist small- and medium-sized companies with the management of their intellectual property portfolios through offering a virtual intellectual property management service.

Prior to forming Tame IP, Alex was global intellectual property rights manager at Vodafone with oversight of the global intellectual property portfolio and associated strategy. Alex led Vodafone's intellectual property team through several periods of business change, influencing senior management and delivering revenue to the business through patent sales and licensing whilst growing the overall size and quality of the portfolio.

During his time at Vodafone, Alex developed a global network of educated intellectual property contacts throughout the organisation and overcame challenges such as cultural differences, portfolio management, reward/recognition and budget management, to ensure the successful delivery of a sustainable programme for managing intellectual property rights.

Richard Turner
Managing Director, FTI Consulting LLP
richard.turner@fticonsulting.com

Richard Turner is a managing director at FTI Consulting based in London. Richard leads tax and innovation services encompassing intellectual property planning, research and development incentives and the UK patent box. He regularly provides input to HM Revenue and Customs and HM Treasury for research and development tax incentives and patent box. Under Richard's leadership, FTI Consulting has established itself as one of the most progressive firms in this area of taxation.

Latterly, Richard was a partner at Deloitte and part of the United Kingdom healthcare and life science leadership. Prior to that, he worked as an international tax director for PowderJect Pharmaceuticals Plc and Chiron Corporation, spending significant time in the United States, Germany and Italy.

Related titles in IP

Globe Law
and Business

Go to **www.globelawandbusiness.com**
for full details including free sample chapters